lonely planet

# MANDARIN

Travel Phrasebook & Dictionary

## Credits

**Production Editor** Joel Cotterell

**Language Writers** Anthony Garnaut, Tim Lu

## Thanks

Sofie Andersen, Piera Chen, Fergal Condon, Gwen Cotter, Kellie Langdon, Saralinda Turner, Clifton Wilkinson

**Published by Lonely Planet Global Limited**
CRN 554153

Digital Depot, Roe Lane off Thomas Street, Dublin
D08 TCV4, Ireland (EU authorised representative)

12th Edition – Sep 2026
ISBN 978 1 80653 183 7

**Cover Images** Traditional fan, Hseena/Shutterstock; Chinese New Year dragon, Catchiangmai/Shutterstock; Ceramic porcelain, The Crunchy Studio/Shutterstock
Printed in Malaysia 10 9 8 7 6 5 4 3 2 1

**Contact** lonelyplanet.com/contact

## Look out for the following icons throughout the book:

**'Shortcut' Phrase**
Easy-to-remember alternative to the full phrase

**Q&A Pair**
'Question-and-answer' pair – we suggest a response to the question asked

**Look for**
Phrases you may see on signs, menus etc

**Listen for**
Phrases you may hear from officials, locals etc

**LANGUAGE TIP**

An insight into Mandarin

**CULTURE TIP**

An insight into the local culture

**How to read the phrases:**

- Coloured words and phrases throughout the book are phonetic guides to help you pronounce Mandarin.
- Lists of phrases with tinted background are options you can choose to complete the phrase above them.

---

**These abbreviations will help you choose the right words and phrases in this book:**

| | | | | | |
|---|---|---|---|---|---|
| inf | informal | pl | plural | sg | singular |
| lit | literal | pol | polite | | |

# CONTENTS

## ABOUT MANDARIN .............. 6

*Learn about Mandarin, build your own sentences and pronounce words correctly.*

Introduction .............................. 6

Top Phrases .............................. 8

Pronunciation ..........................10

Grammar ..................................18

## TRAVEL PHRASES

*Ready-made phrases for every situation – buy a ticket, book a hotel and much more.*

### BASICS ........................... 31

Understanding ...................... 32

Numbers & Amounts ........... 34

Time & Dates ........................ 38

### PRACTICAL ............... 43

Transport ............................... 44

Border Crossing ..................... 61

Directions ............................... 63

Accommodation ..................... 66

Shopping ................................ 78

Communications .................. 88

Money & Banking................ 94
Business................................97
Sightseeing........................100
Seniors & Travellers with Disabilities........................106
Travel with Children..........108

## SOCIAL........................111

Meeting People....................112
Interests..................................123
Feelings & Opinions...........128
Going Out...........................134
Romance.................................140
Beliefs & Culture..................145
Sports.......................................148
Outdoors...................................156

## SAFE TRAVEL.........161

Emergencies........................162
Police........................................164
Health.......................................166

## FOOD..........................175

Eating Out............................176
Self-Catering........................192
Vegetarian & Special Meals......................196

## MENU DECODER............199

*Dishes and ingredients explained – order with confidence and try new foods.*

## TWO-WAY DICTIONARY......209

*Quick reference vocabulary guide – 3500 words to help you communicate.*

English–Mandarin Dictionary..............................209
Mandarin–English Dictionary..............................239

## INDEX.................. 252

# ABOUT Mandarin

普通话 PŬTŌNGHUÀ

## Who speaks Mandarin?

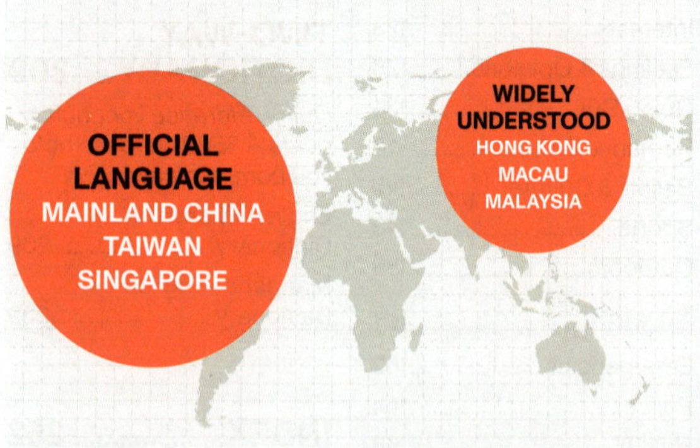


### Why Bother

With more than one billion speakers worldwide, Mandarin is the most widely spoken language on the planet. How can you miss the chance to communicate with one in seven people on Earth?

### Distinctive Sounds

In Mandarin you can change the meaning of a word by raising and lowering the pitch level (tone) on certain syllables. Mandarin has four tones (high, high-rising, high-falling and low falling-rising), plus a fifth, neu-

**990 million** speak Mandarin as their first language

**1.1 billion** Mandarin speakers worldwide

tral tone.

### Pinyin

Pinyin was officially adopted in 1958 as a way of writing Mandarin using the Roman alphabet. Today in Chinese cities you'll see it everywhere: on maps, road and shop signs and in brand names.

### Chinese Script

Many of the basic Chinese characters are pictographs (highly stylised pictures of what they represent), but most have a 'meaning' element and a 'sound' element. Each character represents a syllable, and most words consist of two characters.

### Chinglish

'Chinglish' (Chinese English) provides many entertaining mistranslations – eg a 'Keep Quiet' notice might instead read 'the subliminal of thought has started while the noisy has stopped'.

### Language Family

The term 'Mandarin' refers to one of the seven Chinese dialect groups and is more accurately called Modern Standard Chinese or Pǔtōnghuà 普通话 (literally 'the common dialect'). Close relatives in the Sino-Tibetan family are the other six dialects: Gan, Hakka, Min, Wu, Xiang and Yue.

### Must-Know Grammar

Mandarin doesn't have direct equivalents of 'yes' and 'no' used in isolation. Instead, to answer the question affirmatively, repeate the verb used in the question (eg shì 是 – 'be'). For a negative answer, add bù 不 (not) before the verb.

### Donations to English

Quite a few – for example, *gung-ho, Japan, ketchup, kung fu, silk, t'ai chi, tea.*

# 5 Phrases TO LEARN BEFORE YOU GO

## 01 Where would you go for yum cha?

哪里的早茶好？ Nǎlǐ de zǎochá hǎo?

When in China, make sure you find the right place for what has to be the signature dining experience in Chinatowns the world over.

## 02 Please bring a knife and fork.

请拿一副刀叉来。 Qǐng ná yī fù dāochā lái.

Don't be afraid to ask for cutlery at a restaurant if you haven't quite mastered the art of eating with chopsticks.

## 03 Can I get a discount (for the room)?

这（房间）能打折吗？ Zhè (fángjiān) néng dǎzhé ma?

In China, always bargain for a hotel room – discounts of 10% to 50% off the rack rate are the norm, available by simply asking at reception.

## 04 I'd like to hire a bicycle.

我想租一辆自行车。 Wǒ xiǎng zū yīliàng zìxíngchē.

Bikes are a great option for getting around Chinese cities and tourist sites. They can also be invaluable for exploring the countryside.

## 05 Can you write that in Pinyin for me?

请用拼音写。 Qǐng yòng Pīnyīn xiě.

If you find Chinese script intimidating, Pinyin (the official system for writing Mandarin in the Roman alphabet) is your next best option.

# 10 Phrases TO SOUND LIKE A LOCAL

| | | |
|---|---|---|
| **Great!** | 真棒！ | Zhēnbàng! |
| **Hey!** | 喂！ | Wèi! |
| **It's OK.** | 还行。 | Háixíng. |
| **Just a minute.** | 等一下。 | Děngyīxià.**May-** |
| **be.** | 有可能。 | Yǒu kěnéng. |
| **No problem.** | 没事。 | Méishì. |
| **No way!** | 不可能！ | Bù kěnéng! |
| **Sure, whatever.** | 行，行，行。 | Xíng, xíng, xíng. |
| **That's enough!** | 够了，够了！ | Gòule, gòule! |
| **Just joking.** | 开玩笑。 | Kāiwánxiào. |

# Mandarin Pronunciation

For speakers of English, the sounds of Mandarin are quite easy to produce, as many of them have equivalents in English. One aspect of the language that may prove a little challenging is the use of tones. In Mandarin you can change the meaning of a word by altering the pitch level (tone) at which it is spoken. See **tones** on page 13 for an explanation of how this works.

## THE PINYIN SYSTEM

Pinyin was officially adopted by the Chinese in 1958 as a way of writing Mandarin using the Roman alphabet. It provided access to a common language in a vast country with countless dialects, and so played an important role in communication and development. Today in Chinese cities you'll see Pinyin everywhere: on maps, road signs, shop signs and in brand names. Nevertheless, many Chinese can't read Pinyin and its use is very limited in rural areas, so this book includes the Chinese script characters as well.

You'll find Pinyin an easy system to use once you've learnt the rules on how to pronounce letters. For example, Pinyin c is pronounced like the 'ts' in 'cats' and Pinyin q is pronounced like the 'ch' in 'cheese'.

For information on the Chinese names of the Roman alphabet letters – useful if, for example, you need to spell out your name on check-in – see the box on page 16.

### LANGUAGE TIP: MANDARIN BEIJING-STYLE

The pronunciation given in this book is based on 'Beijingese', the dialect of Mandarin spoken in the capital. This is because Modern Standard Chinese is based on the Beijing dialect. You'll be understood throughout the country as all Chinese have broad exposure to the official language.

One feature of standard Mandarin that's a reflection of a peculiarly Beijing pronunciation is the addition of an 'r' sound at the end of many words. This 'r' sound is represented in this phrasebook by the character 儿. You won't normally hear this 'r' in other parts of China. Also be aware that outside the capital the sibilant (hissing) sounds 's' and 'z' may not match the patterns of the Beijing standard. Generally speaking, the greater the distance from the capital the more you should expect to hear different pronunciations.

## VOWEL SOUNDS

Mandarin vowels are straightforward and you'll notice that there's quite a lot of overlap with English vowel sounds. Be aware that in Pinyin, vowels are often pronounced differently depending on the other letters surrounding them, as shown in the table below.

| PINYIN | ENGLISH SOUND | MANDARIN EXAMPLE |
|---|---|---|
| a (an, ang) | father (fun, sung) | fà (fàn, fǎng) |
| e (en, eng) | her (broken, Deng) | gě (mèn, fěng) |
| i (in, ing) | peel (pin, ping) | pí (pǐn, píng) |
| i (after z, c, or s) | girl | zǐ |
| i (after zh, ch, sh or r) | like the r in Grrr! | shí |
| o (ong) | more (Jung) | bó (tóng) |
| u | tool | shù |
| ü (and u or un after j, q, x or y) | similar to 'new' pronounced with rounded lips | lǚ (qù, yùn) |

## VOWEL/CONSONANT COMBINATIONS

Mandarin has quite a few diphthongs (vowel sound combinations) and vowel and consonant combinations – when the letters i and u occur before other vowels, they are pronounced 'y' and 'w' respectively. Again, you'll notice that most of these have counterparts in English.

| - PINYIN - | - ENGLISH SOUND - | - MANDARIN EXAMPLE - |
|---|---|---|
| ai | aisle | zài |
| ao | now | báo |
| ei | pay | bèi |
| ia | yard | jiā |
| ian | yen | tiān |
| iang | young | xiǎng |
| iao | loud | xiǎo |
| ie | yes | xié |
| iong | Jung | xiōngdì |
| iu | yolk | qiú |
| ou | low | lóu |
| ua | wah! | guā |
| uai | why | kuài |
| uan | one | chuān |
| uan (after j, q, x or y) | went | yuān |
| uang | swung | kuàng |
| ue | you wet | yuè |
| ui | way | tuī |
| uo | war | huǒ |

## CONSONANT SOUNDS

The consonants should be quite easy for you to get your tongue around, as they'll all be familiar from English.

| PINYIN | ENGLISH SOUND | MANDARIN EXAMPLE |
|---|---|---|
| b | bit | bāng |
| c | cats | cè |
| ch | true | chū |
| d | dog | dì |
| f | fun | fēng |
| g | go | gān |
| h | hot | hǎi |
| j | jump | jùn |
| k | kid | kě |
| l | lip | lín |
| m | map | mín |
| n | no | néng |
| ng | sing | máng |
| p | pig | pèi |
| q | churn | qū |
| r | run | rì |
| s | sip | sī |
| sh | shop | shǎo |
| t | top | tú |
| w | win | wàng |
| y | you | yǒu |
| x | sheet | xiá |
| z | lads | zì |
| zh | gem | zhāo |

## TONES

Many words in Mandarin appear to have the same basic pronunciation. What distinguishes these 'homophones' is their tonal quality – the raising and lowering of pitch on certain syllables. Mandarin is usually described as having four tones, (numbered first through to fourth), plus a fifth, neutral tone.

Apart from the unmarked neutral tone, Pinyin uses diacritics (symbols) to indicate each tone, appearing above the vowels as shown below.

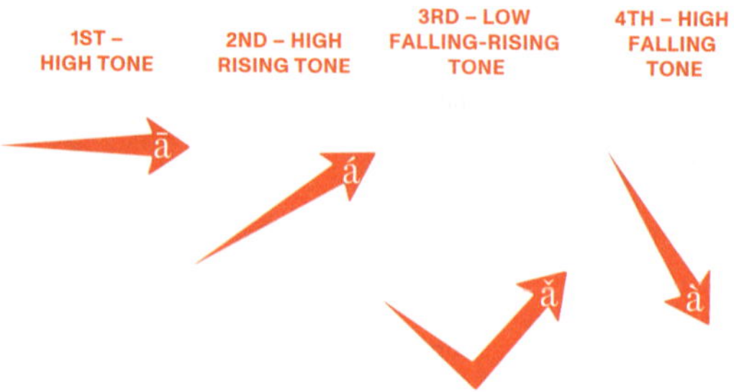


The following table shows how one 'word' ma can have five different meanings which are distinguished by tone only.

| - TONE - | - EXAMPLE - | - MEANING - |
|---|---|---|
| 1st – high | mā | mother |
| 2nd – high rising | má | hemp |
| 3rd – low falling-rising | mǎ | horse |
| 4th – high falling | mà | scold |
| neutral | ma | question marker |

Tones in Mandarin allow for some amusing tone-based tongue twisters. This one uses the example words given above:

**Mother rides a horse. The horse is slow. Mother scolds the horse.**

妈妈骑马，马慢，妈妈骂马。
(lit: mother ride horse, horse slow, mother scold horse)
Māma qí mǎ, mǎ màn, māma mà mǎ.

Bear in mind that tones are not absolute in pitch but are relative to your natural vocal range. So don't feel inhibited – just experiment with the contours of your natural voice. English speakers do this anyway to a small extent. When you pronounce 'What?' you're getting close to a Mandarin high rising tone and when you say 'Damn!' you're approximating a high falling tone.

There's no need to feel daunted by this 'foreign' system. There's nothing obscure or mysterious about tones – over half of the world's languages use them. You might have mixed success in getting your meaning across to start with, but remember that patient repetition is all it takes to learn. Even if your tones are slightly off, the meaning you wish to convey will often be clear from the context. Failing that, you can always point to the word or phrase you're aiming for in this phrasebook.

## Tonal Variations

In spoken Mandarin, tones can sometimes vary with context. The most common change occurs when there are two low falling-rising (3rd) tones in sequence – the first one changes to something more like a high rising (2nd) tone, for example:

| | | |
|---|---|---|
| **at least** | 起码 | qǐ mǎ is pronounced as qí mǎ |

Another common change occurs when the word bù 不 'no/not' is followed by another high falling tone – in that case it's pronounced as a high rising tone, for example:

| | | |
|---|---|---|
| **incorrect** | 不对 | bù duì is pronounced as bú duì |

The common character yī 一 'one' has a couple of tonal variations. It has a high tone when used in isolation, a high rising tone when followed by a high falling tone (as in 一会儿 yīhuìr 'a little while' which is pronounced as yíhuìr), and a high falling tone when followed by any other tone (see the examples on the following page).

| | | |
|---|---|---|
| **ordinary** | 一般 | yībān is pronounced as yìbān |
| **together** | 一同 | yītóng is pronounced as yìtóng |
| **a little** | 一点儿 | yīdiǎnr is pronounced as yìdiǎnr |

In our coloured pronunciation guides throughout the book we show the unmodified version of these tones – the ones mentioned first in the examples above – which is the correct style for written Pinyin.

### ☑ LANGUAGE TIP: SPELLING

Most Chinese are familiar with the Latin alphabet through their knowledge of Pinyin and English. If you want to spell out your name in hotels etc, you should follow the Chinese pronunciation of the alphabet in the chart below as you probably won't be understood if you say the letters as in English. Latin letters can be represented with characters denoting the sounds.

| | | | | | |
|---|---|---|---|---|---|
| **A** | 诶 | ēi | **N** | 恩 | ēn |
| **B** | 必 | bì | **O** | 呕 | ō |
| **C** | 西 | xī | **P** | 披 | pī |
| **D** | 弟 | dì | **Q** | 酷 | kù |
| **E** | 衣 | yī | **R** | 耳 | ěr |
| **F** | 艾付 | àifù | **S** | 艾斯 | àisī |
| **G** | 记 | jì | **T** | 踢 | tī |
| **H** | 爱耻 | àichǐ | **U** | 忧 | yōu |
| **I** | 挨 | āi | **V** | 维 | wéi |
| **J** | 宅 | zhāi | **W** | 大波留 | dàbōliú |
| **K** | 开 | kāi | **X** | 埃克斯 | āikèsī |
| **L** | 饿罗 | èluó | **Y** | 歪 | wāi |
| **M** | 饿母 | èmǔ | **Z** | 再得 | zàide |

## WRITING SYSTEM

Mandarin is often described as a language of pictographs. Many of the basic Chinese characters are in fact highly stylised pictures of what they represent, but the majority are compounds of a 'meaning' element and a 'sound' element. Each character represents a spoken syllable, and most words are comprised of two separate characters.

The bulkiest Chinese dictionaries have some 100,000 characters, but to be able to read a newspaper you 'only' need to know a few thousand. Theoretically, all Chinese dialects use the same writing system and people from all over China should be able to read and understand the characters in the words and phrases in this book. In practice, however, Cantonese adds about 3000 specialised characters and many dialects don't have a written form at all. Note that in this book we've used simplified Chinese characters, along with Pinyin (the official system of writing Mandarin using the Roman alphabet) in the pronunciation guides. Simplified Chinese is used in mainland China and has been adopted by Singapore, Malaysia and other Southeast Asian countries (whereas traditional Chinese characters are used in Taiwan, Hong Kong and Macau).

# Mandarin Grammar

This chapter is designed to explain the main grammatical structures you need in order to make your own sentences. Look under each heading for information on functions which these grammatical categories express in a sentence. For example, demonstratives are used for giving instructions, so you'll need them to tell the taxi driver where your hotel is.

## ADJECTIVES

### Describing People/Things • Comparing People/Things

As in English, words that describe or modify nouns, ie adjectives, come before the noun. Usually, the particle de 的 is placed between an adjective consisting of more than one syllable and the noun.

**a big strawberry** 很大的草莓
(lit: very big de strawberry)
hěn dà de cǎoméi

To compare one thing to another, you insert the word bǐ 比 'compare' between the two objects you wish to compare. The object being compared comes before this term of comparison (which plays the same role as the word 'than' in English).

| | |
|---|---|
| **China is bigger than Australia.** | 中国比澳大利亚大。(lit: China compare Australia big)<br>Zhōngguó bǐ Àodàlìyà dà. |
| **This one's better than that one.** | 这个比那个好。(lit: this-one compare that-one good)<br>Zhège bǐ nàge hǎo. |

# ARTICLES

## Naming People/Things

One thing that you won't have to bother about when putting together a Mandarin sentence are the equivalents for the English articles 'a/an' and 'the': Mandarin has no articles at all. The context indicates whether something indefinite (corresponding to 'a/an') or definite (corresponding to 'the') is meant.

# BE

## Describing People/Things • Making Statements

Although Mandarin has an equivalent of the English verb 'to be', shì 是, it's not used in quite the same way. The verb shì is only ever used with a noun, as in this sentence:

| | |
|---|---|
| **I'm a doctor.** | 我是医生。(lit: I am doctor)<br>Wǒ shì yīshēng. |

The verb shì is dropped altogether with adjectives – a Mandarin speaker says literally 'I thirsty' not 'I am thirsty'. (The particle le 了 indicates a change of state, ie 'I was not thirsty but I am thirsty now'.)

| | |
|---|---|
| **I'm thirsty.** | 我渴了。(lit: I thirsty-le)<br>Wǒ kěle. |

# CLASSIFIERS/COUNTERS

## Counting People/Things

In Mandarin, when you talk about quantities of any noun, it's important to put a classifier or 'measure word' between the number and the noun. This concept is not entirely alien to English. We talk about 'two pairs of trousers', 'two bunches of bananas', 'two sheets of paper' etc. The system is a bit more highly developed in Mandarin and classifiers must be used every time numbers are used with a noun. Different classifiers are used for different kinds of objects, taking into account their shape, or a general category (based on Chinese logic) to which they belong. The full list of classifiers is too long to give here but these are the most common ones:

### – COMMON CLASSIFIERS/COUNTERS –

| | | |
|---|---|---|
| **generic classifier** | 个 | ge |
| **big things (mountains, buildings, etc)** | 座 | zuò |
| **chairs, knives, teapots, tools or implements with handles** | 把 | bǎ |
| **drinking receptacles (cups, glasses etc)** | 杯 | bēi |
| **flat things (tickets, stamps etc)** | 张 | zhāng |
| **flowers (the blossoms, not the plants)** | 朵 | duǒ |
| **long things (fish, snakes, rivers etc)** | 条 | tiáo |
| **nondescript animals (dogs, cats etc)** | 只 | zhī |
| **people** | 位 | wèi |
| **trees** | 棵 | kē |
| **vehicles** | 辆 | liàng |

Don't be intimidated by this system. The good news is that you can get by just using the 'generic' (all-purpose) classifier ge 个. It may not be strictly correct, and you may find people gently correcting you, but you'll be understood.

Classifiers are used with the demonstrative pronouns 'this' (zhè 这) and 'that' (nà 那) and between pronouns and nouns (see also **demonstratives**).

| | |
|---|---|
| **this week** | 这个星期 (lit: this-ge week)<br>zhège xīngqī |
| **that woman** | 那位女士 (lit: that-wèi woman)<br>nàwèi nǚshì |

# CONJUNCTIONS

## Asking Questions • Making Statements

To connect two words or phrases, place a joining word (or conjunction) between the two elements. The most common conjunctions are 'and' hé 和 and 'or' háishì 还是.

| | |
|---|---|
| **I like rice and noodles.** | 我喜欢米饭和面条。<br>(lit: I like rice and noodle)<br>Wǒ xǐhuān mǐfàn hé miàntiáo. |
| **Are you American or English?** | 你是美国人还是英国人？<br>(lit: you are America person or England person)<br>Nǐ shì Měiguó rén háishì Yīngguó rén? |

# DEMONSTRATIVES

## Giving Instructions • Indicating Location • Pointing Things Out

To point things out in Mandarin you can use the following expressions (known as demonstrative pronouns).

| | | |
|---|---|---|
| **that** | 那 | nà |
| **this** | 这 | zhè |

The demonstratives can be combined with the generic classifier ge to give the following expressions:

| | | |
|---|---|---|
| **that one** | 那个 | nàge |
| **this one** | 这个 | zhège |

# HAVE

## Possessing

To say that you have something in Mandarin, you use the word yǒu 有.

| | |
|---|---|
| **I have a ticket.** | 我有票。(lit: I have ticket)<br>Wǒ yǒu piào. |

To say that you don't have something, just place the particle méi 没 'not' before yǒu.

| | |
|---|---|
| **I don't have a ticket.** | 我没有票。(lit: I not-have ticket)<br>Wǒ méiyǒu piào. |

# IMPERATIVES

## Giving Instructions

To express a command in Mandarin you place emphasis on the verb. A positive command is formed by just stating the verb in a commanding tone:

| | |
|---|---|
| **Leave!** | 滚！ (lit: roll (away))<br>Gǔn! |

A negative command is formed by putting 'not want' bùyào 不要 (sometimes abbreviated to bié 别) before a verb. There's also a polite form of a negative command – akin to saying 'needn't' in English. In this case 'not need' bùyòng 不用 is placed before the verb. This has an abbreviated form béng 甭.

| | |
|---|---|
| **not want** | 不要<br>bùyào |
| **not want (abbreviated form)** | 别<br>bié |
| **not need** | 不用<br>bùyòng |
| **not need (abbreviated form)** | 甭<br>béng |
| **Don't shout!** | 不要喊！<br>(lit: not-want shout)<br>Bùyào hăn! |
| **No need for formalities!** | 不用客气！<br>(lit: not-need politeness)<br>Bùyòng kèqi! |

# NEED

## Making Statements

The verb 'need' is expressed by the compound word xūyào 需要, which includes the word yào 要 'to want'.

| | |
|---|---|
| **I need to go to the toilet.** | 我需要上厕所。<br>(lit: I need mount toilet)<br>Wŏ xūyào shàng cèsuŏ. |

As with all negatives, to say you don't need something, just place bù 不 'not' before xūyào.

| | |
|---|---|
| **I don't need money.** | 我不需要钱。<br>(lit: I not-need money)<br>Wŏ bù xūyào qián. |

# NEGATIVES

## Negating

To form negative sentences in Mandarin, you place the particle bù 不 'not' before the verb or adjective that you wish to negate. (Note that when bù appears before a word with the same tone, it changes to a rising tone.)

| | |
|---|---|
| **I'm not hungry.** | 我不饿。(lit: I not hungry)<br>Wǒ bù è. |
| **It's not OK.** | 不行。(lit: not passable)<br>Bù xíng. |

The particle méi 没 is used instead of bù to make a negative of 'have' and also when the sentence refers to past events. Here méi can be thought of as the equivalent of the English 'haven't'.

| | |
|---|---|
| **I haven't eaten lunch.** | 我没吃午饭。(lit: I méi eat lunch)<br>Wǒ méi chī wǔfàn. |

# NOUNS

## Naming People/Things

Nouns are usually compounds made up of two words (characters). Nouns have only one fixed form and they don't show gender (masculine, feminine etc) or number (singular or plural).

| | |
|---|---|
| **lunch/lunches** | 午饭 (lit: noon-rice)<br>wǔfàn |

# PARTICLES

## Doing Things • Making Statements

Mandarin makes use of a number of particles. These are 'function words' which don't necessarily have a definable meaning of their own but serve a grammatical function in a sentence.

The particle le 了, for example, when attached to a verb indicates that an action has been completed.

# PERSONAL PRONOUNS

## Making Statements • Naming People/Things

Pronouns in Mandarin don't change their form according to whether they are the subject (performer of the action, eg 'I') or object (undergoer of the action, eg 'me') of a sentence. Note that whilst 'he/him', 'she/her' and 'it' are represented by different characters they are pronounced in exactly the same way.

- PERSONAL PRONOUNS -

| | | |
|---|---|---|
| **I/me** | 我 | wǒ |
| **you sg** | 你 | nǐ |
| **he/him** | 他 | |
| **she/her** | 她 | tā |
| **it** | 它 | |
| **we/us** | 我们 | wǒmen |
| **you pl** | 你们 | nǐmen |
| **they/them** | 他们 | tāmen |

You'll notice that plural pronouns are formed with the simple addition of men 们 to the singular forms.

# POSSESSIVES

## Possessing

To show possession, simply add de 的 to a personal pronoun, then follow it with the object or person that's possessed.

| | |
|---|---|
| **my passport** | 我的护照 (lit: I-de passport)<br>wǒde hùzhào |
| **your child** | 你的孩子 (lit: you-de child)<br>nǐde háizi |

- POSSESSIVE PRONOUNS -

| | | |
|---|---|---|
| **my/mine** | 我的 | wǒde |
| **your(s) sg** | 你的 | nǐde |
| **his/her(s)/its** | 他的/她的/它的 | tāde |
| **our(s)** | 我们的 | wǒmende |
| **your(s) pl** | 你们的 | nǐmende |
| **their(s)** | 他们的 | tāmende |

# PREPOSITIONS

## Giving Instructions • Indicating Location/Time • Pointing Things Out

A time relationship between a noun and another word in the sentence is reflected by the use of prepositions of time.

| | |
|---|---|
| **I watched TV before eating.** | 我吃饭前看了电视。<br>(lit: I ate-rice before (that I) watch-le television)<br>Wǒ chī fàn qián kànle diànshì. |

- PREPOSITIONS -

| | | |
|---|---|---|
| **after** | 后 | hòu |
| **before** | 前 | qián |
| **until** | 到 | dào |

Location is indicated by the word zài 在, which literally means 'is located'. The word zài is used with almost all prepositions of place (words such as 'opposite' or 'behind' which indicate a spatial relationship). Note that zài comes before, but not necessarily next to, the preposition in the sentence.

| | |
|---|---|
| **The bank is opposite the hotel.** | 银行在酒店对面。<br>(lit: bank is-located hotel opposite)<br>Yínháng zài jiǔdiàn duìmiàn. |

| | |
|---|---|
| **You're sitting behind me.** | 你坐在我的后边。<br>(lit: you sit is-located my behind)<br>Nǐ zuò zài wǒde hòubian. |

# QUESTIONS

## Asking Questions • Answering Questions • Negating

The most common way of forming questions in Mandarin is simply to put the particle ma 吗 at the end of a statement.

| | |
|---|---|
| **He's going to see the Great Wall.** | 他要去长城。<br>(lit: he going Great-Wall)<br>Tā yào qù Chángchéng. |
| **Is he going to see the Great Wall?** | 他要去长城吗？<br>(lit: he going Great-Wall ma)<br>Tā yào qù Chángchéng ma? |

### - QUESTION WORDS -

| | | |
|---|---|---|
| **who** | 谁 | shéi/shuí |
| **which** | 哪个 | năge |
| **what** | 什么 | shénme |
| **where** | 哪儿 | năr |
| **how** | 怎么 | zěnme |
| **when** | 什么时候 | shénme shíhòu |

Mandarin doesn't have words that correspond directly to 'yes' and 'no' when used in isolation. To answer a question in the affirmative, you simply repeat the verb used in the question. To answer a question in the negative, place the negative particle bù 不 'not' before the repeated verb. The particle ma 吗 is a question marker (see above for an explanation).

| | |
|---|---|
| **Are you hungry?** | 你饿吗？<br>(lit: you hungry ma)<br>Nǐ è ma? |

| | |
|---|---|
| **Yes.** | 饿。(lit: hungry)<br>È. |
| **No.** | 不饿。(lit: not hungry)<br>Bù è. |

You're likely to hear the word duì 对 as an equivalent to 'yes' as well. It literally means 'correct'. In the negative, this becomes bù duì 不对 ('not correct').

| | |
|---|---|
| **Are you leaving tomorrow?** | 你明天走吗?<br>(lit: you tomorrow leave ma)<br>Nǐ míngtiān zǒu ma? |
| **Yes, I am.** | 对，明天走。<br>(lit: correct tomorrow leave)<br>Duì, míngtiān zǒu. |
| **No, I'm leaving today.** | 不(对)，我今天走。<br>(lit: not (correct) I today leave)<br>Bù (duì), wǒ jīntiān zǒu. |

## VERBS

### Doing Things • Expressing Past/Future Actions

Mandarin verbs have fixed forms – they don't change form according to who or what the subject (the person or thing performing the action of the verb) is, as they do in English, eg 'I am' vs 'you are' etc. Only one form of each verb exists, so there's no need to memorise long lists of varying verb forms as you may have had to do when learning other languages. To see how this works, look at the following table for the verb chī 吃 'eat'.

**– PRESENT TENSE –**

| | | | |
|---|---|---|---|
| **I eat a meal.** | 我吃饭。<br>Wǒ chī fàn. | **We eat a meal.** | 我们吃饭。<br>Wǒmen chī fàn. |
| **You eat a meal. sg** | 你吃饭。<br>Nǐ chī fàn. | **You eat a meal. pl** | 你们吃饭。<br>Nǐmen chī fàn. |
| **He/She eats a meal.** | 他/她/它吃饭。<br>Tā chī fàn. | **They eat a meal.** | 他们吃饭。<br>Tāmen chī fàn. |

Not only do Mandarin verbs not change according to who or what is performing the action of the verb, but they also remain fixed regardless of when the action took place, ie they don't change according to tense. The time something takes place can be, instead, conveyed by the use of adverbs of time (words that modify a verb and indicate time). So to talk about things in the past, present or future, you place an adverb of time – such as 'a while ago' (yǐqián 以前), 'last year' (qùnián 去年), 'now' (xiànzài 现在), 'tomorrow' (míngtiān 明天) or '(this) morning' (zǎoshàng 早上) – before the verb to specify when the action took place.

| | |
|---|---|
| **Tomorrow I'm going to Beijing.** | 我明天去北京。<br>(lit: I tomorrow go Beijing)<br>Wǒ míngtiān qù Běijīng. |
| **Now she lives in Beijing.** | 她现在住在北京。<br>(lit: she now live in Beijing)<br>Tā xiànzài zhù zài Běijīng. |
| **In the morning I didn't eat anything.** | 我早上什么也没吃。<br>(lit: I morning anything not eat)<br>Wǒ zǎoshàng shénme yě méi chī. |

## Past Tense Alternative Forms

The particle le 了 can be added to a verb to indicate that an action has been completed. In many cases this is just like the past tense in English.

| | |
|---|---|
| **He has gone to Shanghai.** | 他去了上海。<br>(lit: he go-le Shanghai)<br>Tā qùle Shànghǎi. |

For things that have happened some time in the unspecified past, the particle guò 过 is used.

| | |
|---|---|
| **He's been to Taiwan.** | 他去过台湾。<br>(lit: he go-guò Taiwan)<br>Tā qùguò Táiwān. |

### Future Tense Alternative Forms

The verb yào 要 'want', when placed before a verb, can be used to indicate the future. For less certain future actions, it can be replaced with xiǎng 想 'feel like' or dǎsuàn 打算 'plan to'.

| | |
|---|---|
| **I'm going to Hong Kong.** | 我要去香港。<br>(lit: I want go Hong-Kong)<br>Wǒ yào qù Xiānggǎng. |
| **I feel like going to Hong Kong.** | 我想去香港。<br>(lit: I feel-like go Hong-Kong)<br>Wǒ xiǎng qù Xiānggǎng. |
| **I'm planning to go to Hong Kong.** | 我打算去香港。<br>(lit: I plan-to go Hong-Kong)<br>Wǒ dǎsuàn qù Xiānggǎng. |

## WANT

### Making Statements

The equivalent of 'to want' in Mandarin is the verb xiǎng 想. To say you don't want something, just place the negative particle bù 不 'not' before xiǎng.

| | |
|---|---|
| **I want to eat.** | 我想吃。(lit: I want eat)<br>Wǒ xiǎng chī. |
| **I don't want to eat.** | 我不想吃。(lit: I not want eat)<br>Wǒ bù xiǎng chī. |

## WORD ORDER

### Making Statements

Word order of basic sentences in Mandarin is the same as in English, ie subject-verb-object.

| | |
|---|---|
| **I eat a meal.** | 我吃饭。(lit: I eat rice)<br>Wǒ chī fàn. |

# BASICS

| | |
|---|---|
| UNDERSTANDING | 32 |
| NUMBERS & AMOUNTS | 34 |
| TIME & DATES | 38 |

# Understanding

## KEY PHRASES

| | | |
|---|---|---|
| **Do you speak English?** | 你会说英文吗？ | Nǐ huìshuō Yīngwén ma? |
| **I don't understand.** | 我不明白。 | Wǒ bù míngbai. |
| **What does ... mean?** | ……是什么意思？ | ... shì shénme yìsi? |

| | |
|---|---|
| (Q) **Do you speak English?** | 你会说英文吗？<br>Nǐ huìshuō Yīngwén ma? |
| (Q) **Does anyone speak English?** | 有谁会说英文吗？<br>Yǒu shéi huìshuō Yīngwén ma? |
| (A) **I speak a little.** | 我会说一点。<br>Wǒ huìshuō yīdiǎn. |
| (Q) **Do you understand?** | 你明白吗？<br>Nǐ míngbai ma? |
| (A) **I understand.** | 明白。<br>Míngbai. |
| (A) **I don't understand.** | 我不明白。<br>Wǒ bù míngbai. |
| **Could you write that in Pinyin for me?** | 请用拼音写。<br>Qǐng yòng Pīnyīn xiě. |
| **Could you write that down for me in Chinese characters?** | 请用中文写下来。<br>Qǐng yòng Zhōngwén xiěxiàlái. |
| **Please point to the phrase in this book.** | 请指出书上的范句。<br>Qǐng zhǐchū shūshàng de fànjù. |

### LANGUAGE TIP: TONES & TONGUE TWISTERS

Mandarin is a tonal language (see **pronunciation**, p13). While this can be a challenge for the foreign visitor to China, it's also a source of mirth for locals who happen upon outsiders. For example, foreign diplomats (wàijiāoguān 外交官) often introduce themselves in Mandarin as wāijiāoguǎn 歪胶管 (lit: 'rubber U-bend pipes').

Fortunately, not only foreigners have trouble with Mandarin pronunciation. Southerners, particularly Cantonese speakers, are notorious in Beijing for getting their sibilants (the sounds 's', 'sh' and 'z') mixed up. Practice with tongue twisters, such as this one:

| | |
|---|---|
| 四十四只石狮子是死的。 | sìshísì zhī shíshīzǐ shì sǐde<br>Forty-four stone lions are dead. |

| | |
|---|---|
| **What does ... mean?** | ……是什么意思?<br>... shì shénme yìsi? |
| **How do you pronounce this?** | 怎么念这个?<br>Zěnme niàn zhège? |
| **How do you write ...?** | 怎么写...?<br>Zěnme xiě ......? |
| **Could you please repeat that?** | 请你再说一遍?<br>Qǐng nǐ zài shuō yībiàn? |
| **Could you please write it down?** | 请你写下来?<br>Qǐng nǐ xiěxiàlái? |
| **Could you please speak more slowly?** | 请你慢一点说?<br>Qǐng nǐ màn yīdiǎn shuō? |

| **Slowly, please.** | 请慢点。 | Qǐng màndiǎn. |
|---|---|---|

# Numbers & Amounts

## KEY PHRASES

| | | |
|---|---|---|
| **How much?** | 多少？ | Duōshǎo? |
| **a few** | 一些 | yīxiē |
| **many** | 许多 | xǔduō |

## CARDINAL NUMBERS

Numbers in Mandarin are easy to learn. Multiples of 10 are made by stating the multiple followed by 10 – so 20 is literally 'two ten'. Two is a tricky number, generally pronounced èr unless it's joined with a classifier, in which case it will be pronounced liǎng (see **classifiers/counters**, page 20).

| | | |
|---|---|---|
| **0** | 零 | líng |
| **1** | 一 | yī |
| **2** | 二/两 | èr/liǎng |
| **3** | 三 | sān |
| **4** | 四 | sì |
| **5** | 五 | wǔ |
| **6** | 六 | liù |
| **7** | 七 | qī |
| **8** | 八 | bā |
| **9** | 九 | jiǔ |
| **10** | 十 | shí |
| **11** | 十一 | shíyī |
| **12** | 十二 | shí'èr |
| **13** | 十三 | shísān |

| | | |
|---|---|---|
| **14** | 十四 | shísì |
| **15** | 十五 | shíwǔ |
| **16** | 十六 | shíliù |
| **17** | 十七 | shíqī |
| **18** | 十八 | shíbā |
| **19** | 十九 | shíjiǔ |
| **20** | 二十 | èrshí |
| **21** | 二十一 | èrshíyī |
| **22** | 二十二 | èrshí'èr |
| **30** | 三十 | sānshí |
| **40** | 四十 | sìshí |
| **50** | 五十 | wǔshí |
| **60** | 六十 | liùshí |
| **70** | 七十 | qīshí |
| **80** | 八十 | bāshí |
| **90** | 九十 | jiǔshí |
| **100** | 一百 | yībǎi |
| **101** | 一百零一 | yībǎi língyī |
| **103** | 一百零三 | yībǎi língsān |
| **113** | 一百一十三 | yībǎi yīshísān |
| **122** | 一百二十二 | yībǎi èrshí'èr |
| **200** | 两百 | liǎngbǎi |
| **1000** | 一千 | yīqiān |
| **10,000** | 一万 | yīwàn |
| **1,000,000** | 一百万 | yībǎiwàn |
| **100,000,000** | 一亿 | yīyì |

## ORDINAL NUMBERS

| | | |
|---|---|---|
| **1st** | 第一 | dìyī |
| **2nd** | 第二 | dì'èr |
| **3rd** | 第三 | dìsān |
| **4th** | 第四 | dìsì |
| **5th** | 第五 | dìwǔ |

## FRACTIONS

| | | |
|---|---|---|
| **a quarter** | 四分之一 | sìfēnzhīyī |
| **a third** | 三分之一 | sānfēnzhīyī |
| **a half** | 一半 | yībàn |
| **three-quarters** | 四分之三 | sìfēnzhīsān |
| **all** | 所有 | suǒyǒu |
| **none** | 没有 | méiyǒu |

## CLASSIFIERS/COUNTERS

The following are the most commonly used classifiers or 'counters', used when counting things (see also **grammar**, page 20).

| | | |
|---|---|---|
| **generic classifier** | 个 | gè |
| **flat things (tickets, stamps etc)** | 张 | zhāng |
| **long things (fish, snakes, rivers etc)** | 条 | tiáo |
| **people** | 位 | wèi |
| **nondescript animals (dogs, chickens etc)** | 只 | zhī |
| **big things (buildings, mountains, etc)** | 座 | zuò |

# AMOUNTS

China uses a complete set of words for imperial weights and measures. In mainland China (though not in Hong Kong or Taiwan) these have all been recast in metric mould, so that foreign visitors are, at most, required to multiply by two to yield a standard international metric measure.

| | |
|---|---|
| **How much?** | 多少？<br>Duōshǎo? |
| **How many?** | 几个？<br>Jǐge? |
| **Please give me ...** | 请给我……<br>Qǐng gěi wǒ ... |

| | | |
|---|---|---|
| **(50) grams** | (50)克 | (wǔshí) kè |
| **one Chinese ounce (50 grams)** | 1两 | yīliǎng |
| **one *jīn* (about 0.6kg)** | 1斤 | yījīn |
| **(two) *jīn*** | (两)斤 | (liǎng) jīn |
| **a kilo** | 1公斤 | yìgōngjīn |
| **(two) kilos** | (两)公斤 | (liǎng) gōngjīn |
| **a few** | 一些 | yīxiē |
| **less** | 少一点 | shǎoyīdiǎn |
| **a little** | 一小块 | yīxiǎokuài |
| **a lot** | 好多 | hǎoduō |
| **many** | 许多 | xǔduō |
| **more** | 多一些 | duōyīxiē |
| **some** | 一些 | yīxiē |

# Time & Dates

## KEY PHRASES

| | | |
|---|---|---|
| **What time is it?** | 现在几点钟？ | Xiànzài jǐdiǎn zhōng? |
| **At what time?** | 什么时候？ | Shénme shíhòu? |
| **What date is it?** | 今天几号？ | Jīntiān jǐhào? |

## TELLING THE TIME

Telling the time in Mandarin is simple. To express a time on the hour, simply give the hour followed by diǎn 点 'point' and zhōng 钟 'clock'. For all other times, give the hour followed by diǎn 点 and then the number of minutes past the hour followed by the word fēn 分 'minutes'. For example, the literal translation of 'quarter past 10' is '10 points 15 minutes'.

| | | |
|---|---|---|
| Q **What time is it?** | 现在几点钟？ | Xiànzài jǐdiǎn zhōng? |
| A **It's (10) o'clock.** | (十)点钟。 | (Shí)diǎn zhōng. |
| **Five past (10).** | (十)点零五分。 | (Shí)diǎn língwǔfēn. |
| **Quarter past (10).** | (十)点十五分。 | (Shí)diǎn shíwǔfēn. |
| **Half past (10).** | (十)点三十分。 | (Shí)diǎn sānshífēn. |
| **Twenty to (11).** | (十)点四十分。 | (Shí)diǎn sìshífēn. |
| **Quarter to (11).** | (十)点四十五分。 | (Shí)diǎn sìshíwǔfēn. |
| **am** | 早上 | zǎoshàng |
| **pm** | 晚上 | wǎnshàng |

| | | |
|---|---|---|
| **Q At what time (does it start)?** | 什么时候（开始）？ | Shénme shíhòu (kāishǐ)? |
| **A (It starts) At 10.** | 十点钟（开始）。 | Shídiǎn zhōng (kāishǐ). |
| **A It starts at (9:57pm).** | （晚上9点57分）开始。 | (Wǎnshàng jiǔdiǎn wǔshíqīfēn) kāishǐ. |

Time during the day is divided up slightly differently in Mandarin than it is in English. In China, meals are considered so important that parts of the day are defined as falling before or after meals.

| | | |
|---|---|---|
| **afternoon** | 下午 | xiàwǔ |
| **dawn (before breakfast)** | 黎明 | límíng |
| **day** | 白天 | báitiān |
| **early morning (after breakfast)** | 早上 | zǎoshàng |
| **evening (after dinner)** | 晚上 | wǎnshàng |
| **late morning (before lunch)** | 上午 | shàngwǔ |
| **midday (lunch & siesta time)** | 中午 | zhōngwǔ |
| **night (sleep time)** | 深夜 | shēnyè |
| **sunrise** | 日出 | rìchū |
| **sunset** | 日落 | rìluò |

## THE CALENDAR

The days of the week follow a simple pattern in Mandarin. The word 'week' (xīngqī 星期) comes first, followed by numbers one to six (starting with Monday). Sunday is the 'day of heaven' – the day of worship in the Western world, from which the seven-day week was introduced.

| | | |
|---|---|---|
| **Monday** | 星期一 | xīngqī yī |
| **Tuesday** | 星期二 | xīngqī èr |
| **Wednesday** | 星期三 | xīngqī sān |
| **Thursday** | 星期四 | xīngqī sì |
| **Friday** | 星期五 | xīngqī wǔ |
| **Saturday** | 星期六 | xīngqī liù |
| **Sunday** | 星期天 | xīngqī tiān |

As with the days of the week, the months in Mandarin follow a system of pure logic. The word 'month' (yuè 月) is prefaced with the numbers one to twelve starting with January. The Western-style calendar was only imported in China some 200 years ago and, as this new calendar was felt to be foreign enough, further complicated linguistic terms were thought best avoided.

| | | |
|---|---|---|
| **January** | 一月 | yīyuè |
| **February** | 二月 | èryuè |
| **March** | 三月 | sānyuè |
| **April** | 四月 | sìyuè |
| **May** | 五月 | wǔyuè |
| **June** | 六月 | liùyuè |
| **July** | 七月 | qīyuè |
| **August** | 八月 | bāyuè |
| **September** | 九月 | jiǔyuè |
| **October** | 十月 | shíyuè |
| **November** | 十一月 | shíyīyuè |
| **December** | 十二月 | shí'èryuè |

| | | |
|---|---|---|
| Q **What date is it?** | 今天几号？ | Jīntiān jǐhào? |
| A **It's (18 October).** | （十月十八号）。 | (Shíyuè shíbā hào). |

| | | |
|---|---|---|
| **spring** | 春天 | chūntiān |
| **summer** | 夏天 | xiàtiān |
| **autumn** | 秋天 | qiūtiān |
| **winter** | 冬天 | dōngtiān |

## PRESENT

| | | |
|---|---|---|
| **now** | 现在 | xiànzài |
| **today** | 今天 | jīntiān |
| **this morning (after breakfast)** | 这个早上 | zhège zǎoshàng |
| **this morning (before lunch)** | 这个上午 | zhège shàngwǔ |
| **this afternoon** | 这个下午 | zhège xiàwǔ |
| **tonight** | 今天晚上 | jīntiān wǎnshàng |
| **this week** | 这个星期 | zhège xīngqī |
| **this month** | 这个月 | zhège yuè |
| **this year** | 今年 | jīnnián |

## PAST

| | | |
|---|---|---|
| **(three days) ago** | (三天) 以前 | (sāntiān) yǐqián |
| **day before yesterday** | 前天 | qiántiān |
| **yesterday morning (after breakfast)** | 昨天早上 | zuótiān zǎoshàng |
| **yesterday morning (before lunch)** | 昨天上午 | zuótiān shàngwǔ |
| **yesterday afternoon** | 昨天下午 | zuótiān xiàwǔ |
| **yesterday evening (after dinner)** | 昨天晚上 | zuótiān wǎnshàng |

| | | |
|---|---|---|
| **last night** | 昨天晚上 | zuótiān wǎnshàng |
| **last week** | 上个星期 | shàngge xīngqī |
| **last month** | 上个月 | shàngge yuè |
| **last year** | 去年 | qùnián |
| **since (May)** | 从(五月)以来 | cóng (wǔyuè) yǐlái |

# FUTURE

| | | |
|---|---|---|
| **in (six days)** | (六天)以后 | (liùtiān) yǐhòu |
| **day after tomorrow** | 后天 | hòutiān |
| **tomorrow morning (after breakfast)** | 明天早上 | míngtiān zǎoshàng |
| **tomorrow morning (before lunch)** | 明天上午 | míngtiān shàngwǔ |
| **tomorrow afternoon** | 明天下午 | míngtiān xiàwǔ |
| **tomorrow evening (after dinner)** | 明天晚上 | míngtiān wǎnshàng |
| **next week** | 下个星期 | xiàge xīngqī |
| **next month** | 下个月 | xiàge yuè |
| **next year** | 明年 | míngnián |
| **until (June)** | 到(六月)为止 | dào (liùyuè) wéizhǐ |

# PRACTICAL

TRANSPORT 44

BORDER CROSSING 61

DIRECTIONS 63

ACCOMMODATION 66

SHOPPING 78

COMMUNICATIONS 88

MONEY & BANKING 94

BUSINESS 97

SIGHTSEEING 100

SENIORS & TRAVELLERS WITH DISABILITIES 106

TRAVEL WITH CHILDREN 108

# Transport

## KEY PHRASES

| | | |
|---|---|---|
| **When's the next bus?** | 下一趟车几点走? | Xià yītàng chē jǐdiǎn zǒu? |
| **A ticket to ...** | 一张到……的票。 | Yīzhāng dào ... de piào. |
| **Can you tell me when we get to ...?** | 到了……请叫我,好吗? | Dàole ... qǐng jiào wǒ, hǎoma? |
| **Please take me to this address.** | 请带我到这个地址。 | Qǐng dàiwǒ dào zhège dìzhǐ. |
| **I'd like to hire a self-drive car.** | 我想租一辆轿车。 | Wǒ xiǎng zū yīliàng jiàochē. |

## GETTING AROUND

| | |
|---|---|
| **Which ... goes to (Hangzhou)?** | 到(杭州)坐什么……?<br>Dào (Hángzhōu) zuò shénme ... ? |
| **Is this the ... to (Hangzhou)?** | 这个……到(杭州)去吗?<br>Zhège ... dào (Hángzhōu) qù ma? |

| | | |
|---|---|---|
| **boat** | 船 | chuán |
| **bus** | 车 | chē |
| **plane** | 飞机 | fēijī |
| **train** | 火车 | huǒchē |

| | |
|---|---|
| **When's the first (bus)?** | 首班(车)几点走?<br>Shǒubān (chē) jǐdiǎn zǒu? |
| **When's the last (bus)?** | 末班(车)几点走?<br>Mòbān (chē) jǐdiǎn zǒu? |
| **When's the next (bus)?** | 下一趟(车)几点走?<br>Xià yītàng (chē) jǐdiǎn zǒu? |
| **What time does it leave?** | 几点钟出发?<br>Jǐdiǎnzhōng chūfā? |
| **What time does it get to (Hangzhou)?** | 几点钟到(杭州)?<br>Jǐdiǎnzhōng dào (Hángzhōu)? |
| **How long will it be delayed?** | 推迟多久?<br>Tuīchí duōjiǔ? |
| **Is this seat free?** | 这儿有人吗?<br>Zhèr yǒurén ma? |

| **Is it free?** | 有人? | Yǒurén? |
|---|---|---|

| | |
|---|---|
| **That's my seat.** | 那是我的座。<br>Nà shì wǒde zùo. |
| **Can you tell me when we get to (Hangzhou)?** | 到了(杭州)请叫我, 好吗?<br>Dàole (Hángzhōu) qǐng jiào wǒ, hǎoma? |
| **I want to get off here.** | 我想这儿下车。<br>Wǒ xiǎng zhèr xiàchē. |
| **How long do we stop here?** | 在这里停多久?<br>Zài zhèlǐ tíng duōjiǔ? |
| **Are you waiting for more people?** | 还等人吗?<br>Háiděng rén ma? |
| **Can you take us around the city, please?** | 请带我到城里转一圈?<br>Qǐng dàiwǒ dào chénglǐ zhuàn yī quān. |
| **How many people can ride on this?** | 车上能坐多少人?<br>Chēshàng néngzùo duōshǎo rén? |

# BUYING TICKETS

On Chinese trains there are no classes, instead the options are: hard seat (yìngzuò 硬座) or soft seat (ruǎnzuò 软座) and hard sleeper (yìngwò 硬卧) or soft sleeper (ruǎnwò 软卧). Classes do exist on long-distance boat services in China.

**Where do I buy a ticket?**
哪里买票？
Nǎli mǎi piào?

**Do I need to book?**
要先订票吗？
Yào xiān dìngpiào ma?

**A ... ticket to (Dalian).**
一张到(大连)的……票。
Yīzhāng dào (Dàlián) de ... piào.

| | | |
|---|---|---|
| **1st-class** | 头等 | tóuděng |
| **2nd-class** | 二等 | èrděng |
| **3rd-class** | 三等 | sānděng |
| **child's** | 儿童 | értóng |
| **one-way** | 单程 | dānchéng |
| **return** | 来回 | láihuí |
| **student** | 学生 | xuéshēng |

**I want to travel by ... train.**
我想坐……
Wǒxiǎng zuò ...

| | | |
|---|---|---|
| **direct** | 直达车 | zhídá chē |
| **express** | 特快车 | tèkuài chē |
| **fast** | 快车 | kuài chē |
| **local** | 普通车 | pǔtōng chē |
| **slow** | 慢车 | màn chē |

**I'd like a hard-seat ticket.**
我想买硬座票。
Wǒ xiǎng mǎi yìngzuò piào.

**I'd like a soft-seat ticket.**
我想买软座票。
Wǒ xiǎng mǎi ruǎnzuò piào.

# Buying a Ticket

WHAT TIME IS THE NEXT ...?
下一趟……几点走?
Xià yītàng ... jǐdiǎn zǒu?

BOAT
船
chuán

BUS
车
chē

TRAIN
火车
huǒchē

ONE ... TICKET, PLEASE.
一张到的……票。
Yīzhāng dào de ... piào.

ONE-WAY
单程
dānchéng

RETURN
来回
láihuí

I'D LIKE A/AN ... SEAT.
我想要……的座位。
Wǒ xiǎngyào ... de zuòwèi.

AISLE
靠走廊
kào zǒuláng

WINDOW
靠窗户
kào chuānghu

WHICH PLATFORM DOES IT DEPART FROM?
这列火车从几号站台出发?
Zhèliè huǒchē cóng jǐhào zhàntái chūfā?

## CULTURE TIP: BUYING TICKETS

Trains, particularly high-speed trains, are the best way to travel long distances in China. Tickets are usually released 15 days in advance. Reserve online as early as possible. Trip.com has an English interface. Don't buy them at the last minute. You can buy at the stations but expect to queue. Ticket windows may sometimes be unstaffed and you may have to find someone to serve you. If you decide to buy at the station, bring your passport and ask around with these phrases:

| | |
|---|---|
| **Do you speak English?** | 你会说英文吗？<br>Nǐ huìshuō Yīngwén ma? |
| **Does anyone speak English?** | 有谁会说英文吗？<br>Yǒu shéi huìshuō Yīngwén ma? |

Even better, you could show the staff a screenshot of your ticket details in Mandarin script. Use these phrases to help devise your message:

| | |
|---|---|
| **Could you write down the ticket details in Chinese characters for me?** | 请帮我用中文写车票的详细情况。<br>Qǐng bāngwǒ yòng zhōngwén xiě chēpiào de xiángxì qíngkuàng. |
| **Could you write down (Dalian) in Chinese characters?** | 请帮我用中文写下(大连)。<br>Qǐng bāngwǒ yòng zhōngwén xiěxià (Dàlián). |

With this in hand, you should be assured of obtaining your ticket to ride.

For regular trains, you can say:

| | |
|---|---|
| **I'd like a hard-sleeper berth.** | 我想坐硬卧。<br>Wǒ xiǎng zuò yìngwò. |
| **I'd like a soft-sleeper berth.** | 我想坐软卧。<br>Wǒ xiǎng zuò ruǎnwò. |
| **I'd like a bottom berth.** | 我想睡下铺。<br>Wǒ xiǎng shuì xiàpù. |
| **I'd like a middle berth.** | 我想睡中铺。<br>Wǒ xiǎng shuì zhōngpù. |
| **I'd like an upper berth.** | 我想睡上铺。<br>Wǒ xiǎng shuì shàngpù. |
| **I'd like an aisle seat.** | 我想要靠走廊的座位。<br>Wǒ xiǎngyào kào zǒuláng de zuòwèi. |
| **I'd like a window seat.** | 我想要靠窗户的座位。<br>Wǒ xiǎngyào kào chuānghu de zuòwèi. |
| **I'd like a (non)smoking seat.** | 我想要(不)吸烟的座位。<br>Wǒ xiǎngyào (bù) xīyān de zuòwèi. |

## LISTEN FOR

| | | |
|---|---|---|
| 到哪里? | Dào nǎli? | Where to? |
| 旅行社 | lǚxíng shè | travel agent |
| 满 | mǎn | full |
| 取消 | qǔxiāo | cancelled |
| 时刻表 | shíkè biǎo | timetable |
| 售票窗 | shòupiào chuāng | ticket window |
| 晚点 | wǎndiǎn | delayed |
| 站台 | zhàntái | platform |
| 这个/那个 | zhège/nàge | this one/that one |

| | |
|---|---|
| **Is there (a) ...?** | 有……吗？<br>Yǒu ... ma? |

| | | |
|---|---|---|
| **air-conditioning** | 空调 | kōngtiáo |
| **blanket** | 毛毯 | máotǎn |
| **sick bag** | 呕吐袋 | ǒutù dài |
| **toilet** | 厕所 | cèsuǒ |

| | |
|---|---|
| **I'd like to cancel my ticket.** | 我想退票。<br>Wǒ xiǎng tuì piào. |
| **I'd like to change my ticket.** | 我想改票。<br>Wǒ xiǎng gǎi piào. |
| **I'd like to confirm my ticket.** | 我想确定票。<br>Wǒ xiǎng quèdìng piào. |
| **Can I get a stand-by ticket?** | 能买站台票吗？<br>Néng mǎi zhàntái piào ma? |
| **How much is a (soft-seat) fare to ...?** | 到……的（软座票）多少钱？<br>Dào ... de (ruǎnzuò piào) duōshǎo qián? |
| **How long does the trip take?** | 几个小时到站？<br>Jǐge xiǎoshí dàozhàn? |
| **Is it a direct route?** | 是直达的吗？<br>Shì zhídáde ma? |
| **What time should I check in?** | 什么时候检票？<br>Shénme shíhou jiǎnpiào? |
| **Which platform does it depart from?** | 这列火车从几号站台出发？<br>Zhèliè huǒchē cóng jǐhào zhàntái chūfā? |

## LUGGAGE

| | |
|---|---|
| **Can I have some coins/tokens?** | 我想换一些硬币？<br>Wǒ xiǎng huàn yīxiē yìngbì. |

LISTEN FOR

| | | |
|---|---|---|
| 超重行李 | chāozhòng xíngli | excess baggage |
| 手提行李 | shǒutí xíngli | carry-on baggage |
| 行李票 | xíngli piào | ticket |

**Where can I find ...?** ……在哪里？ ... zài nǎli?

| | | |
|---|---|---|
| **the baggage claim** | 取行李 | qǔ xíngli |
| **the left-luggage office** | 行李寄存处 | xíngli jìcún chù |
| **a luggage locker** | 行李暂存箱 | xíngli zàncúnxiāng |
| **a trolley** | 小推车 | xiǎo tuīchē |

| | |
|---|---|
| **My luggage has been damaged.** | 我的行李被摔坏了。<br>Wǒde xíngli bèi shuāihuài le. |
| **My luggage has been lost.** | 我的行李被弄丢了。<br>Wǒde xíngli bèi nòngdiū le. |
| **My luggage has been stolen.** | 我的行李被偷走了。<br>Wǒde xíngli bèi tōuzǒu le. |

## PLANE

| | |
|---|---|
| **Where does flight (BJ8) depart?** | (BJ8) 飞机在哪里起飞？<br>(BJ8)* bā fēijī zài nǎli qǐfēi? |
| **Where does flight (BJ8) arrive?** | (BJ8) 飞机在哪里抵达？<br>(BJ8)* bā fēijī zài nǎli dǐdá? |

* use English pronunciation for flight number

| Where's ...? | ……在哪里？<br>... zài nǎli? |
|---|---|

| | | |
|---|---|---|
| the airport shuttle | 机场巴士 | jīchǎng bāshì |
| arrivals | 入境口 | rùjìng kǒu |
| departures | 出境口 | chūjìng kǒu |
| the duty-free shop | 免税店 | miǎnshuì diàn |
| gate (8) | (8号)登机口 | (bā hào) dēngjī kǒu |

## BUS

| | |
|---|---|
| How often do buses come? | 多久来一班车？<br>Duōjiǔ lái yībān chē? |
| Which number bus goes to (Harbin)? | 到(哈尔滨)坐几号车？<br>Dào (Hā'ěrbīn) zuò jǐhào chē? |
| Does it stop at (Harbin)? | 在(哈尔滨)能下车吗？<br>Zài (Hā'ěrbīn) néng xià chē ma? |
| What's the next stop? | 下一站是哪里？<br>Xiàyī zhàn shì nǎli? |
| I'd like to get off at (Harbin). | 我在(哈尔滨)下车。<br>Wǒ zài (Hā'ěrbīn) xià chē. |
| Please stop pushing! | 不要挤！<br>Bùyào jǐ! |
| boarding pass | 登机牌<br>dēngjī pái |
| passport | 护照<br>hùzhào |
| transfer | 转机<br>zhuǎnjī |
| transit | 过境<br>guòjìng |

| | |
|---|---|
| **city** a | 市内<br>shìnèi |
| **city bus** | 市内大巴<br>shìnèi dàbā |
| **intercity** a | 长途<br>chángtú |
| **intercity bus** | 长途车<br>chángtú chē |
| **local** a | 本地<br>běndì |
| **private-run bus** | 小巴<br>xiǎobā |
| **sleeper bus** | 卧铺长途车<br>wòpù chángtú chē |

## SUBWAY & TRAIN

| | |
|---|---|
| **Which platform for the ... train?** | ……列火车到几号站台?<br>... liè huǒchē dào jǐhào zhàntái? |
| **What station is this?** | 这是哪个站?<br>Zhè shì nǎge zhàn? |
| **What's the next station?** | 下一站是哪里?<br>Xiàyī zhàn shì nǎli? |
| **Does it stop at (Tianjin)?** | 在(天津)能下车吗?<br>Zài (Tiānjīn) néng xià chē ma? |
| **Do I need to change?** | 需要换车吗?<br>Xūyào huànchē ma? |
| **Which line goes to ...?** | 到……坐哪条线?<br>Dào ... zuò nǎtiáo xiàn? |
| **How many stops to ...?** | 到……坐几站?<br>Dào ... zuò jǐzhàn? |

| | |
|---|---|
| **Is it direct?** | 是直达车吗？<br>Shì zhítōng chē ma? |
| **Is it express?** | 是特快车吗？<br>Shì tèkuài chē ma? |
| **Which carriage is for dining?** | 吃饭到几号车厢？<br>Chīfàn dào jǐhào chēxiāng? |
| **Which carriage has the soft-sleeper seats?** | 软卧在几号车厢？<br>Ruǎnwò zài jǐhào chēxiāng? |

## BOAT

| | |
|---|---|
| **How long is the trip to ...?** | 几个小时到……？<br>Jǐge xiǎoshí dào ...? |
| **Is there a fast boat?** | 有快艇吗？<br>Yǒu kuàitǐng ma? |
| **How long will we stop here?** | 这里停留多久？<br>Zhèlǐ tíngliú duōjiǔ? |
| **What time should we be back on board?** | 几点钟再上船？<br>Jǐdiǎnzhōng zài shàngchuán? |
| **Is there karaoke on the boat?** | 船上有卡拉ＯＫ吗？<br>Chuánshàng yǒu kǎlā ōkèi ma? |
| **Are there life jackets on the boat?** | 船上有救生衣吗？<br>Chuánshàng yǒu jiùshēng yī ma? |
| **Is there a toilet on the boat?** | 船上有厕所吗？<br>Chuánshàng yǒu cèsuǒ ma? |
| **What's the sea like today?** | 今天海浪大不大？<br>Jīntiān hǎilàng dàbùdà? |
| **I feel seasick.** | 我有点恶心。<br>Wǒ yǒudiǎn ěxin. |

| | |
|---|---|
| **cabin** | 船舱<br>chuáncāng |
| **captain** | 船长<br>chuánzhǎng |
| **deck** | 甲板<br>jiǎbǎn |
| **ferry** | 渡船<br>dùchuán |
| **lifeboat** | 救生艇<br>jiùshēng tǐng |
| **life jacket** | 救生衣<br>jiùshēng yī |
| **yacht** | 帆船<br>fānchuán |

还等人吗？
Háiděng rén ma?
***Are you waiting for more people?***

# HIRE CAR & TAXI

| | |
|---|---|
| **I'd like a taxi to depart at (9am).** | 我要订一辆出租车,(早上9点钟)出发。<br>Wǒ yào dìng yīliàng chūzū chē, (zǎoshàng jiǔ diǎn zhōng) chūfā. |
| **I'd like a taxi now.** | 我要订一辆出租车,现在。<br>Wǒ yào dìng yīliàng chūzū chē, xiànzài. |
| **I'd like a taxi tomorrow.** | 我要订一辆出租车,明天。<br>Wǒ yào dìng yīliàng chūzū chē, míngtiān. |
| **Where's the taxi rank?** | 在哪里打出租车?<br>Zài nǎli dǎ chūzū chē? |
| **Is this taxi free?** | 这出租车有人吗?<br>Zhè chūzū chē yǒurén ma? |

| **Is it free?** | 有人? | Yǒurén? |
|---|---|---|

| | |
|---|---|
| **Please put the meter on.** | 请打表。<br>Qǐng dǎbiǎo. |
| **(The Great Wall), if that's OK.** | (长城),好吗?<br>(Chángchéng), hǎo ma? |
| **How much is it to (the Great Wall)?** | 到(长城)多少钱?<br>Dào (Chángchéng) duōshǎo qián? |
| **I'd like to hire a self-drive car.** | 我想租一辆轿车。<br>Wǒ xiǎng zū yīliàng jiàochē. |
| **I'd like to hire a car with a driver.** | 我想包一辆车。<br>Wǒ xiǎng bāo yīliàng chē. |
| **How much to hire a car with a driver to ...?** | 包一辆车到……多少钱?<br>Bāo yīliàng chē dào ... duōshǎo qián? |

| | |
|---|---|
| **Is it air-conditioned?** | 有空调吗？<br>Yǒu kōngtiáo ma? |
| **Is petrol/gas included?** | 包括汽油吗？<br>Bāokuò qìyóu ma? |
| **Are tolls included?** | 包括路费吗？<br>Bāokuò lùfèi ma? |
| **Could I have a receipt for the toll?** | 请给我发票？<br>Qǐng gěi wǒ fāpiào. |
| **How much is it (to this address)?** | （到这个地址）<br>多少钱？<br>(Dào zhège dìzhǐ)<br>duōshǎo qián? |
| **Please take me to (this address).** | 请带我到（这个地址）。<br>Qǐng dàiwǒ dào (zhège dìzhǐ). |

| **To ...** | 去…… | Qù ... |
|---|---|---|

| | |
|---|---|
| **Something's wrong with your meter.** | 你的表有问题。<br>Nǐde biǎo yǒuwèntí. |
| **I'll write down your licence number and call 110.** | 我会记下你的车号，<br>打110。<br>Wǒ huì jìxià nǐde chēhào,<br>dǎ yāo yāo líng. |
| **Where are we going?** | 我们到哪儿去？<br>Wǒmen dào nǎr qù? |
| **Please slow down.** | 请慢点开。<br>Qǐng màndiǎn kāi. |
| **Please stop here.** | 请在这儿停。<br>Qǐng zài zhèr tíng. |
| **Please wait here.** | 请在这儿等。<br>Qǐng zài zhèr děng. |

# BICYCLE

Bicycles are an excellent method for getting around Chinese cities or visiting tourist sites. In a country with more than 300 million bikes, some organisation is required to prevent cycle chaos. In cities you'll be required to park your bike at a bicycle parking lot known as a cúnchēchù 存车处 overseen by an attendant.

| | |
|---|---|
| **I'd like my bicycle repaired.** | 我想修这辆自行车。<br>Wǒ xiǎng xiū zhèliàng zìxíng chē. |
| **I'd like to buy a bicycle.** | 我想买一辆自行车。<br>Wǒ xiǎng mai yiliàng zìxíng chē. |
| **I'd like to hire a bicycle.** | 我想租一辆自行车。<br>Wǒ xiǎng zū yīliàng zìxíngchē |
| **I'd like a mountain bike.** | 我要辆山地车。<br>Wǒ yàoliàng shāndì chē. |
| **I'd like a racing bike.** | 我要辆赛车。<br>Wǒ yàoliàng sài chē. |
| **I'd like a second-hand bike.** | 我要辆二手车。<br>Wǒ yàoliàng èrshǒu chē. |
| **How much is it per day?** | 一天多少钱?<br>Yī tiān duōshǎo qián? |
| **How much is it per hour?** | 一小时多少钱?<br>Yī xiǎoshí duōshǎo qián? |
| **Do I have to pay a deposit?** | 要给押金吗?<br>Yào gěi yājīn ma? |
| **How much is the deposit?** | 押金多少?<br>Yājīn duōshǎo? |
| **I have a puncture.** | 车胎被戳破了。<br>Chētāi bèi chūopò le. |

| | |
|---|---|
| **Could you pump up my tyres, please?** | 能帮我打气吗？<br>Néng bāngwǒ dǎqì ma? |
| **How much to have this repaired?** | 修这些多少钱？<br>Xiū zhèxiē duōshǎo qián? |
| **Where's the bicycle parking lot?** | 存车处在哪儿？<br>Cúnchēchù zài nǎr? |
| **My bike's been stolen.** | 我的自行车被偷走了。<br>Wǒde zìxíngchē bèi tōu zǒu le |

## ☑ CULTURE TIP: CHINESE DYNASTIES

The abbreviations BCE and CE stand for 'Before Common Era' and 'Common Era' and are equivalent to the terms BC and AD.

| | |
|---|---|
| **Xia dynasty (2070–1600BCE)** | 夏朝<br>Xiàcháo |
| **Shang dynasty (1600–1046BCE)** | 商朝<br>Shāngcháo |
| **Zhou dynasty (1046–256BCE)** | 周朝<br>Zhōucháo |
| **Spring and Autumn period (770–476BCE)** | 春秋时期<br>Chūnqiū shíqī |
| **Warring States period (475–221BCE)** | 战国时期<br>Zhànguó shíqī |
| **Qin dynasty (221–207BCE)** | 秦朝<br>Qíncháo |
| **Han dynasty (206BCE–220CE)** | 汉朝<br>Hàncháo |
| **Tang dynasty (618–907CE)** | 唐朝<br>Tángcháo |
| **Song dynasty (960–1279CE)** | 宋朝<br>Sòngcháo |
| **Yuan dynasty (1279–1368)** | 元朝<br>Yuáncháo |
| **Ming dynasty (1368–1644)** | 明朝<br>Míngcháo |
| **Qing dynasty (1644–1911)** | 清朝<br>Qīngcháo |
| **Republic of China (1911–1949)** | 民国时期<br>Mínguó shíqī |
| **People's Republic (1949–present)** | 解放后<br>Jiěfàng hòu |

# Border Crossing

## KEY PHRASES

| | | |
|---|---|---|
| **I'm here for ... days.** | 我要住……天。 | Wǒ yào zhù ... tiān. |
| **I'm staying at ...** | 我住…… | Wǒ zhù ... |
| **I have nothing to declare.** | 我没有东西申报。 | Wǒ méiyǒu dōngxi shēnbào. |

## PASSPORT CONTROL

| | |
|---|---|
| **I'm ...** | 我是……来的。<br>Wǒ shì ... láide. |

| | | |
|---|---|---|
| **in transit** | 过境 | guòjìng |
| **on business** | 出差 | chūchāi |
| **on holiday** | 度假 | dùjià |
| **on a student visa** | 持学生签证 | chí xuéshēng qiānzhèng |

| | |
|---|---|
| **I'm here for (three) days.** | 我要住(三)天。<br>Wǒ yào zhù (sān) tiān. |
| **I'm here for (three) weeks.** | 我要住(三)个星期。<br>Wǒ yào zhù (sān)ge xīngqī. |
| **I'm here for (three) months.** | 我要住(三)个月。<br>Wǒ yào zhù (sān)ge yuè. |
| **I'm going to (Beijing).** | 我到(北京)去。<br>Wǒ dào (Běijīng) qù. |
| **I'm staying at (the Pujiang Hotel).** | 我住(浦江宾馆)。<br>Wǒ zhù (Pǔjiāng Bīnguǎn). |

LISTEN FOR

| | | |
|---|---|---|
| 一家 | yījiā | family |
| 团体 | tuántǐ | group |
| 护照 | hùzhào | passport |
| 签证 | qiānzhèng | visa |

| | |
|---|---|
| **The children are on this passport.** | 孩子在这个护照上。<br>Háizi zài zhège hùzhào shàng. |
| **My visa is in order.** | 我的签证办好了。<br>Wǒde qiānzhèng bànhǎole. |
| **Do I have to pay extra for that?** | 这样要加钱吗？<br>Zhèyàng yào jiāqián ma? |

## CUSTOMS

| | |
|---|---|
| **I have nothing to declare.** | 我没有东西申报。<br>Wǒ méiyǒu dōngxi shēnbào. |
| **I have something to declare.** | 我有东西申报。<br>Wǒ yǒu dōngxi shēnbào. |
| **Do I have to declare this?** | 这个要申报吗？<br>Zhège yào shēnbào ma? |
| **I didn't know I had to declare it.** | 我不知道这个要申报。<br>Wǒ bù zhīdào zhège yào shēnbào. |

LOOK FOR

| | | |
|---|---|---|
| 海关 | hǎiguān | Customs |
| 免税 | miǎnshuì | Duty Free |
| 入境 | rùjìng | Immigration |
| 护照检查 | hùzhào jiǎnchá | Passport Control |
| 检疫 | jiǎnyì | Quarantine |

# Directions

## KEY PHRASES

| | | |
|---|---|---|
| **Where's ...?** | ……在哪儿? | ... zài nǎr? |
| **What's the address?** | 什么地址? | Shénme dìzhǐ? |
| **How far is it?** | 有多远? | Yǒu duō yuǎn? |

| | |
|---|---|
| **What's the address?** | 什么地址?<br>Shénme dìzhǐ? |
| Q **Where's (a bank)?** | (银行)在哪儿?<br>(Yínháng) zài nǎr? |
| A **It's ...** | 在……<br>Zài ... |
| **It's straight ahead.** | 一直往前。<br>Yīzhí wǎngqián. |
| **It's close.** | 离这儿不远。<br>Lí zhèr bù yuǎn. |
| **Turn at the corner.** | 在拐角拐弯。<br>Zài guǎijiǎo guǎiwān. |
| **Turn at the intersection.** | 在十字路口拐弯。<br>Zài shízì lùkǒu guǎiwān. |
| **Turn at the traffic lights.** | 在红绿灯拐弯。<br>Zài hónglǜdēng guǎiwān. |
| **Turn towards the left.** | 往左拐。<br>Wǎng zuǒ guǎi. |
| **Turn towards the right.** | 往右拐。<br>Wǎng yòu guǎi. |

## LISTEN FOR

| | | |
|---|---|---|
| ……的对面 | ... de duìmiàn | opposite ... |
| ……的前面 | ... de qiánmian | in front of ... |
| ……的后面 | ... de hòumian | behind ... |
| ……附近 | ... fùjìn | near ... |
| 拐角 | guǎijiǎo | on the corner |
| 那里 | nàli | there |
| ……旁边 | ... pángbiān | next to ... |
| 这里 | zhèli | here |

| | |
|---|---|
| **How do I get there?** | 怎么走？<br>Zěnme zǒu? |
| **How far is it?** | 有多远？<br>Yǒu duō yuǎn? |
| **Can you show me on the map where I am?** | 请帮我找我在地图上的位置。<br>Qǐng bāngwǒ zhǎo wǒ zài dìtú shàng de wèizhi. |
| **Can you show me on the map where it is?** | 请帮我找它在地图上的位置。<br>Qǐng bāngwǒ zhǎo tā zài dìtú shàng de wèizhi. |
| **by bus** | 坐车去<br>zuòchē qù |
| **by subway** | 坐地铁去<br>zuò dìtiě qù |
| **by taxi** | 打车去<br>dǎchē qù |
| **by train** | 坐火车去<br>zuò huǒchē qù |
| **on foot** | 走路去<br>zǒulù qù |

| | |
|---|---|
| **north** | 北<br>běi |
| **south** | 南<br>nán |
| **east** | 东<br>dōng |
| **west** | 西<br>xī |

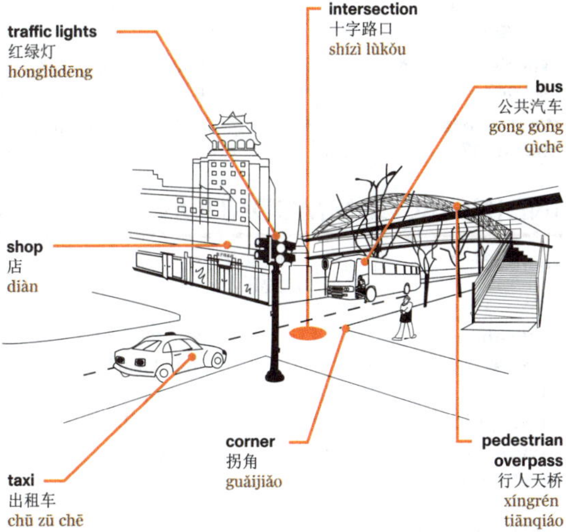

# Accommodation

## KEY PHRASES

| | | |
|---|---|---|
| **Where's a hotel?** | 哪里有酒店? | Nǎli yǒu jiǔdiàn? |
| **Do you have a double room?** | 有没有套房? | Yǒuméiyǒu tào fáng? |
| **How much is it per night?** | 每晚多少钱? | Měi wǎn duōshǎo qián? |
| **When's breakfast served?** | 几点钟吃早饭? | Jǐdiǎn zhōng chī zǎofàn? |
| **What time is checkout?** | 几点钟退房? | Jǐdiǎnzhōng tuìfáng? |

## FINDING ACCOMMODATION

**Where's a ...?** 哪里有……? Nǎli yǒu ...?

| | | |
|---|---|---|
| **guesthouse** | 宾馆 | bīnguǎn |
| **hostel** | 招待所 | zhāodàisuǒ |
| **hotel** | 酒店 | jiǔdiàn |
| **luxury hotel** | 高级酒店 | gāojí jiǔdiàn |
| **university dormitory** | 学校招待所 | xuéxiào zhāodàisuǒ |

For addresses, see **directions**, page 63.

| | |
|---|---|
| **Can you recommend somewhere ...?** | 你能推荐一个……的地方住吗？<br>Nǐ néng tuījiàn yīge ... de dìfang zhù ma? |

| | | |
|---|---|---|
| **cheap** | 便宜 | piányi |
| **good** | 好 | hǎo |
| **luxurious** | 舒服 | shūfu |
| **nearby** | 比较近 | bǐjiào jìn |
| **romantic** | 有情调 | yǒu qíngdiào |

## BOOKING AHEAD & CHECKING IN

| | |
|---|---|
| **Can foreigners stay here?** | 外国人能住这里吗？<br>Wàiguó rén néng zhù zhèlǐ ma? |
| **I'll arrange it with the PSB (Public Security Bureau).** | 我到公安局跟他们协商。<br>Wǒ dào gōng'ānjú gēn tāmen xiéshāng. |
| **I'd like to book a room, please.** | 我想订房间。<br>Wǒ xiǎng dìng fángjiān. |

| | | |
|---|---|---|
| **Are there rooms?** | 有空房吗？ | Yǒu kōngfáng ma? |

| | |
|---|---|
| **I have a reservation.** | 我有预订。<br>Wǒ yǒu yùdìng. |
| **For (three) nights.** | 住(三)天。<br>Zhù (sān) tiān. |
| **For (three) weeks.** | 住(三)个星期。<br>Zhù (sān)ge xīngqī. |
| **From (2 July) to (6 July).** | 从(7月2号)到(7月6号)。<br>Cóng (qīyuè èrhào) dào (qīyuè liùhào). |
| **Do you have a room with a bathroom?** | 有带浴室的房间吗？<br>Yǒu dài yùshì de fángjiān ma? |

## LISTEN FOR

| | | |
|---|---|---|
| 住几天? | Zhù jǐtiān? | How many nights? |
| 护照 | hùzhào | passport |
| 住满 | zhùmǎn | full |
| 前台 | qiántái | reception |
| 钥匙 | yàoshi | key |

| | |
|---|---|
| **Do you have a double room?** | 有没有套房?<br>Yǒuméiyǒu tào fáng? |
| **Do you have a single room?** | 有没有单人房?<br>Yǒuméiyǒu dānrén fáng? |
| **Do you have a twin room?** | 有没有双人房?<br>Yǒuméiyǒu shuāngrén fáng? |
| **Can I see the room?** | 能看房间吗?<br>Néng kàn fángjiān ma? |
| **I'll take it.** | 我订这间。<br>Wǒ dìng zhèjiān. |
| **I won't take it.** | 我不要。<br>Wǒ bùyào. |
| **How much is it per night?** | 每晚多少 钱?<br>Měi wǎn duōshǎo qián? |
| **How much is it per person?** | 每人多少钱?<br>Měi rén duōshǎo qián? |
| **How much is it per week?** | 每星期多少钱?<br>Měi xīngqī duōshǎo qián? |
| **Is breakfast included?** | 早餐包括在内吗?<br>Zǎocān bāokuò zàinèi ma? |
| **Do I need to pay upfront?** | 预先付钱吗?<br>Yùxiān fù qián ma? |
| **Do you give student discounts?** | 学生可以打折吗?<br>Xuéshēng kěyǐ dǎzhé ma? |

For methods of payment, see **money & banking**, page 94.

# Finding a Room

DO YOU HAVE A … ROOM?
有没有……房？
Yǒuméiyǒu ... fáng?

DOUBLE
套
tào

SINGLE
单人
dānrén

HOW MUCH IS IT PER …?
每……多少钱？
Měi ... duōshǎo qián?

NIGHT
晚
wǎn

PERSON
人
rén

IS BREAKFAST INCLUDED?
早餐包括在内吗？
Zǎocān bāokuò zàinèi ma?

CAN I SEE THE ROOM?
能看房间吗？
Néng kàn fángjiān ma?

'LL TAKE IT.
订这间。
ǒ dìng zhèjiān.

I WON'T TAKE IT.
我不要。
Wǒ bùyào.

### LOOK FOR

| | | |
|---|---|---|
| 浴室 | Yù shì | Bathroom |
| 入口 | Rù kǒu | Entry |
| 出口 | Chū kǒu | Exit |
| 女 | Nǚ | Female |
| 男 | Nán | Male |
| 前台 | Qiántái | Reception |

## REQUESTS & QUERIES

| | |
|---|---|
| **When is breakfast served?** | 几点钟吃早饭?<br>Jǐdiǎn zhōng chī zǎofàn? |
| **Where is breakfast served?** | 在哪里吃早饭?<br>Zài nǎli chī zǎofàn? |
| **Please wake me at (7am).** | (早上七点钟)<br>请叫醒我。<br>(Zǎoshàng qīdiǎnzhōng)<br>qǐng jiàoxǐng wǒ. |
| **Is there hot water all day?** | 全天有热水吗?<br>Quántiān yǒu rèshuǐ ma? |
| **Is there heating?** | 有暖气吗?<br>Yǒu nuǎnqì ma? |
| **What times does the heating come on?** | 暖气几点钟开?<br>Nuǎnqì jǐdiǎnzhōng kāi? |
| **What times does the hot water come on?** | 热水几点钟开?<br>Rèshuǐ jǐdiǎnzhōng kāi? |
| **Can I use the kitchen?** | 能用一下厨房吗?<br>Néng yòng yī xià chúfáng ma? |
| **Can I use the laundry?** | 能用一下洗衣房吗?<br>Néng yòng yī xià xǐyīfáng ma? |
| **Can I use the telephone?** | 能用一下电话吗?<br>Néng yòng yī xià diànhuà ma? |

**Do you have a/an ...?** 有没有……？ Yǒuméiyǒu ...?

| | | |
|---|---|---|
| **lift/elevator** | 电梯 | diàntī |
| **laundry service** | 洗衣服务 | xǐyī fúwù |
| **message board** | 信息栏 | xìnxī lán |
| **safe** | 保险箱 | bǎoxiǎn xiāng |
| **swimming pool** | 游泳池 | yǒuyǒng chí |

**Do you arrange tours here?** 你们能安排旅行团吗？ Nǐmen néng ānpái lǚxíng tuán ma?

**Do you change money here?** 你们能换钱吗？ Nǐmen néng huànqián ma?

**Could I have ..., please?** 能不能给我……？ Néngbùnéng gěi wǒ ...?

| | | |
|---|---|---|
| **an extra blanket** | 多一条毛毯 | duō yītiáo máotǎn |
| **my key** | 房间钥匙 | fángjiān yàoshi |
| **a mosquito net** | 一顶蚊帐 | yīdǐng wénzhàng |
| **a receipt** | 发票 | fāpiào |
| **some soap** | 一块肥皂 | yīkuài féizào |
| **a towel** | 一块毛巾 | yīkuài máojīn |

**Is there a message for me?** 有人给我留言吗？ Yǒu rén gěi wǒ liúyán ma?

**Can I leave a message for someone?** 我能留个条吗？ Wǒ néng liú ge tiáo ma?

**I'm locked out of my room.** 我进不了房间。 Wǒ jìnbùliǎo fángjiān.

## COMPLAINTS

| The room's too ... | 房间太……了。<br>Fángjiān tài ... le. |
|---|---|

| | | |
|---|---|---|
| bright | 亮 | liàng |
| cold | 冷 | lěng |
| dark | 暗 | àn |
| expensive | 贵 | guì |
| noisy | 吵 | chǎo |
| small | 小 | xiǎo |

| The ... doesn't work. | ……有毛病。<br>... yǒu máobìng. |
|---|---|

| | | |
|---|---|---|
| air-conditioning | 空调 | kōngtiáo |
| fan | 电风扇 | diànfēngshàn |
| light | 电灯 | diàndēng |
| shower | 淋浴头 | línyù tóu |
| tap/faucet | 水龙头 | shuǐlóngtóu |
| toilet | 厕所 | cèsuǒ |

| | |
|---|---|
| I saw a big rat in my room. | 我房间里有一个大老鼠。<br>Wǒ fángjiānlǐ yǒu yīge dà lǎoshǔ. |
| I saw cockroaches in my room. | 我房间里有蟑螂。<br>Wǒ fángjiānlǐ yǒu zhāngláng. |
| I saw mice in my room. | 我房间里有耗子。<br>Wǒ fángjiānlǐ yǒu hàozi. |
| Can I get an extra (blanket)? | 我能多拿一条(毛毯)吗?<br>Wǒ néng duōná yītiáo (máotǎn) ma? |
| This (pillow) isn't clean. | 这个(枕头)有点脏。<br>Zhège (zhěntou) yǒudiǎn zāng. |

# ANSWERING THE DOOR

| | |
|---|---|
| **Who is it?** | 是谁？<br>Shì shéi? |
| **Just a moment.** | 等一下。<br>Děng yī xià. |
| **Come in.** | 请进。<br>Qǐng jìn. |
| **Come back later, please.** | 请过一会儿再来。<br>Qǐng guòyīhuìr zài lái. |

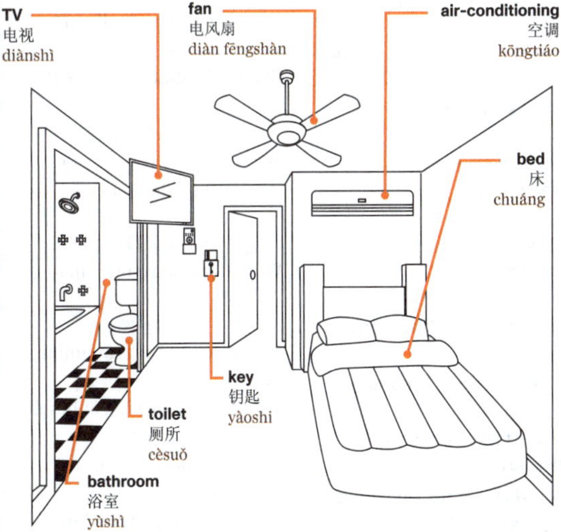

# CHECKING OUT

| | |
|---|---|
| **What time is checkout?** | 几点钟退房？<br>Jǐdiǎnzhōng tuìfáng? |
| **Can I have a late checkout?** | 我能晚点退房吗？<br>Wǒ néng wǎndiǎn tuìfáng ma? |
| **Can you call a taxi for me (for 11am)?** | 请帮我订一辆<br>(早上十一点的)车??<br>Qǐng bāng wǒ dìng yīliàng<br>(zǎoshàng shíyīdiǎn de) chē. |
| **I'm leaving now.** | 我现在走。<br>Wǒ xiànzài zǒu. |
| **Can I leave my bags here?** | 能放一下行李吗？<br>Néng fàngyīxià xíngli ma? |
| **There's a mistake in the bill.** | 帐单上有问题。<br>Zhàngdān shàng yǒu wèntí. |
| **What's that charge for?** | 这项是什么？<br>Zhè xiàng shì shénme? |
| **I had a great stay, thank you.** | 我在这儿住得很开心，谢谢。<br>Wǒ zài zhèr zhùde hěn kāixīn, xièxie. |
| **I'll recommend it to my friends.** | 我会给朋友推荐这个地方。<br>Wǒ huì gěi péngyou tuījiàn zhège dìfāng. |
| **I'll be back in (three) days.** | 我过(三)天再回来。<br>Wǒ guò (sān) tiān zài huílái. |
| **I'll be back on (Tuesday).** | 我下个(星期二)再回来。<br>Wǒ xiàge (xīngqī èr)zài huílái. |
| **Could I have my deposit, please?** | 我想拿回我的押金？<br>Wǒ xiǎng náhuí wǒde yājīn. |
| **Could I have my passport, please?** | 我想拿回我的护照？<br>Wǒ xiǎng náhuí wǒde hùzhào. |

| | |
|---|---|
| **Could I have my valuables, please?** | 我想拿回我的贵重物品？<br>Wǒ xiǎng náhuí wǒde guìzhòng wùpǐn. |

## CAMPING

| | |
|---|---|
| **Where can we spend the night?** | 晚上我们住哪里？<br>Wǎnshang wǒmen zhù nǎli? |
| **Can we camp here?** | 我们能在这里露营吗？<br>Wǒmen néng zài zhèlǐ lùyíng ma? |
| **Can we light a fire here?** | 能在这里生火吗？<br>Néng zài zhèlǐ shēnghuǒ ma? |
| **Is it safe to sleep in this place?** | 住这里安全吗？<br>Zhù zhèlǐ ānquán ma? |

哪里有酒店？

Nǎli yǒu jiǔdiàn?

***Where's a hotel?***

## RENTING

| | |
|---|---|
| **I'm here about the ... for rent.** | 我是租……来的。<br>Wǒ shì zū ... lái de. |
| **Do you have a/an ... for rent?** | 你有……出租吗?<br>Nǐyǒu ... chūzū ma? |

| | | |
|---|---|---|
| **apartment** | 公寓 | gōngyù |
| **house (basic)** | 房子 | fángzi |
| **room** | 房间 | fángjiān |
| **villa (luxurious)** | 别墅 | biéshù |

| | |
|---|---|
| **furnished** | 带家具的<br>dài jiājù de |
| **partly furnished** | 带部分家具的<br>dài bùfen jiājù de |
| **unfurnished** | 不带家具的<br>bù dài jiājù de |

## STAYING WITH LOCALS

| | |
|---|---|
| **Can I stay at your place?** | 我能在你家住吗?<br>Wǒ néng zài nǐ jiā zhù ma? |
| **Is there anything I can do to help?** | 有什么事能帮你吗?<br>Yǒu shénme shì néng bāng nǐ ma? |
| **I have my own mattress.** | 我带了自己的褥子。<br>Wǒ dàile zìjǐ de rùzi. |
| **I have my own sleeping bag.** | 我带了自己的睡袋。<br>Wǒ dàile zìjǐ de shuìdài. |
| **Can I bring anything for the meal?** | 我能带一些吃的来吗?<br>Wǒ néng dài yīxiē chī de lái ma? |

### CULTURE TIP: THANKING HOSTS

Food has great significance in Chinese culture. If you're staying in a Chinese home or have just been invited to share a meal, the surest way to gladden the hearts of your hosts is to express your appreciation of their culinary prowess. Here are two handy phrases:

| | |
|---|---|
| **The food was delicious!** | 真好吃！<br>Zhēn hǎochī! |
| **My stomach is very happy.** | 吃的真饱。<br>Chīde zhēn bǎo. |

In return, you can expect to hear this constant encouragement from your hosts to overindulge yourself:

| | |
|---|---|
| **Eat up!** | 多吃一点！<br>Duō chī yīdiǎn! |

For more dining-related phrases, see **eating out**, page 176.

| | |
|---|---|
| **Can I do the dishes?** | 我能帮你洗盘子吗？<br>Wǒ néng bāng nǐ xǐ pánzi ma? |
| **Thanks for your hospitality.** | 谢谢你的款待。<br>Xièxie nǐ de kuǎndài. |

# Shopping

## KEY PHRASES

| | | |
|---|---|---|
| **I'd like to buy ...** | 我想买…… | Wǒ xiǎng mǎi ... |
| **Can I look at it?** | 我能看看吗？ | Wǒ néng kànkan ma? |
| **Can I try it on?** | 能穿上试试吗？ | Néng chuān shàng shìshi ma? |
| **How much is it?** | 多少钱？ | Duōshǎo qián? |
| **That's too expensive.** | 太贵了。 | Tàiguì le. |

## LOOKING FOR ...

**Where's a/an ...?**
……在哪儿?
... zài nǎr?

| | | |
|---|---|---|
| **antique market** | 古董市场 | gǔdǒng shìchǎng |
| **market** | 市场 | shìchǎng |
| **shopping centre** | 商场 | shāngchǎng |
| **supermarket** | 超市 | chāoshì |

**Where can I buy (a padlock)?**
哪里能买到（锁）？
Nǎli néng mǎidào (suǒ)?

For phrases on directions, see **directions**, page 63.

## MAKING A PURCHASE

**I'm just looking.**
我先看看。
Wǒ xiān kànkan.

| | |
|---|---|
| **I'd like to buy (an adaptor plug).** | 我想买(一个插座)。<br>Wǒ xiǎng mǎi (yīge chāzuò). |
| **How much is it?** | 多少钱?<br>Duōshǎo qián? |
| **Can I look at it?** | 我能看看吗?<br>Wǒ néng kànkan ma? |
| **Please write down the price.** | 请把价钱写下来。<br>Qǐng bǎ jiàqián xiěxià lái. |
| **Do you have any others?** | 有没有别的?<br>Yǒuméiyǒu biéde? |
| **Do you accept credit cards?** | 你们收信用卡吗?<br>Nǐmen shōu xìnyòng kǎ ma? |
| **Do you accept debit cards?** | 你们收借记卡吗?<br>Nǐmen shōu jièjìkǎ ma? |
| **Can I have a bag, please?** | 请给我一个袋子?<br>Qǐng gěi wǒ yīge dàizi. |
| **Can I have a receipt, please?** | 请给我发票?<br>Qǐng gěi wǒ fāpiào. |

**Receipt, please.** 发票，谢谢。 Fāpiào, xièxie.

| | |
|---|---|
| **Could I have it wrapped?** | 能包装一下吗?<br>Néng bāozhuāng yīxià ma? |
| **Does it have a guarantee?** | 有保修期吗?<br>Yǒu bǎoxiūqī ma? |
| **Can I have it sent overseas?** | 你能寄到国外吗?<br>Nǐ néng jìdàoguówài ma? |
| **Will I be allowed to take this out of the country?** | 我能带出境吗?<br>Wǒ néng dài chūjìng ma? |
| **Can you order one for me?** | 能帮我定购一个吗?<br>Néng bāngwǒ dìnggòuyīge ma? |

| | |
|---|---|
| **Can I pick it up later?** | 过一会儿来拿，好吗？<br>Guò yīhuìr lái ná, hǎo ma? |
| **It's faulty.** | 有毛病。<br>Yǒu máobìng. |
| **This item is a fake.** | 这是假货。<br>Zhèshì jiǎhuò. |
| **I don't want to pay the full price.** | 请帮我打个折扣。<br>Qǐng bāngwǒ dǎ ge zhékòu. |
| **I'd like my change, please.** | 可以找零钱吗？<br>Kěyǐ zhǎo língqián ma? |
| **I'd like a refund, please.** | 可以退钱吗？<br>Kěyǐ tuì qián ma? |
| **I'd like to return this, please.** | 可以退换这个吗？<br>Kěyǐ tuìhuàn zhège ma? |

## BARGAINING

| | |
|---|---|
| **You're kidding!** | 开什么玩笑！<br>Kāi shénme wánxiào! |
| **That's too expensive.** | 太贵了。<br>Tàiguì le. |
| **Can you lower the price?** | 能便宜一点吗？<br>Néng piányi yīdiǎn ma? |
| **Do you have something cheaper?** | 有便宜一点的吗？<br>Yǒu piányi yīdiǎn de ma? |
| **I'll give you (five kuai).** | 给你（五块）钱。<br>Gěinǐ (wǔkuài) qián. |
| **That's my final offer.** | 就给这么多。<br>Jiù gěi zhème duō. |

# Making a Purchase

I'D LIKE TO BUY ...
我想买……
Wǒ xiǎng mǎi ...

HOW MUCH IS IT?
多少钱?
Duōshǎo qián?

**OR**

CAN YOU WRITE DOWN THE PRICE?
请把价钱写下来。
Qǐng bǎ jiàqián xiěxià lái.

DO YOU ACCEPT CREDIT CARDS?
你们收信用卡吗?
Nǐmen shōu xìnyòng kǎ ma?

COULD I HAVE A ..., PLEASE?
请给我……
Qǐng gěi wǒ ...

RECEIPT
发票
fāpiào

BAG
一个袋子
yīge dàizi

LISTEN FOR

| | | |
|---|---|---|
| 实惠 | shíhuì | a bargain |
| 大甩卖 | dàshuǎimài | grand sale |
| 打折扣 | dǎ zhékòu | on special |
| 真宰人 | zhēn zǎirén | a rip-off |
| 砍价 | kǎnjià | to bargain |

## BOOKS & READING

| | |
|---|---|
| **Is there an English-language bookshop?** | 附近有英文书店吗？ Fùjìn yǒu Yīngwén shūdiàn ma? |
| **Is there an English-language section?** | 附近有英文书吗？ Fùjìn yǒu Yīngwén shū ma? |
| **Do you have a book by (Jin Yong)?** | 有没有(金庸)的书？ Yǒuméiyǒu (Jīn Yōng) de shū? |
| **Do you have an entertainment guide?** | 有没有娱乐指南？ Yǒuméiyǒu yúlè zhǐnán? |
| **Can you recommend a book to me?** | 你能给我推荐一本好书吗？ Nǐ néng gěi wǒ tuījiàn yīběn hǎo shū ma? |

### ☑ CULTURE TIP: CHINESE WRITERS

China has a rich literary tradition. Unfortunately, unless would-be readers master the language, most of it is inaccessible to foreigners. That said, an increasing number of Chinese classics are available in translation. Look out for the works of Shen Congwen, Wang Shuo, Lao She, Ba Jin, Feng Jicai and Gao Xingjian.

# CLOTHES

| | |
|---|---|
| **My size is ...** | 我穿……号。<br>Wǒ chuān ... hào. |

| | | |
|---|---|---|
| **(40)** | (40) | (sìshí) |
| **extra large** | 特大 | tèdà |
| **large** | 大 | dà |
| **medium** | 中 | zhōng |
| **small** | 小 | xiǎo |

| | |
|---|---|
| **Can I try it on?** | 能穿上试试吗？<br>Néng chuān shàng shìshi ma? |
| **Is there a mirror?** | 有镜子吗？<br>Yǒu jìngzi ma? |
| **It doesn't fit.** | 穿得不合身。<br>Chuānde bù héshēn. |
| **Where can I find a tailor?** | 哪里能找个裁缝？<br>Nǎli néng zhǎoge cáifeng? |

For clothing items, see the **dictionary**, page 209.

# PHOTOGRAPHY

| | |
|---|---|
| **Can you print digital photos?** | 你能打印数码照片吗？<br>Nǐ néng dǎyìn shùmǎ zhàopiān ma? |
| **Can you recharge the battery?** | 你能给电池充电吗？<br>Nǐ néng gěi diànchí chōngdiàn ma? |
| **Do you have batteries for this camera?** | 你有这个相机的电池吗？<br>Nǐ yǒu zhègè xiàngjī de diànchí ma? |

多少钱？
Duōshǎo qián?
***How much is it?***

| | |
|---|---|
| **Do you have memory cards for this camera?** | 你有这个相机的内存卡吗？<br>Nǐ yǒu zhègè xiàngjī de nèicún kǎ ma? |
| **When will it be ready?** | 什么时候来取？<br>Shénme shíhòu lái qǔ? |
| **I need a passport photo taken.** | 我想拍一张护照照片。<br>Wǒ xiǎng pāi yīzhāng hùzhào zhàopiān. |
| **I'm not happy with these photos.** | 这卷洗得不好。<br>Zhè juǎn xǐde bùhǎo. |

# REPAIRS

| | |
|---|---|
| **Can I have my ... repaired here?** | 你能修我的……吗？<br>Nǐ néngxiū wǒde ... ma? |
| **When will my ... be ready?** | 什么时候来拿……？<br>Shénme shíhòu láiná ...? |

## LISTEN FOR

| | |
|---|---|
| 还要别的吗？ | Hái yào biéde ma?<br>Anything else? |
| 我能帮你吗？ | Wǒ néng bāng nǐ ma?<br>Can I help you? |
| 没有。 | Méiyǒu.<br>No, we don't have any. |

| | | |
|---|---|---|
| **backpack** | 背包 | bèibāo |
| **camera** | 照相机 | zhàoxiàngjī |
| **glasses** | 眼镜 | yǎnjìng |
| **shoes** | 鞋子 | xiézi |
| **sunglasses** | 墨镜 | mòjìng |

## SOUVENIRS

| | |
|---|---|
| **bronze** | 青铜器<br>qīngtóngqì |
| **calligraphy** | 书法<br>shūfǎ |
| **ink painting** | 水墨画/国画<br>shuǐmòhuà/guóhuà |
| **jade** | 玉器<br>yùqì |
| **oil painting** | 油画<br>yóuhuà |
| **scroll** | 挂轴<br>guàzhóu |
| **woodblock print** | 木刻<br>mùkè |

# Communications

Public wi-fi accessibility is generally good in the cities. However, some places may require a Chinese phone number to register. You can rent a mobile hotspot or buy an eSIM online before you go.

## KEY PHRASES

| | | |
|---|---|---|
| **I want to send a parcel.** | 我想寄一个包裹。 | Wǒ xiǎng jì yī gè bāoguǒ. |
| **I want to call ...** | 我想打电话到…… | Wǒ xiǎng dǎ diànhuà dào ... |
| **I'd like a SIM card.** | 我想买一张SIM卡。 | Wǒ xiǎng mǎi yī zhāng SIM kǎ. |

## THE INTERNET

| | |
|---|---|
| **Do you have internet access?** | 你这儿能上网吗？<br>Nǐ zhè'er néng shàngwǎng ma? |
| **Is there wireless internet access here?** | 这里有无线网络讯号吗？<br>Zhèlǐ yǒu wúxiàn wǎngluò xùnhào ma? |
| **Can I get an account with a local internet provider?** | 我能开一个 IP账户吗？<br>Wǒ néng kāiyīge IP zhànghù ma? |

**I'd like to ...** 我想…… Wǒ xiǎng ...

| | | |
|---|---|---|
| **check my email** | 查一下电子信箱 | chá yīxiàdiànzǐ xìnxiāng |
| **download my photos** | 下载我的照片 | xiàzǎi wǒde zhàopiān |
| **get internet access** | 上网 | shàngwǎng |
| **use a printer** | 打印 | dǎyìn |
| **use a scanner** | 扫描 | sǎomiáo |

**Do you have PCs?** 有个人电脑吗？ Yǒu gèrén diànnǎo ma?

**Do you have Macs?** 有苹果电脑吗？ Yǒu píngguǒ diànnǎo ma?

**Can I connect my laptop here?** 我能在这里连接我的笔记本电脑吗？ Wǒ néng zài zhèlǐ liánjiē wǒde bǐjìběn diànnǎo ma?

**Do you have headphones (with a microphone)?** 你有耳机（耳麦）吗？ Nǐ yǒu ěrjī (ěrmài) ma?

| | |
|---|---|
| **Please change it to English-language preference.** | 请帮我换成英文格式。<br>Qǐng bāngwǒhuànchéng Yīngwén géshì. |
| **This connection's really slow.** | 网速太慢了。<br>Wǎngsù tài màn le. |
| **It's crashed.** | 死机了。<br>Sǐjī le. |
| **I've finished.** | 上完了。<br>Shàng wán le. |

## MOBILE/CELL PHONE

| | |
|---|---|
| **I'd like a ...** | 我想买一……<br>Wǒ xiáng mǎi yī ... |

| | | |
|---|---|---|
| **charger for my phone** | 个充电器 | ge chōngdiàn qì |
| **mobile/cell phone** | 个手机 | ge shǒujī |
| **(100 yuan) prepaid card** | 张(一百块的)预付卡 | zhāng (yībǎi kuài de) yùfùkǎ |
| **SIM card** | 张SIM卡 | zhāng SIM kǎ |

| | |
|---|---|
| **What are the rates?** | 电话费怎么算?<br>Diànhuàfèi zěnme suàn? |
| **(30 fen) per minute.** | 每分钟(三毛钱)。<br>Měifēnzhōng (sānmáoqián). |

## PHONE

| | |
|---|---|
| Q **What's your phone number?** | 您的电话号码是多少?<br>Nín de diànhuà hàomǎ shì duōshǎo? |
| A **The number is ...** | 号码是……<br>Hàomǎ shì ... |

| | |
|---|---|
| **Can you help me find the number for ...?** | 请帮我找一下……的号码。<br>Qǐng bāngwǒ zhǎoyīxià ... de hàomǎ. |
| **I want to ...** | 我想……<br>Wǒ xiǎng ... |

| | | |
|---|---|---|
| **call (Singapore)** | 打电话到(新加坡) | dǎ diànhuà dào (Xīnjiāpō) |
| **make a (local) call** | 打(市内)电话 | dǎ (shìnèi) diànhuà |
| **reverse the charges** | 打对方付款的电话 | dǎ duìfāng fùkuǎn de diànhuà |
| **speak for (three) minutes** | 讲(三)分钟 | jiǎng (sān) fēnzhōng |

| | |
|---|---|
| **What's the code for (New Zealand)?** | (新西兰)的区号是多少?<br>(Xīnxīlán) de qūhào shì duōshǎo? |
| **It's engaged.** | 占线了。<br>Zhànxiàn le. |
| **I've been cut off.** | 断掉了。<br>Duàndiào le. |
| **The connection's bad.** | 线路不好。<br>Xiànlù bùhǎo. |
| **Hello.** | 喂。<br>Wèi. |

### LISTEN FOR

| | | |
|---|---|---|
| 打错了。 | Dǎcuò le. | Wrong number. |
| 你是谁？ | Nǐ shì shéi? | Who's calling? |
| 你找谁？ | Nǐ zhǎo shéi? | Who do you want to speak to? |
| (他/她)不在。 | (Tā) bùzài. | (He/She) is not here. |
| 等一下。 | Děngyīxià. | One moment. |

| | |
|---|---|
| **Can I speak to ...?** | 我找……<br>Wǒ zhǎo ... |
| **It's ...** | 这是……<br>Zhè shì ... |
| **Is ... there?** | ……在吗？<br>... zài ma? |
| **Please tell him/her I called.** | 请告诉他/她我打过电话。<br>Qǐng gàosù tā wǒ dǎguò diànhuà. |
| **Can I leave a message?** | 我能留言吗？<br>Wǒ néng liúyán ma? |
| **My number is ...** | 我的号码是……<br>Wǒde hàomǎ shì ... |
| **I don't have a contact number.** | 我在这儿没有联系电话。<br>Wǒ zài zhèr méiyǒu liánxì diànhuà. |
| **I'll call back later.** | 我晚点再打过来。<br>Wǒ wǎndiǎn zài dǎguòlái. |

## POST OFFICE

| | |
|---|---|
| **I want to send a letter.** | 我想寄一封信。<br>Wǒ xiǎng jì yī fēng xìn. |
| **I want to send a parcel.** | 我想寄一个包裹。<br>Wǒ xiǎng jì yī gè bāoguǒ. |

| | |
|---|---|
| **I want to send a postcard.** | 我想寄一张明信片。<br>Wǒ xiǎng jì yī zhāng míngxìnpiàn. |
| **I want to buy an envelope.** | 我想买一个信封。<br>Wǒ xiǎng mǎi yī ge xìnfēng. |
| **I want to buy a stamp.** | 我想买一张邮票。<br>Wǒ xiǎng mǎi yī zhāng yóupiào. |
| **Please send it by airmail/surface mail to (Australia).** | 请寄航空信/平信到(澳大利亚)。<br>Qǐng jì hángkōng xìn/píngxìn dào (Àodàlìyà). |
| **It contains (souvenirs).** | 里面有(纪念品)。<br>Lǐmian yǒu (jìniànpǐn). |
| **Is there any mail for me?** | 有没有我的信?<br>Yǒuméiyǒu wǒde xìn? |
| **customs declaration** | 海关报税<br>hǎiguān bàoshuì |
| **domestic** | 国内<br>guónèi |
| **international** | 国际<br>guójì |
| **postal service** | 信件<br>xìnjiàn |

## LISTEN FOR

| | | |
|---|---|---|
| 航空信 | hángkōng xìn | air |
| 特快 | tèkuài | express |
| 挂号 | guàhào | registered |
| (陆运)平信 | (lùyùn) píngxìn | surface (land) |
| (海运)平信 | (hǎiyùn) píngxìn | surface (sea) |

# Money & Banking

## KEY PHRASES

| | | |
|---|---|---|
| **How much is it?** | 多少钱? | Duōshǎo qián? |
| **What's the exchange rate?** | 兑换率是多少? | Duìhuànlǜ shì duōshǎo? |
| **Where's an ATM?** | 自动取款机在哪儿? | Zìdòng qǔkuǎnjī zài nǎr? |
| **I'd like to change money.** | 我要换钱。 | Wǒ yào huànqián. |
| **What's the charge for that?** | 手续费是多少? | Shǒuxùfèi shì duōshǎo? |

## PAYING THE BILL

| | |
|---|---|
| Q **How much is it?** | 多少钱?<br>Duōshǎo qián? |
| A **It's (1200) RMB.** | 是(1200)元。<br>Shì (yīqiān liǎngbǎi) yuán. |
| A **It's free.** | 是免费的。<br>Shì miǎnfèi de. |
| **Please write down the price.** | 请把价钱写下来。<br>Qǐng bǎ jiàqián xiě xiàlái. |
| **Do you accept credit cards?** | 你们收信用卡吗?<br>Nǐmen shōu xìnyòng kǎ ma? |
| **Do you accept debit cards?** | 你们收借记卡吗?<br>Nǐmen shōu jièjìkǎ ma? |

## LISTEN FOR

| | | |
|---|---|---|
| 护照 | hùzhào | passport |
| 证件 | zhèngjiàn | identification |
| 签字。 | Qiānzì. | Sign here. |
| 你的帐户没有钱。 | Nǐde zhànghù méiyǒu qián. | You have no funds left. |
| 我们不能办。 | Wǒmen bùnéng bàn. | We can't do that. |
| 有问题。 | Yǒu wèntí. | There's a problem. |

**There's a mistake in the bill.** 帐单上有问题。
Zhàngdān shàng yǒu wèntí.

**I'd like my change, please.** 可以找零吗？
Kěyǐ zhǎo líng ma?

**I'd like a refund, please.** 可以退款吗？
Kěyǐ tuì kuǎn ma?

# BANKING

**What time does the bank open?** 银行什么时候开门？
Yínháng shénme shíhòu kāimen?

**Where can I ...?** 我在哪里能……？
Wǒ zài nǎli néng ...?

**I'd like to ...** 我要……
Wǒ yào ...

| | | |
|---|---|---|
| **cash a cheque** | 兑现一张支票 | duìxiàn yīzhāng zhīpiào |
| **change money** | 换钱 | huànqián |
| **get a cash advance** | 现金透支 | xiànjīn tòuzhī |
| **withdraw money** | 取现金 | qǔ xiànjīn |

## CULTURE TIP: CHINESE CURRENCY

RMB (Renminbi rénmínbì) – 'People's Money' – is the official term for the Chinese currency.

| | | |
|---|---|---|
| 元 | yuán | the official name for the basic unit of RMB |
| 块 | kuài | commonly used colloquial term for a yuan |
| 角 | jiǎo | the official term; 10 jiao make up one yuan |
| 毛 | máo | commonly used colloquial term for a jiao |
| 分 | fēn | the official term; 10 fen make up one jiao |

| | |
|---|---|
| **Where's an ATM?** | 自动取款机在哪儿？<br>Zìdòng qǔkuǎnjī zài nǎr? |
| **Where's a place to change foreign money?** | 换外币的地方在哪儿？<br>Huàn wàibì de dìfang zài nǎr? |
| **What's the exchange rate?** | 兑换率是多少？<br>Duìhuànlǜ shì duōshǎo? |
| **What's the charge for that?** | 手续费是多少？<br>Shǒuxùfèi shì duōshǎo? |
| **The ATM took my card.** | 取款机吃了我的卡。<br>Qǔkuǎnjī chīle wǒde kǎ. |
| **I've forgotten my PIN.** | 我忘了我的密码。<br>Wǒ wàngle wǒde mìmǎ. |
| **Can I use my credit card to withdraw money?** | 能用信用卡取现金吗？<br>Néng yòng xìnyòngkǎ qǔ xiànjīn ma? |
| **Has my money arrived yet?** | 我的汇款到了没有？<br>Wǒde huìkuǎn dàole méiyǒu? |
| **How long will it take to arrive?** | 还要等多久？<br>Háiyàoděng duōjiǔ? |

# Business

## KEY PHRASES

| | | |
|---|---|---|
| **I'm attending a conference.** | 我来参加一个研讨会。 | Wǒ lái cānjiā yīge yántǎohuì. |
| **I have an appointment with ...** | 我跟……有约。 | Wǒ gēn ... yǒuyuē. |
| **Shall we go for a meal?** | 咱们是不是出去吃顿饭？ | Zánmen shìbùshì chūqù chīdùnfàn? |

| | |
|---|---|
| **Where's the business centre?** | 商务中心在哪儿？<br>Shāngwù zhōngxīn zài nǎr? |
| **Where's the conference?** | 研讨会在哪儿？<br>Yántǎohuì zài nǎr? |
| **Where's the meeting?** | 会议在哪儿？<br>Huìyì zài nǎr? |
| **I'm attending a ...** | 我来参加一个……<br>Wǒ lái cānjiā yīge ... |

| | | |
|---|---|---|
| **conference** | 研讨会 | yántǎohuì |
| **course** | 培训班 | péixùnbān |
| **meeting** | 会议 | huìyì |
| **trade fair** | 交易会 | jiāoyìhuì |

| | |
|---|---|
| **I'm here for (two) days.** | 我要呆(两)天。<br>Wǒ yào dāi (liǎng)tiān. |
| **I'm here for (two) weeks.** | 我要呆(两)个星期。<br>Wǒ yào dāi (liǎng)ge xīngqī. |

## CULTURE TIP: TIME IN CHINA

The Chinese tend to view punctuality as a virtue and you should find that people arrive on time for meetings and social events. They may even arrive a little ahead of time, just to be on the safe side. In business dealings, punctual attendance at appointments can be interpreted as a sign of earnestness.

When planning events, note that the Chinese are very superstitious about numbers. When setting a date, you might be wise to check with your Chinese counterparts that the numbers contained in the proposed date are favourable. The number four (sì 四), in particular, is considered unlucky as it sounds a lot like the word for 'death' (sǐ 死).

| | |
|---|---|
| **I'm staying at ..., room ...** | 我住在……，<br>……号房间。<br>Wǒ zhù zài ...,<br>... hào fángjiān. |
| **I'm with (China Travel Co).** | 我跟（中旅公司）<br>一块来的。<br>Wǒ gēn (Zhōnglǚ gōngsī)<br>yīkuàilái de. |
| **I'm with my colleague(s).** | 我跟（几个）<br>同事一块来的。<br>Wǒ gēn (jǐge)<br>tóngshì yīkuàilái de. |
| **I'm with (two) others.** | 我跟（两个）<br>人一块来的。<br>Wǒ gēn (liǎngge)<br>rén yīkuàilái de. |
| **I'm alone.** | 我一个人来的。<br>Wǒ yīgerén lái de. |
| **I have an appointment with ...** | 我跟……有约。<br>Wǒ gēn ... yǒuyuē. |

**I need ...** 我需要……
Wǒ xūyào ...

| | | |
|---|---|---|
| **a computer** | 一个电脑 | yīge diànnǎo |
| **an internet connection** | 上网 | shàng wǎng |
| **an interpreter** | 一位翻译 | yīwèi fānyì |

**That went very well.** 刚才开得很好。
Gāngcái kāide hénhǎo.

**Thank you for your time.** 谢谢你们的关照。
Xièxie nǐmende guānzhào.

**Shall we go for a drink?** 咱们是不是出去喝杯酒?
Zánmen shìbùshì chūqù hēbēijiǔ?

**Shall we go for a meal?** 咱们是不是出去吃顿饭?
Zánmen shìbùshì chūqù chīdùnfàn?

**It's on me.** 我请客。
Wǒ qǐng kè.

## CULTURE TIP: DOING BUSINESS IN CHINA

The notion of guānxì 关系 (connections) is central to doing business in China. In a country where people often have to compete for goods and services in short supply, a network of advantageous reciprocal connections in places of power is all-important. Obtaining goods and services through such channels is colloquially known as 'going through the back door' (zǒuhòumén 走后门). Typical displays of guānxì are lavish banquets fuelled with Chinese spirit (báijiǔ 白酒). If you want to cut any deals while in China, you may be wise to adopt the local custom in this regard.

# Sightseeing

## KEY PHRASES

| | | |
|---|---|---|
| **I'd like a guide.** | 我想买一本指南。 | Wǒ xiǎng mǎi yī běn zhǐnán. |
| **Can I take photos?** | 可以照相吗？ | Kěyǐ zhàoxiàng ma? |
| **When does the museum open?** | 博物馆几点开门？ | Bówùguǎn jǐdiǎn kāimén? |
| **I'm interested in ...** | 我对……感兴趣。 | Wǒ duì ... gǎnxìngqù. |
| **When's the next (tour)?** | 下一个（向导游）是什么时候？ | Xiàyīge (xiàngdǎoyóu) shì shénme shíhòu? |

## REQUESTS & QUERIES

**I'd like a/an ...**
我想买一……
Wǒ xiǎng mǎi yī ...

| | | |
|---|---|---|
| **audio set** | 语音导览 | yǔyīn dǎolǎn |
| **catalogue** | 本画册 | běn huàcè |
| **guide** | 本指南 | běn zhǐnán |
| **guidebook in English** | 本英文指南 | běn Yīngwén zhǐnán |
| **(local) map** | 张（本地）地图 | zhāng (běndì) dìtú |

**Do you have information on local culture?**
有没有关于地方文化的资料？
Yǒuméiyǒu guānyú dìfāng wénhuà de zīliào?

几点回来？
Jǐdiǎn huílái?
***What time should we be back?***

| | |
|---|---|
| **Do you have information on local history?** | 有没有关于地方史的资料？<br>Yǒuméiyǒu guānyú dìfāng shǐ de zīliào? |
| **Do you have information on local religion?** | 有没有关于地方宗教的资料？<br>Yǒuméiyǒu guānyú dìfāng zōngjiào de zīliào? |
| **I'd like to see ...** | 我想看……<br>Wǒ xiǎng kàn ... |
| **What's that?** | 那是什么？<br>Nà shì shénme? |
| **Who made it?** | 是谁做的？<br>Shì shéi zuòde? |
| **How old is it?** | 有多久的历史？<br>Yǒu duōjiǔ de lìshì? |

| | |
|---|---|
| **Can I take photos?** | 可以照相吗？<br>Kěyǐ zhàoxiàng ma? |
| **Could you take a photo of me?** | 你能帮我照相吗？<br>Nǐ néng bāng wǒ zhàoxiàng ma? |
| **Can I take a photo (of you)?** | 我能拍(你)吗？<br>Wǒ néng pāi(nǐ) ma? |
| **I'll send you the photograph.** | 我会把照片寄给你。<br>Wǒ huì bǎ zhàopiàn jìgěi nǐ. |
| **Please write down your name and address.** | 请写下你的名字和地址。<br>Qǐng xiěxià nǐde míngzì hé dìzhǐ. |
| **I've been to ...** | 我去过……<br>Wǒ qùguò ... |
| **I'm planning to go to (the) ...** | 我打算去……<br>Wǒ dǎsuàn qù ... |

| | | |
|---|---|---|
| **Army of Terracotta Warriors in Xi'an** | 西安兵马俑 | Xī'ān Bīngmǎyǒng |
| **Forbidden City** | 故宫 | Gùgōng |
| **Great Wall** | 长城 | Chángchéng |
| **Guilin** | 桂林 | Guìlín |
| **Pingyao** | 平遥 | Píngyáo |
| **Tai Shan** | 泰山 | Tàishān |
| **West Lake of Hangzhou** | 杭州西湖 | Hángzhōu Xīhú |

## GETTING IN

| | |
|---|---|
| **What time does it open?** | 几点开门？<br>Jǐdiǎn kāimén? |
| **What time does it close?** | 几点关门？<br>Jǐdiǎn guānmén? |

| | |
|---|---|
| **What's the admission charge?** | 门票多少钱？<br>Ménpiào duōshǎo qián? |
| **Is there a discount for ...?** | 给……打折扣吗？<br>Gěi ... dǎzhékòu ma? |

| | | |
|---|---|---|
| **children** | 儿童 | értóng |
| **families** | 家庭 | jiātíng |
| **groups** | 团体 | tuántǐ |
| **older people** | 老年人 | lǎoniánrén |
| **students** | 学生 | xuéshēng |

# GALLERIES & MUSEUMS

| | |
|---|---|
| **When does the gallery open?** | 艺术馆几点开门？<br>Yìshùguǎn jǐdiǎn kāimén? |
| **When does the museum open?** | 博物馆几点开门？<br>Bówùguǎn jǐdiǎn kāimén? |
| Q **What kind of art are you interested in?** | 你喜欢什么样的艺术？<br>Nǐ xǐhuān shénmeyàng de yìshù? |
| A **I'm interested in ...** | 我对……感兴趣。<br>Wǒ duì ... gǎnxìngqù. |
| Q **What's in the collection?** | 这里收藏了什么？<br>Zhè lǐ shōucáng le shénme? |
| A **It's a/an ... exhibition.** | 是一个……展览。<br>Shì yīge ... zhǎnlǎn. |
| Q **What do you think of ...?** | 你觉得……怎么样？<br>Nǐ juéde ... zěnmeyàng? |
| A **I like the works of ...** | 我喜欢……的作品。<br>Wǒ xǐhuān ... de zuòpǐn. |
| A **It reminds me of ...** | 让我想到……<br>Ràng wǒ xiǎngdào ... |

| **... art** | ……艺术<br>... yìshù |
|---|---|

| | | |
|---|---|---|
| **comic** | 漫画 | mànhuà |
| **graphic** | 版画 | bǎnhuà |
| **modern** | 现代派 | xiàndài pài |
| **realist** | 现实主义 | xiànshí zhǔyì |

## TOURS

| | |
|---|---|
| **Can you recommend a (boat trip)?** | 你能推荐一个（游船）吗？<br>Nǐ néng tuījiàn yīge (yóuchuān) ma? |
| **Can you recommend a (day trip)?** | 你能推荐一个（一日游）吗？<br>Nǐ néng tuījiàn yīge (yīrìyóu) ma? |
| **When's the next (tour)?** | 下一个（向导游）是什么时候？<br>Xiàyīge (xiàngdǎoyóu) shì shénme shíhòu? |
| **Is ... included?** | 包括……吗？<br>Bāokuò ... ma? |

| | | |
|---|---|---|
| **accommodation** | 住宿 | zhùsù |
| **the admission price** | 门票钱 | ménpiàoqián |
| **food** | 饮食 | yǐnshí |
| **transport** | 交通 | jiāotōng |

| | |
|---|---|
| **The guide will pay.** | 导游会付钱。<br>Dǎoyóu huì fùqián. |
| **The guide has paid.** | 导游已经付了钱。<br>Dǎoyóu yǐjīng fùle qián. |

## CULTURE TIP: HEY OLD STRANGER!

One of the mild annoyances you're likely to face on the road, if you venture outside the cosmopolitan centres, is the incessant exclamation 老外 lǎowài, or even 'Hello lǎowài, hello!' The first character means 'old' and is a mark of respect in Mandarin. The second character literally means 'outside'.

The expression is not exactly polite, but it shouldn't cause offence. You could think of it as something like 'Hey Old Stranger!' It's certainly a lot better than outmoded forms of address such as 'Foreign Devil' or 'American Spy'. If you answer with 'Hello!' be prepared for your audience to break into hysterical laughter.

| | |
|---|---|
| **How long is the tour?** | 向导游要多长时间？<br>Xiàngdǎoyóu yào duōcháng shíjiān? |
| **What time should we be back?** | 几点回来？<br>Jǐdiǎn huílái? |
| **I'm with them.** | 我跟他们在一块。<br>Wǒ gēn tāmen zài yīkuài. |
| **I've lost my group.** | 我找不到我的团队。<br>Wǒ zhǎobùdào wǒde tuánduì. |

# Seniors & Travellers with Disabilites

## KEY PHRASES

| | | |
|---|---|---|
| **I need assistance.** | 我需要帮助。 | Wǒ xūyào bāngzhù. |
| **Is there wheelchair access?** | 轮椅能进门吗？ | Lúnyǐ néng jìn mén ma? |
| **Could you help me cross the street safely?** | 能帮我过马路吗？ | Néng bāngwǒ guò mǎlù ma? |

In China older people are revered. To be called an 'old man' (dàye 大爷 – literally 'great father') or an 'old woman' (lǎo tàitài 老太太 – literally 'elderly married woman') is a compliment, a tribute to your maturity and wisdom. Disabled people, on the other hand, will not find getting around China easy as there are precious few facilities for the disabled.

| | |
|---|---|
| **I'm deaf.** | 我耳朵聋了。<br>Wǒ ěrduō lóng le. |
| **I have a hearing aid.** | 我带有助听器。<br>Wǒ dàiyǒu zhùtīngqì. |
| **I have a disability.** | 我有残疾。<br>Wǒ yǒu cánjí. |
| **I need assistance.** | 我需要帮助。<br>Wǒ xūyào bāngzhù. |
| **Is there wheelchair access?** | 轮椅能进门吗？<br>Lúnyǐ néng jìn mén ma? |
| **How wide is the entrance?** | 门口有多宽？<br>Ménkǒu yǒu duōkuān? |

| | |
|---|---|
| **How many steps are there?** | 有多少台阶？<br>Yǒu duōshǎo táijiē? |
| **Is there a lift/elevator?** | 有电梯吗？<br>Yǒu diàntī ma? |
| **Are there rails in the bathroom?** | 浴室里有扶手吗？<br>Yùshì lǐ yǒu fúshǒu ma? |
| **Is there somewhere I can sit down?** | 哪里可以坐下休息？<br>Nǎli kěyǐ zuòxià xiūxi? |
| **Could you help me cross the street safely?** | 能帮我过马路吗？<br>Néng bāngwǒ guò mǎlù ma? |
| **older person** | 老年人<br>lǎoniánrén |
| **person with a disability** | 残疾人<br>cánjí rén |
| **ramp** | 坡道<br>pōdào |
| **walking frame** | 拐杖架子<br>guǎizhàng jiàzi |
| **walking stick** | 拐杖<br>guǎizhàng |
| **wheelchair** | 轮椅<br>lúnyǐ |

# Travel with Children

## KEY PHRASES

| | | |
|---|---|---|
| **Are children allowed?** | 能带小孩去吗？ | Néng dài xiǎohái qù ma? |
| **Is there a child discount?** | 这儿有没有给儿童打折扣？ | Zhèr yǒuméiyǒu gěi értóng dǎ zhékòu? |
| **Are there any good places to take children around here?** | 附近有孩子玩的地方吗？ | Fùjìn yǒu háizi wánde dìfang ma? |

Chinese people find foreign children fascinating. You may find that travelling with kids greatly facilitates striking up conversations with locals and getting to know them.

| | | |
|---|---|---|
| **Is there a ...?** | 这儿有没有……？ | Zhèr yǒuméiyǒu ...? |
| **child discount** | 给儿童打折扣 | gěi értóng dǎ zhékòu |
| **child-minding service** | 保姆服务 | bǎomǔ fúwù |
| **child's portion** | 儿童份量（的饭菜） | értóng fènliàng (de fàncài) |
| **creche** | 幼儿园 | yòu'éryuán |
| **family ticket** | 家庭票 | jiātíng piào |

**I need a/an ...** 我在找一……
Wǒ zài zhǎo yī ...

| | | |
|---|---|---|
| **baby seat** | 个婴儿座 | ge yīng'ér zuò |
| **(English-speaking) babysitter** | 位(会说英文的)保姆 | wèi (huì shuō Yīngwén de) báomǔ |
| **cot** | 张婴儿床 | zhāng yīng'ér chuáng |
| **highchair** | 张高凳子 | zhāng gāodèngzi |
| **plastic bag** | 个塑料袋 | ge sùliào dài |
| **plastic sheet** | 块塑料布 | kuài sùliào bù |
| **potty** | 个婴儿马桶 | ge yīng'ér mǎtǒng |
| **pram** | 辆小推车 | liǎng xiǎotuīchē |
| **sick bag** | 个呕吐袋 | ge ǒutù dài |
| **stroller** | 辆婴儿推车 | liǎng yīng'ér tuīchē |

**Do you sell ...?** 你们卖……吗?

| | | |
|---|---|---|
| **baby wipes** | 婴儿纸巾 | yīng'ér zhǐjīn |
| **disposable nappies/diapers** | 一次性尿裤 | yīcìxìng niàokù |
| **painkillers for infants** | 孩子止痛药 | háizi zhǐtòng yào |
| **tissues** | 纸巾 | zhǐjīn |

**Where's the nearest ...?** 最近的……在哪里?
Zuìjìn de ... zài nǎli?

| | | |
|---|---|---|
| **park** | 公园 | gōngyuán |
| **playground** | 孩子活动地方 | háizi huódòng dìfang |
| **swimming pool** | 游泳池 | yóuyǒng chí |
| **tap** | 水龙头 | shuǐlóngtóu |
| **theme park** | 游乐园 | yóulèyuán |
| **toyshop** | 玩具店 | wánjù diàn |

| | |
|---|---|
| **Do you hire prams/ strollers?** | 这儿能租用婴儿推车吗？<br>Zhèr néng zūyòng yīng'ér tuīchē ma? |
| **Is there space for a pram/ stroller?** | 有地方放推车吗？<br>Yǒu dìfang fàng tuīchē ma? |
| **Are children allowed?** | 能带小孩去吗？<br>Néng dài xiǎohái qù ma? |
| **Are there any good places to take children around here?** | 附近有孩子玩的地方吗？<br>Fùjìn yǒu háizi wánde dìfang ma? |
| **Is this suitable for ...-year-old children?** | 对……岁孩子合适吗？<br>Duì ... suì háizi héshì ma? |
| **Do you mind if I breastfeed here?** | 这儿喂奶你介意吗?<br>Zhèr wèinǎi nǐ jièyì ma? |
| **Could I have some paper and pencils, please?** | 能借用纸和笔吗？<br>Néng jièyòng zhǐ hé bǐ ma? |
| **Do you know a dentist who's good with children?** | 哪个儿科牙医比较好?<br>Nǎge érkē yáyī bǐjiào hǎo? |
| **Do you know a doctor who's good with children?** | 哪个儿科医生比较好?<br>Nǎge érkē yīshēng bǐjiào hǎo? |

If your child is sick, see **health**, page 166.

# SOCIAL

| | |
|---|---|
| MEETING PEOPLE | 112 |
| INTERESTS | 123 |
| FEELINGS & OPINIONS | 128 |
| GOING OUT | 134 |
| ROMANCE | 140 |
| BELIEFS & CULTURE | 145 |
| SPORTS | 148 |
| OUTDOORS | 156 |

# Meeting People

## KEY PHRASES

| | | |
|---|---|---|
| **My name is ...** | 我叫…… | Wǒ jiào ... |
| **I'm from ...** | 我从……来。 | Wǒ cóng ... lái. |
| **I'm ...** | 我是个…… | Wǒ shì gè ... |
| **I'm ... years old.** | 我……岁。 | Wǒ ... suì. |
| **And you?** | 你呢？ | Nǐ ne? |

## BASICS

Note that in Mandarin, the word 'please' (qǐng 请) always precedes a request. You're likely to become familiar with the two phrases at the top of the opposite page as Chinese people use them a lot.

| | |
|---|---|
| **Yes.** | 是。<br>Shì. |
| **No.** | 不是。<br>Bùshì. |
| **Please ...** | 请……<br>Qǐng ... |
| **Thank you (very much).** | (非常) 谢谢你。<br>(Fēicháng) xièxie nǐ. |
| **You're welcome.** | 不客气。<br>Bù kèqi. |
| **Excuse me. (to get attention)** | 劳驾。<br>Láojià. |
| **Excuse me. (to get past)** | 借光。<br>Jièguāng. |
| **Sorry.** | 对不起。<br>Duìbùqǐ. |

| | |
|---|---|
| **As you please.** | 随便。<br>Suíbiàn. |
| **No problem.** | 没关系。<br>Méiguānxi. |

## GREETINGS & GOODBYES

In common parlance, nǐ 你 ('you' singular) can have the polite form nín 您. This polite form is particularly common in Beijing. You'll encounter it as part of some common greetings.

| | |
|---|---|
| **Greetings all.** | 大家好。<br>Dàjiā hǎo. |
| **Hello. (general)** | 你好。<br>Nǐhǎo. |
| **Hello. (Beijing)** | 您好。<br>Nínhǎo. |

我很喜欢这里。
Wǒ hěn xǐhuān zhèlǐ.
***I love it here!***

| | |
|---|---|
| **Hi. (lit: Have you eaten?)** | 吃饭了吗？<br>Chīfàn le ma? |
| **Good afternoon.** | 下午好。<br>Xiàwǔ hǎo. |
| **Good evening.** | 晚上好。<br>Wǎnshàng hǎo. |
| **Good morning. (after breakfast)** | 早上好。<br>Zǎoshàng hǎo. |
| Q **How are you? (general)** | 你好吗？<br>Nǐhǎo ma? |
| A **How are you? (Beijing)** | 您好吗？<br>Nínhǎo ma? |
| A **Fine. And you?** | 好。你呢？<br>Hǎo. Nǐ ne? |
| **What's your name?** | 你叫什么名字？<br>Nǐ jiào shénme míngzi? |
| **My name is ...** | 我叫……<br>Wǒ jiào ... |
| **I'd like to introduce you to ...** | 给你介绍……<br>Gěi nǐ jièshào ... |

| **This is ...** | 这是…… | Zhèshì ... |
|---|---|---|

| | |
|---|---|
| **I'm pleased to meet you.** | 幸会。<br>Xìnghuì. |
| **This is my ...** | 这是我的……<br>Zhè shì wǒde ... |

| | | |
|---|---|---|
| **child** | 孩子 | háizi |
| **colleague** | 同事 | tóngshì |
| **friend** | 朋友 | péngyou |
| **partner (intimate)** | 对象 | duìxiàng |

For other family members, see **family**, page 120.

| | |
|---|---|
| **Goodbye.** | 再见。<br>Zàijiàn. |
| **Bye.** | 拜拜。<br>Bàibai. |
| **See you later.** | 回头见。<br>Huítóu jiàn. |
| **Good night.** | 晚安。<br>Wǎn'ān. |

## TITLES & ADDRESSING PEOPLE

China is host to a wealth of titles and terms of address, reflecting the richness of its feudal past. Travellers to the country can get by using the three titles given below. The last term xiǎojiě 小姐 is becoming the generic term for women of unspecified marital status. Be aware that it can carry a derogatory overtone of 'prostitute', but only if used in sexually suggestive contexts.

| | |
|---|---|
| **Mr/Sir (lit: first-born)** | 先生<br>xiānsheng |
| **Mrs/Madam** | 女士<br>nǚshì |
| **Ms/Miss (lit: little sister)** | 小姐<br>xiǎojiě |

## MAKING CONVERSATION

Here are some common greetings and conversation starters that you may encounter or that may help you to break the ice.

| | |
|---|---|
| **Have you eaten?** | 吃饭了吗？<br>Chīfàn le ma? |
| **Stepping out?** | 出去吗？<br>Chūqù ma? |
| **You've arrived!** | 你来啦！<br>Nǐ lái la! |

### ☑ CULTURE TIP: FAMILY & FRIENDS

In China, the friendliest way to address people is by using kinship terms. You can call a woman of an older generation āyí 阿姨 (auntie). It's polite to give people the benefit of the doubt on the upwards side when guessing their age.

In Beijing, gēmenr 哥们儿 (buddy) and jiěmenr 姐们儿 (sis) are popular for men and women respectively, reflecting the capital's laid-back youth culture. Elsewhere, the terms dàgē 大哥 (big brother) and jiějie 姐姐 (big sister) are commonly used. On the less friendly side, to call one of your peers sūnzi 孙子 (grandchild) – a rank two full generations below yours – is a popular insult.

| | |
|---|---|
| **Off to the market?** | 买菜去？<br>Mǎicài qù? |
| **Do you live here?** | 你住这里吗？<br>Nǐ zhù zhèlǐ ma? |
| **Where are you going?** | 上哪儿去？<br>Shàngnǎr qù? |
| **What are you doing?** | 你在干吗？<br>Nǐ zài gànma? |
| Q **Do you like it here?** | 喜欢这里吗？<br>Xǐhuān zhèlǐ ma? |
| A **I love it here.** | 我很喜欢这里。<br>Wǒ hěn xǐhuān zhèlǐ. |
| Q **Are you here on holiday?** | 你来这里旅游吗？<br>Nǐ lái zhèlǐ lǚyóu ma? |
| A **I'm here for a holiday.** | 我来这里旅游。<br>Wǒ lái zhèlǐ lǚyóu. |
| A **I'm here on business.** | 我来这里出差。<br>Wǒ lái zhèlǐ chūchāi. |

| | |
|---|---|
| Ⓐ **I'm here to study.** | 我来这里留学。<br>Wǒ lái zhèlǐ liúxué. |
| Ⓠ **How long are you here for?** | 你在这里住多久？<br>Nǐ zài zhèlǐ zhù duōjiǔ? |
| Ⓐ **I'm here for (four) weeks.** | 我住（四）个星期。<br>Wǒ zhù (sì)ge xīngqī. |
| **Can I take a photo (of you)?** | 我可以拍（你）吗？<br>Wǒ kěyǐ pāi (nǐ) ma? |
| **That's (beautiful), isn't it?** | 太（好看）了！<br>Tài (hǎokàn) le! |
| **Just joking.** | 开玩笑。<br>Kāiwánxiào. |
| **What's this called?** | 这个叫什么？<br>Zhège jiào shénme? |

# NATIONALITIES

| | |
|---|---|
| Ⓠ **Where are you from?** | 你从哪儿来？<br>Nǐ cóngnǎr lái? |
| Ⓐ **I'm from Australia.** | 我从澳大利亚来。<br>Wǒ cóng Àodàlìyà lái. |
| Ⓐ **I'm from Canada.** | 我从加拿大来。<br>Wǒ cóng Jiānádà lái. |
| Ⓐ **I'm from Singapore.** | 我从新加坡来。<br>Wǒ cóng Xīnjiāpō lái. |

For more nationalities, see the **dictionary**, page 209.

# AGE

Try not to be too ruffled if everyone asks how many years you've managed to pack into your life's journey. They don't mean to cause offence, but are simply curious to know how old you are – age is an indication of status and wealth in traditional China.

### LISTEN FOR

People are often curious to know how foreigners get over their initial culture shock. You may well have locals ask you this question.

| | |
|---|---|
| 你在这儿习惯吗? | Nǐ zài zhèr xíguàn ma? Are you accustomed to life here? |

| | |
|---|---|
| Q **How old are you?** | 你多大了? Nǐ duōdà le? |
| A **I'm ... years old.** | 我……岁。 Wǒ ... suì. |
| Q **How old is your daughter?** | 你的女儿多大了? Nǐde nǚ'ér duōdà le? |
| Q **How old is your son?** | 你的儿子多大了? Nǐde érzi duōdà le? |
| A **He/She is ... years old.** | 他/她……岁。 Tā ... suì. |
| **Too old!** | 太老了! Tài lǎo le! |
| **I'm younger than I look.** | 我还小了。 Wǒ hái xiǎo le. |

For your age, see **numbers & amounts**, page 34.

## OCCUPATIONS & STUDIES

Expect inquisitive locals to ask 'How much do you earn?' (Nǐ zhèng duōshǎo qián? 你挣多少钱? ), as this is one of the top 10 questions asked of foreigners. This curiosity is probably explained by the rise of the free market and free-market jobs in China – a new and exciting phenomenon.

| | |
|---|---|
| Q **What's your occupation?** | 你做什么工作? Nǐ zuò shénme gōngzuò? |

Ⓐ **I'm a/an ...** 我是个……
Wǒ shì gè ...

| | | |
|---|---|---|
| **accountant** | 会计 | kuàijì |
| **chef** | 厨师 | chúshī |
| **engineer** | 工程师 | gōngchéngshī |
| **journalist** | 记者 | jìzhě |
| **teacher** | 老师 | lǎoshī |

Ⓐ **I do business.** 我做生意。
Wǒ zuò shēngyì.

Ⓐ **I do casual work.** 我打工。
Wǒ dǎgōng.

Ⓐ **I work in administration.** 我做秘书工作。
Wǒ zuò mìshū gōngzuò.

Ⓐ **I work in health.** 我做卫生工作。
Wǒ zuò wèishēng gōngzuò.

Ⓐ **I work in sales and marketing.** 我做销售工作。
Wǒ zuò xiāoshòu gōngzuò.

Ⓐ **I'm retired.** 我退休了。
Wǒ tuìxiū le.

### LANGUAGE TIP: CONVERSATION STARTERS

When trying to start up a conversation in China, never be afraid to ask, or state, the obvious. If a friend is coming out of a restaurant with braised pork smeared all over their face, best check to see whether they've eaten by asking Chīfàn le ma? 吃饭了吗？('Have you eaten?'). If you can't think of an obvious question to ask, try stating the obvious. It's as easy as talking about the weather. If a friend has just arrived at your house, let them know they've arrived with a gleeful Nǐ lái la! 你来啦！('You've arrived!').

| | |
|---|---|
| (A) **I'm self-employed.** | 我下海了。<br>Wǒ xiàhǎi le. |
| (A) **I'm unemployed.** | 我下岗了。<br>Wǒ xiàgǎng le. |
| (Q) **What are you studying?** | 你学什么？<br>Nǐ xué shénme? |
| (A) **I'm studying humanities.** | 我学文科。<br>Wǒ xué wénkē. |
| (A) **I'm studying (Mandarin) Chinese.** | 我学中文。<br>Wǒ xué Zhōngwén. |
| (A) **I'm studying science.** | 我学理科。<br>Wǒ xué lǐkē. |

For more occupations and studies, see the **dictionary**, page 209.

## FAMILY

Mandarin kinship terms can get very complicated as there are different titles according to age, hierarchy and whether the relationship is maternal or paternal. Included here are the terms for immediate family members and a selection of extended-family terms.

| | |
|---|---|
| (Q) **Are you married?** | 你结婚了吗？<br>Nǐ jiéhūn le ma? |
| (A) **I live with someone.** | 我有伴儿。<br>Wǒ yǒu bànr. |
| (A) **I'm ...** | 我……<br>Wǒ ... |

| | | |
|---|---|---|
| **divorced** | 离婚了 | líhūn le |
| **in a relationship** | 有伴 | yǒubàn |
| **married** | 结婚了 | jiéhūn le |
| **separated** | 分手了 | fēnshǒu le |
| **single** | 单身 | dānshēn |

| | |
|---|---|
| Q **Do you have a family of your own?** | 你成家了吗？<br>Nǐ chéngjiā le ma? |
| A **Do you have a/an ...?** | 你有……吗？<br>Nǐ yǒu ... ma? |
| A **I (don't) have a/an ...** | 我(没)有……<br>Wǒ (méi) yǒu ... |

| | | |
|---|---|---|
| **brother** | 兄弟 | xiōngdì |
| **daughter** | 女儿 | nǚ'ér |
| **father** | 父亲 | fùqīn |
| **granddaughter** | 孙女 | sūnnǚ |
| **grandson** | 孙子 | sūnzi |
| **husband** | 丈夫 | zhàngfu |
| **mother** | 母亲 | mǔqīn |
| **partner (intimate)** | 对象 | duìxiàng |
| **sister** | 姐妹 | jiěmèi |
| **son** | 儿子 | érzi |
| **wife** | 太太 | tàitai |

# FAREWELLS

| | |
|---|---|
| **I'm leaving tomorrow.** | 明天我要走了。<br>Míngtiān wǒ yào zǒu le. |
| **If you come to (Scotland), you can stay with me.** | 有机会来(苏格兰)，可以住我那儿。<br>Yǒu jīhuì lái (Sūgélán) kěyǐ zhù wǒ nàr. |
| **Keep in touch!** | 保持联系！<br>Bǎochí liánxì! |
| **It's been great meeting you.** | 认识你实在很高兴。<br>Rènshi nǐ shízài hěn gāoxìng. |

| | |
|---|---|
| Ⓠ **What's your (email address)?** | 你的(网址)是什么？<br>Nǐde (wǎngzhǐ)shì shénme? |
| Ⓐ **Here's my (address).** | 给你我的(地址)。<br>Gěi nǐ wǒde (dìzhǐ). |
| Ⓐ **Here's my (phone number).** | 给你我的(电话号码)。<br>Gěi nǐ wǒde (diànhuà hàomǎ). |

## WELL-WISHING

| | |
|---|---|
| **Bon voyage!** | 一路平安！<br>Yīlù píngān! |
| **Congratulations!** | 恭喜，恭喜！<br>Gōngxǐ, gōngxǐ! |
| **Good luck!** | 祝你好运！<br>Zhù nǐ hǎoyùn! |
| **Happy birthday!** | 生日快乐！<br>Shēngrì kuàilè! |
| **Happy (Chinese) New Year!** | 新年好！<br>Xīnnián hǎo! |
| **Congratulations! May you make lots of money!** | 恭喜发财！<br>Gōngxǐ fācái! |

This last expression is a popular Chinese New Year greeting, especially in southern China.

# Interests

## KEY PHRASES

| | | |
|---|---|---|
| **What do you do in your spare time?** | 你有什么爱好吗？ | Nǐ yǒu shénme àihào ma? |
| **Do you like ...?** | 你喜欢……吗？ | Nǐ xǐhuān ... ma? |
| **I (don't) like ...** | 我（不）喜欢…… | Wǒ (bù) xǐhuān ... |

## COMMON INTERESTS

Q **What do you do in your spare time?**
你有什么爱好吗？
Nǐ yǒu shénme àihào ma?

Q **Do you like ...?**
你喜欢……吗？
Nǐ xǐhuān ... ma?

| | | |
|---|---|---|
| **calligraphy** | 书法 | shūfǎ |
| **climbing mountains** | 爬山 | páshān |
| **computer games** | 电子游戏 | diànzǐ yóuxì |
| **films** | 看电影 | kàn diànyǐng |
| **music** | 听音乐 | tīngyīnyuè |
| **photography** | 摄影 | shèyǐng |
| **sport** | 体育 | tǐyù |
| **surfing the internet** | 上网 | shàngwǎng |
| **window shopping** | 逛商店 | guàngshāngdiàn |

**Ⓐ I (don't) like ...** 我(不)喜欢…… Wǒ (bù) xǐhuān ...

| | | |
|---|---|---|
| **cooking** | 做饭 | zuòfàn |
| **dancing** | 跳舞 | tiàowǔ |
| **drawing** | 画画 | huàhuà |
| **drinking** | 喝酒 | hējiǔ |
| **eating** | 吃饭 | chīfàn |
| **gardening** | 养花 | yǎnghuā |
| **reading** | 看书 | kànshū |
| **talking** | 聊天 | liáotiān |
| **travelling** | 旅游 | lǚyóu |
| **walking** | 散步 | sànbù |
| **watching TV** | 看电视 | kàn diànshì |

For sporting activities, see **sports**, page 148.

## MUSIC

**Do you like to ...?** 你爱……吗？ Nǐ ài ... ma?

| | | |
|---|---|---|
| **dance** | 跳舞 | tiàowǔ |
| **go to concerts** | 参加音乐会 | cānjiā yīnyuèhuì |
| **listen to music** | 听音乐 | tīngyīnyuè |
| **play an instrument** | 弹乐器 | tán yuèqì |
| **sing** | 唱歌 | chànggē |

**Which bands do you like?** 你喜欢什么乐队？ Nǐ xǐhuān shénme yuèduì?

**What music do you like?** 你喜欢什么音乐？ Nǐ xǐhuān shénme yīnyuè?

**Which singers do you like?** 你喜欢什么歌手？ Nǐ xǐhuān shénme gēshǒu?

| | |
|---|---|
| **alternative music** | 非主流音乐<br>fēizhǔliú yīnyuè |
| **blues** | 蓝调音乐<br>lándiào yīnyuè |
| **Chinese traditional music** | 中国传统音乐<br>Zhōngguó chuántǒng yīnyuè |
| **classical music** | 古典音乐<br>gǔdiǎn yīnyuè |
| **easy listening** | 轻音乐<br>qīng yīnyuè |
| **electronic music** | 电子音乐<br>diànzǐ yīnyuè |
| **folk music** | 民谣<br>mínyáo |
| **heavy metal** | 重金属音乐<br>zhòngjīnshǔ yīnyuè |
| **hip hop** | 说唱音乐<br>shuōchàng yīnyuè |
| **jazz** | 爵士乐<br>juéshì yuè |
| **Peking opera** | 京剧<br>jīngjù |
| **pop** | 流行音乐<br>liúxíng yīnyuè |
| **rock** | 摇滚<br>yāogǔn |
| **world music** | 国际民谣音乐<br>guójì mínyáo yīnyuè |

Planning to go to a concert? See **buying tickets**, page 46, and **going out**, page 134.

# CINEMA & THEATRE

| | |
|---|---|
| **I feel like going to a (ballet).** | 我想去看(芭蕾)。<br>Wǒ xiǎngqù kàn (bālěi). |
| **I feel like going to a (film).** | 我想去看(电影)。<br>Wǒ xiǎngqù kàn (diànyǐng). |
| **What's showing tonight?** | 今晚有什么节目?<br>Jīnwǎn yǒu shénme jiémù? |
| **Is it in English?** | 是英文版吗?<br>Shì Yīngwén bǎn ma? |
| **Does it have (English) subtitles?** | 有(英文)字幕吗?<br>Yǒu (Yīngwén) zìmù ma? |
| **Is this seat taken?** | 这座有人吗?<br>Zhè zuò yǒu rén ma? |
| **Have you seen ...?** | 你看过……吗?<br>Nǐ kànguò ... ma? |
| Q **Who's in it?** | 是谁演的?<br>Shì shéi yǎnde? |
| A **It stars ...** | 主角是……<br>Zhǔjué shì ... |
| Q **Did you like the (play)?** | 你喜欢(戏剧)吗?<br>Nǐ xǐhuān (xìjù) ma? |
| A **I thought it was excellent.** | 我觉得很好看。<br>Wǒ juéde hěn hǎokàn. |
| A **I thought it was long.** | 我觉得有点长。<br>Wǒ juéde yǒu diǎn cháng. |
| A **I thought it was OK.** | 我觉得还行。<br>Wǒ juéde háixíng. |
| **I (don't) like ...** | 我(不)喜欢……<br>Wǒ (bù) xǐhuān ... |

### ☑ CULTURE TIP: GAMES & ENTERTAINMENT

In China you won't go far without seeing groups of people (often retired men) playing board games or cards in public places like teahouses or parks. The most popular game is mahjong májiàng 麻将. The shuffling of mahjong tiles is often accompanied by the hum of conversation, which sometimes becomes animated as money is won or lost on the game.

Some claim that chess was invented in China. While this is hard to prove, it is true that both Chinese chess xiàngqí 象棋 and international chess guójì xiàngqí 国际象棋 are very popular. The Chinese love of gambling extends to numerous forms of card games pūkè pái 扑克牌, with bridge being very popular.

| | | |
|---|---|---|
| **action movies** | 动作片 | dòngzuò piàn |
| **animated films** | 动画片 | dònghuà piàn |
| **Chinese cinema** | 中国电影 | Zhōngguó diànyǐng |
| **comedies** | 喜剧片 | xǐjù piàn |
| **documentaries** | 纪录片 | jìlù piàn |
| **drama** | 戏剧 | xìjù |
| **Hong Kong cinema** | 香港电影 | Xiānggǎng diànyǐng |
| **horror movies** | 恐怖片 | kǒngbù piàn |
| **kung fu movies** | 武打片 | wǔdǎ piàn |
| **sci-fi movies** | 科幻片 | kēhuàn piàn |
| **short films** | 短篇电影 | duǎnpiān diànyǐng |
| **thrillers** | 惊险片 | jīngxiǎn piàn |
| **war movies** | 战争片 | zhànzhēng piàn |

# Feelings & Opinions

## KEY PHRASES

| | | |
|---|---|---|
| **Are you ...?** | 你……吗？ | Nǐ ... ma? |
| **I'm (not) ...** | 我(不)…… | Wǒ (bù) ... |
| **What do you think of it?** | 你觉得怎么样？ | Nǐ juéde zěnme yàng? |
| **I thought it was OK.** | 我觉得还行。 | Wǒ juéde háixíng. |
| **Did you hear about ...?** | 你听说过……吗？ | Nǐ tīngshuōguò ... ma? |

## FEELINGS

Physical sensations (hot, hungry, etc) are expressed in the form 'I am ...', while sentiments (depressed, disappointed, etc) are expressed in the form 'I feel ...' . These phrases could come in handy in China as friendliness is often expressed through an exaggerated concern for the welfare of others.

| | |
|---|---|
| Q **Are you ...?** | 你……吗？<br>Nǐ ... ma? |
| A **I'm (not) ...** | 我(不)……<br>Wǒ (bù) ... |

| | | |
|---|---|---|
| **cold** | 冷 | lěng |
| **hot** | 热 | rè |
| **hungry** | 饿 | è |
| **thirsty** | 渴 | kě |
| **tired** | 累 | lèi |

| | | |
|---|---|---|
| Ⓠ **Do you feel ...?** | 你感到……吗？<br>Nǐ gǎndào ... ma? | |
| Ⓐ **I (don't) feel ...** | 我(不)感到……<br>Wǒ (bù) gǎndào ... | |

| | | |
|---|---|---|
| **annoyed** | 生气 | shēngqì |
| **depressed** | 郁闷 | yùmèn |
| **disappointed** | 失望 | shīwàng |
| **embarrassed** | 不好意思 | bùhǎo yìsi |
| **happy** | 高兴 | gāoxìng |
| **sad** | 难过 | nánguò |
| **surprised** | 惊讶 | jīngyà |
| **worried** | 着急 | zháojí |

If you're feeling unwell, see **health**, page 166.

# OPINIONS

| | |
|---|---|
| Ⓠ **Did you like it?** | 你觉得好吗？<br>Nǐ juéde hǎo ma? |
| Ⓐ **I thought it was ...** | 我觉得……<br>Wǒ juéde ... |
| Ⓠ **What do you think of it?** | 你觉得怎么样？<br>Nǐ juéde zěnme yàng? |
| Ⓐ **It's ...** | 它……<br>Tā ... |

| | | |
|---|---|---|
| **awful** | 很差劲 | hěn chàjìn |
| **beautiful** | 好美 | hǎoměi |
| **boring** | 很无聊 | hěn wúliáo |
| **great** | 很棒 | hěn bàng |
| **interesting** | 很有意思 | hěn yǒu yìsi |
| **strange** | 奇怪 | qíguài |

| | |
|---|---|
| **a little** | 有一点<br>yǒu yīdiǎn |
| **I'm a little sad.** | 我有一点难过。<br>Wǒ yǒu yīdiǎn nánguò. |
| **very** | 很<br>hěn |
| **I'm very surprised.** | 我很惊讶。<br>Wǒ hěn jīngyà. |
| **extremely** | 非常<br>fēicháng |
| **I'm extremely happy.** | 我非常高兴。<br>Wǒ fēicháng gāoxìng. |

## POLITICS & SOCIAL ISSUES

When talking about social, political and environmental issues, keep in mind that certain issues are too politically sensitive to discuss with strangers. In addition, your status as a foreigner who can afford to travel may affect how your questions are understood. Unqualified criticism of things Chinese is not likely to win you any friends.

| | |
|---|---|
| Q **Who do you vote for?** | 你投票给哪个党？<br>Nǐ tóupiào gěi nǎge dǎng? |
| A **I support the ... party.** | 我支持……党。<br>Wǒ zhīchí ... dǎng. |
| A **I'm a member of the ... party.** | 我是……人士。<br>Wǒ shì ... rénshì. |
| **communist party** | 共产党<br>gòngchǎndǎng |
| **conservative** | 保守派<br>bǎoshǒu pài |
| **green activists** | 环保人士<br>huánbǎo rénshì |
| **leftist** | 左翼<br>zuǒyì |

它好美
Tā hǎoměi.
***It's beautiful.***

| | |
|---|---|
| **reformist** | 改革派<br>gǎigé pài |
| **rightist** | 右翼<br>yòuyì |
| **social democratic party** | 社会民主党<br>shèhuì mínzhǔdǎng |
| **socialist** | 社会党<br>shèhuì dǎng |
| **Did you hear about ...?** | 你听说过……吗？<br>Nǐ tīngshuōguò ... ma? |
| Q **Do you agree?** | 你同意吗？<br>Nǐ tóngyì ma? |
| A **I (don't) agree with ...** | 我(不)同意……<br>Wǒ (bù) tóngyì ... |

### CULTURE TIP: SMOOTHING SOCIAL SITUATIONS

If someone looks worried that they may have offended you, try letting them know that everything is OK with a long, slow méishì 没事 ('No problem.'). If you're worried that you may have caused offence, turn this into a question Méishì ba? 没事吧？('There's no problem, is there?'). If you're worried that they might have meant to cause offence, then ask Yǒushì ma? 有事吗？('Got a problem?') to find out for sure. Armed with these phrases you should be able to remedy any awkward situations that you might find yourself in.

| | |
|---|---|
| **How do people feel about ...?** | 人们觉得……怎么样？<br>Rénmen juéde ... zěnmeyàng? |
| **crime** | 犯罪活动<br>fànzuì huódòng |
| **the economy** | 经济<br>jīngjì |
| **education** | 教育<br>jiàoyù |
| **the environment** | 环境<br>huánjìng |

## THE ENVIRONMENT

You may find that concern about many issues, including environmental ones, tends to be very far removed from the minds of most Chinese, who generally contend with more pressing issues of local importance.

| | |
|---|---|
| **Is this a protected forest?** | 这个是被保护的森林吗？<br>Zhège shì bèibǎohù de sēnlín ma? |
| **Is this a protected park?** | 这个是被保护的公园吗？<br>Zhège shì bèibǎohù de gōngyuán ma? |

| | |
|---|---|
| **Is this a protected species?** | 这个是被保护的物种吗？<br>Zhège shì bèibǎohù de wùzhǒng ma? |
| **Is there a ... problem here?** | 本地有……问题吗？<br>Běn dì yǒu ... wèntí ma? |
| **What should be done about ...?** | ……应该怎么处理？<br>... yīnggāi zěnme chǔlǐ? |
| **ozone layer** | 臭氧层<br>chòuyǎngcéng |
| **pollution** | 污染<br>wūrǎn |
| **recycling programme** | 回收措施<br>huíshōu cuòshī |

# Going Out

## KEY PHRASES

| | | |
|---|---|---|
| **What's on tonight?** | 今天晚上有什么活动？ | Jīntiān wǎnshàng yǒu shénme huódòng? |
| **Where can I find clubs?** | 夜店怎么找？ | Yèdiàn zěnme zhǎo? |
| **Would you like to go for a coffee?** | 你想去喝咖啡吗？ | Nǐ xiǎng qù hē kāfēi ma? |
| **When will we meet?** | 几点钟碰头？ | Jǐdiǎnzhōng pèngtóu? |
| **Where will we meet?** | 在哪里碰头？ | Zài nǎli pèngtóu? |

## WHERE TO GO

| | |
|---|---|
| **What's there to do in the evenings?** | 晚上有什么好玩的吗？ Wǎnshàng yǒu shénme hǎowán de ma? |
| **What's on ...?** | ……有什么活动？ ... yǒu shénme huódòng? |

| | | |
|---|---|---|
| **locally** | 这儿附近 | zhèr fùjìn |
| **this weekend** | 这个周末 | zhège zhōumò |
| **today** | 今天 | jīntiān |
| **tonight** | 今天晚上 | jīntiān wǎnshàng |

| | |
|---|---|
| **Where can I find ...?** | ……怎么找？<br>... zěnme zhǎo? |

| | | |
|---|---|---|
| **clubs** | 夜店 | yèdiàn |
| **gay venues** | 同志吧 | tóngzhìbā |
| **places to eat** | 吃饭的地方 | chīfàn de dìfang |
| **pubs** | 酒吧 | jiǔbā |

| | |
|---|---|
| **Is there a local entertainment guide?** | 有没有本地的娱乐指南？<br>Yǒuméiyǒu běndì de yúlè zhǐnán? |
| **Is there a local film guide?** | 有没有本地的电影指南？<br>Yǒuméiyǒu běndì de diànyǐng zhǐnán? |
| **Is there a local music guide?** | 有没有本地的音乐指南？<br>Yǒuméiyǒu běndì de yīnyuè zhǐnán? |
| **I feel like going to a ...** | 我想到……去。<br>Wǒ xiǎng dào ... qù. |

| | | |
|---|---|---|
| **bar/pub** | 酒吧 | jiǔbā |
| **cafe** | 咖啡店 | kāfēi diàn |
| **club** | 夜店 | yèdiàn |
| **party (any lively gathering)** | 趴体 | pātǐ |
| **restaurant** | 饭馆 | fànguǎn |

| **I feel like going to ...** | 我想去…… Wǒ xiǎng qù ... |
|---|---|

| | | |
|---|---|---|
| **listen to a concert** | 听音乐会 | tīng yīnyuè huì |
| **see a film** | 看电影 | kàn diànyǐng |
| **see a show** | 看演出 | kàn yǎnchū |
| **sing karaoke** | 唱卡拉OK | chàng kālā ōkèi |
| **see Peking opera** | 看京剧 | kàn jīngjù |
| **see some acrobats** | 看杂技 | kàn zájì |
| **watch a ballet** | 看芭蕾 | kàn bālěi |

For more on bars and drinks, see **romance**, page 140, and **eating out**, page 176.

# INVITATIONS

| | |
|---|---|
| **What are you doing now?** | 你现在做什么？<br>Nǐ xiànzài zuò shénme? |
| **What are you doing this weekend?** | 你这个周末做什么？<br>Nǐ zhège zhōumò zuò shénme? |
| **What are you doing tonight?** | 你今天晚上做什么？<br>Nǐ jīntiān wǎnshàng zuò shénme? |
| **Do you know a good restaurant?** | 你知道哪里有好饭店？<br>Nǐ zhīdào nǎli yǒu hǎo fàndiàn? |
| **Do you want to come to the concert with me?** | 你想跟我去音乐会吗？<br>Nǐ xiǎng gēn wǒ qù yīnyuè huì ma? |
| **We're having a party/ banquet.** | 我们要开聚会/宴会。<br>Wǒmen yàokāi jùhuì/yànhuì. |
| **You should come.** | 你应该来。<br>Nǐ yīnggāi lái. |

| | |
|---|---|
| **The drinks are on me.** | 我请客。<br>Wǒ qǐngkè. |
| Q **Would you like to go (for a) ...?** | 你想去……吗？<br>Nǐ xiǎng qù ... ma? |
| A **I feel like going (for a) ...** | 我想去……<br>Wǒ xiǎng qù ... |

| | | |
|---|---|---|
| **banquet** | 大吃大喝 | dàchī dàhē |
| **coffee** | 喝咖啡 | hē kāfēi |
| **dancing** | 跳舞 | tiàowǔ |
| **drink** | 喝酒 | hējiǔ |
| **meal** | 吃饭 | chīfàn |
| **out somewhere** | 外面玩儿 | wàimian wánr |
| **walk** | 散步 | sànbù |

## RESPONDING TO INVITATIONS

| | |
|---|---|
| **Sure!** | 好！<br>Hǎo! |
| **Yes, I'd love to.** | 好，我愿意。<br>Hǎo, wǒ yuànyì. |
| **That's very kind of you.** | 你太客气了。<br>Nǐ tài kèqi le. |
| **Where shall we go?** | 我们到哪儿去？<br>Wǒmen dàonǎr qù? |
| **No, I'm afraid I can't.** | 不行，我不能来。<br>Bùxíng, wǒ bùnéng lái. |
| **Sorry, I can't sing/dance.** | 不好意思，我不会唱歌/跳舞。<br>Bùhǎo yìsi, wǒ bùhuì chànggē/tiàowǔ. |
| **What about tomorrow?** | 明天行吗？<br>Míngtiān xíng ma? |

# ARRANGING TO MEET

| | |
|---|---|
| Ⓠ **When will we meet?** | 几点钟碰头？<br>Jǐdiǎnzhōng pèngtóu? |
| Ⓐ **Let's meet at (eight) o'clock.** | 我们在（八）点钟见面。<br>Wǒmen zài (bā)diǎn zhōng jiànmiàn. |
| Ⓠ **Where will we meet?** | 在哪里碰头？<br>Zài nǎli pèngtóu? |
| Ⓐ **Let's meet at (the entrance).** | 我们在（门口）见面。<br>Wǒmen zài (ménkǒu) jiànmiàn. |
| **I'll pick you up.** | 我来接你。<br>Wǒ lái jiē nǐ. |
| Ⓠ **Are you ready?** | 准备好了吗？<br>Zhǔnbèi hǎo le ma? |
| Ⓐ **I'm ready.** | 准备好了。<br>Zhǔnbèi hǎo le. |
| Ⓐ **I'll be coming later.** | 我要晚一点来。<br>Wǒ yào wǎnyīdiǎn lái. |
| **Where will you be?** | 我在哪里找你？<br>Wǒ zài nǎli zhǎo nǐ? |
| **If I'm not there by (nine) o'clock, don't wait for me.** | 如果到了（九）点钟我还没来，就不要等我。<br>Rúguǒ dàole (jiǔ)diǎn zhōng wǒ hái méilái, jiù bùyào děngwǒ. |
| **I'll see you then.** | 不见不散。<br>Bùjiàn bùsàn. |
| **See you later.** | 回头见。<br>Huítóu jiàn. |
| **See you tomorrow.** | 明天见。<br>Míngtiān jiàn. |

**CULTURE TIP: STREET LIFE**

In China's crowded cities, a lot of life – particularly in summer – is lived out on the streets and in the precious open spaces and parks. An evening's entertainment might consist of activities such as kite flying (fàng fēngzheng 放风筝) or playing pool (dǎtáiqiú 打台球). In the warmer months, young people indulge in open-air dancing to rock music (bēngdí 蹦迪) while older people gather in the parks for ballroom dancing sessions (tiào jiāoyì wǔ 跳交谊舞).

| | |
|---|---|
| **I'm looking forward to it.** | 我期待它的到来。<br>Wǒ qīdài tāde dàolái. |
| **Sorry I'm late.** | 不好意思，来晚了。<br>Bùhǎo yìsi, láiwǎn le. |
| **Never mind.** | 没事。<br>Méishì. |

## DRUGS

| | |
|---|---|
| **I don't take drugs.** | 我不吸毒。<br>Wǒ bù xīdú. |
| **I take ... occasionally.** | 我偶尔吃……<br>Wǒ ǒu'ěr chī ... |
| **Do you want to have a smoke?** | 想抽一点吗？<br>Xiǎng chōuyīdiǎn ma? |
| **Do you have a light?** | 有火吗？<br>Yǒu huǒ ma? |

# Romance

## KEY PHRASES

| | | |
|---|---|---|
| **Would you like to do something (tomorrow)?** | (明天)想出去玩吗? | (Míngtiān) xiǎng chūqù wán ma? |
| **I love you.** | 我爱你。 | Wǒ ài nǐ. |
| **Leave me alone!** | 别烦我! | Bié fán wǒ! |

## ASKING SOMEONE OUT

| | |
|---|---|
| **Where would you like to go (tonight)?** | (今天晚上)想去哪里玩?<br>(Jīntiān wǎnshàng) xiǎng qù nǎli wán? |
| Q **Would you like to do something (tomorrow)?** | (明天)想出去玩吗?<br>(Míngtiān) xiǎng chūqù wán ma? |
| A **Yes, I'd love to.** | 好啊, 很想去。<br>Hǎo a, hěn xiǎngqù. |
| A **I'm busy.** | 对不起, 我有事。<br>Duìbùqǐ, wǒ yǒushì. |

## PICK-UP LINES

| | |
|---|---|
| **Would you like a drink?** | 你想喝点什么?<br>Nǐ xiǎng hē diǎn shénme? |
| **You look like some cousin of mine.** | 你长得像我的表妹。<br>Nǐ zhǎngde xiàng wǒde biǎomèi. |
| **You're a fantastic dancer.** | 你跳得真好。<br>Nǐ tiàode zhēnhǎo. |

| | |
|---|---|
| **Can I be with you forever?** | 我能陪你一起到老吗？<br>Wǒ néng péinǐ yīqǐ dàolǎo ma? |
| **Can I dance with you?** | 我能跟你跳个舞吗？<br>Wǒ néng gēnnǐ tiàogewǔ ma? |
| **Can I sit here?** | 我能坐这儿吗？<br>Wǒ néng zuò zhèr ma? |

## REJECTIONS

| | |
|---|---|
| **I'm here with my boyfriend/girlfriend.** | 我同男朋友/女朋友一起来的。<br>Wǒ tóng nánpéngyou/nǚpéngyou yīqǐ lái de. |
| **Excuse me, I have to go now.** | 对不起，我要走了。<br>Duìbùqǐ, wǒ yào zǒule. |
| **I'd rather not.** | 我不想。<br>Wǒ bù xiǎng. |
| **No, thank you.** | 不行，谢谢。<br>Bùxíng, xièxie. |
| **Go and play somewhere else!** | 到一边玩去！<br>Dào yībiān wán qù! |
| **Leave me alone!** | 别烦我！<br>Bié fán wǒ! |

## GETTING CLOSER

| | |
|---|---|
| **I like you very much.** | 我很喜欢你。<br>Wǒ hěn xǐhuān nǐ. |
| **You're great.** | 你真棒。<br>Nǐ zhēn bàng. |
| **Let's kiss!** | 咱们亲一下！<br>Zánmen qīnyīxià! |

### CULTURE TIP: BODY LANGUAGE

Beware of inadvertently sending the wrong signals with your body language while in China. Squeezing hard on people's hands when shaking hands is an attribute only of foreigners. Chinese handshakes are soft – more of a gentle clasp really. Foreigners' habit of looking at locals while they speak to them is also off-putting, as the norm in China is not to look people in the eye when talking to them. When someone is addressing you, however, it's all right to look at them.

Don't be put off by people gesturing at their noses as if they have an itch. The nose, as opposed to the heart, is the symbolic centre of the self in China. Don't kiss anyone by way of greeting unless you want to frighten or titillate: it's not socially acceptable.

| | |
|---|---|
| **Do you want to come inside for a while?** | 想进来坐坐吗？<br>Xiǎng jìnlái zuòzuo ma? |
| **Do you want a massage?** | 你想按摩吗？<br>Nǐ xiǎng ànmó ma? |

## SEX

| | |
|---|---|
| **Do you have a (condom)?** | 你带（避孕套）了吗？<br>Nǐ dài (bìyùntào) le ma? |
| **Let's use a (condom).** | 咱们用（避孕套）吧。<br>Zánmen yòng (bìyùntào) ba. |
| **I won't do it without protection.** | 没有防备，我不玩。<br>Méiyǒu fángbèi, wǒ bù wán. |
| **Kiss me!** | 亲我！<br>Qīn wǒ! |
| **I want you.** | 我要你。<br>Wǒ yào nǐ. |

| | |
|---|---|
| **I want to make love to you.** | 我想跟你做爱。<br>Wǒ xiǎng gēnnǐ zuò'ài. |
| **It's my first time.** | 这是我的第一次。<br>Zhè shì wǒde dìyīcì. |
| **How about going to bed?** | 咱们上床，好吗？<br>Zánmen shàngchuáng, hǎo ma? |
| **Touch me here.** | 摸我这儿。<br>Mō wǒ zhèr. |
| Q **Do you like this?** | 喜欢这样吗？<br>Xǐhuān zhèyàng ma? |
| A **I (don't) like that.** | 我（不）喜欢这样。<br>Wǒ (bù) xǐhuān zhèyàng. |
| **I think we should stop now.** | 我想我们现在该结束了。<br>Wǒ xiǎng wǒmen xiànzài gāi jiéshù le. |
| **Oh yeah!** | 真是！<br>Zhēn shì! |
| **That's great!** | 真棒！<br>Zhēnbàng! |
| **Easy tiger!** | 慢点来！<br>Màndiǎn lái! |
| **That was amazing.** | 刚才真不可思议。<br>Gāngcái zhēn bùkě sīyì. |
| **That was weird.** | 刚才真有点奇怪。<br>Gāngcái zhēn yǒudiǎn qíguài. |
| **That was wild.** | 刚才真疯狂。<br>Gāngcái zhēn fēngkuáng. |
| **Can I call you?** | 我可以给你打电话吗？<br>Wǒ kěyǐ gěi nǐ dǎ diànhuà ma? |
| **Can I see you?** | 我可以见你吗？<br>Wǒ kěyǐ jiànnǐ ma? |
| **Can I stay over?** | 我可以在这儿过夜吗？<br>Wǒ kěyǐ zài zhèr guòyè ma? |

### LANGUAGE TIP: TERMS FOR GAYS & LESBIANS

Following the Communist Revolution, the officially sanctioned term of address for both men and women was 'comrade' (tóngzhì 同志). In today's China this word isn't commonly used as a term of address and has undergone a shift in meaning – yesterday's 'comrade' is now a slang word for 'gay'. It's a kind of play on words, as the literal meaning of 'comrade' in Chinese is 'of the same mindset'. While in revolutionary circles this mindset entailed a vision of a new society, today's mindset is a particular vision of sexuality. The self-appellation of tóngzhì as used by China's gay community can be seen as a subversive means of challenging the more official tag of 'homosexual' (tóngxìng liàn 同性恋, literally 'same-sex love').

## LOVE

| | |
|---|---|
| **I love you.** | 我爱你。<br>Wǒ ài nǐ. |
| **I think we're good together.** | 我觉得我们俩挺般配。<br>Wǒ juéde wǒmen liǎ tǐng bānpèi. |
| **Will you go out with me?** | 你能跟我谈朋友吗？<br>Nǐ néng gēn wǒ tán péngyou ma? |
| **Will you live with me?** | 你能跟我住一起吗？<br>Nǐ néng gēn wǒ zhù yīqǐ ma? |
| **Will you marry me?** | 你能跟我结婚吗？<br>Nǐ néng gēn wǒ jiéhūn ma? |

# Beliefs & Culture

## KEY PHRASES

| | | |
|---|---|---|
| **What's your religion?** | 你信什么教? | Nǐ xìn shénme jiào? |
| **I'm ...** | 我信…… | Wǒ xìn ... |
| **I'm sorry, it's against my beliefs.** | 不好意思，这是违背我的信仰的。 | Bùhǎo yìsi, zhèshì wéibèi wǒde xìnyǎng de. |

## RELIGION

| | |
|---|---|
| Q **Are you religious?** | 你信教吗? Nǐ xìnjiào ma? |
| Q **What's your religion?** | 你信什么教? Nǐ xìn shénme jiào? |
| A **I'm ...** | 我信…… Wǒ xìn ... |

| | | |
|---|---|---|
| **agnostic** | 不可知论 | bùkězhī lùn |
| **an atheist** | 无神论 | wúshénlùn |
| **Buddhist** | 佛教 | Fójiào |
| **Catholic** | 天主教 | Tiānzhǔjiào |
| **Christian** | 基督教 | Jīdūjiào |
| **Hindu** | 印度教 | Yìndùjiào |
| **Jewish** | 犹太教 | Yóutàijiào |
| **Muslim** | 伊斯兰教 | Yīsīlánjiào |

| | |
|---|---|
| **I (don't) believe in ...** | 我(不)信…… Wǒ (bù) xìn ... |

| | | |
|---|---|---|
| **astrology** | 星象 | xīngxiàng |
| **Confucianism** | 儒教 | Rújiào |
| **Daoism** | 道教 | Dàojiào |
| **fate** | 命运 | mìngyùn |
| **fengshui** | 风水 | fēngshuǐ |
| **God** | 上帝 | shàngdì |

| | |
|---|---|
| **Can I attend a service here?** | 我能在这里做礼拜吗？ Wǒ néng zài zhèlǐ zuò lǐbài ma? |
| **Where can I pray?** | 我在哪里可以祈祷? Wǒ zài nǎli kěyǐ qídǎo? |
| **Where can I meditate?** | 我在哪里可以静坐? Wǒ zài nǎli kěyǐ jìngzuò? |

## CULTURAL DIFFERENCES

| | |
|---|---|
| **Is this a local custom?** | 这是地方风俗吗？ Zhè shì dìfāng fēngsú ma? |
| **I don't want to offend you.** | 我不想得罪你们。 Wǒ bù xiǎng dézuì nǐmen. |
| **I'm not used to this.** | 我没有这个习惯。 Wǒ méiyǒu zhège xíguàn. |
| **I'd rather not join in.** | 我最好不参加。 Wǒ zuìhǎo bù cānjiā. |
| **I'll try it.** | 我可以试试。 Wǒ kěyǐ shìshi. |
| **I didn't mean to do anything wrong.** | 我不想做错什么。 Wǒ bùxiǎng zuòcuò shénme. |

### ☑ CULTURE TIP: COMMUNICATING WITH THE CHINESE

Whether you're wheeling and dealing in China, or just trying to get a few yuan knocked off the price of a portrait of Mao, there are a few points to keep in mind to help your negotiations go smoothly.

The concept of 'saving face' (miànzi 面子) is important in Chinese culture. Essentially it's about avoiding being made to look stupid or to back down in front of others – a concept which isn't limited to the Chinese, of course. Negotiated settlements that provide benefits to both parties are preferable to confrontation. A desire to save face may lead people to disguise uncomfortable truths.

Chinese men and women are generally reserved with hand and facial movements. The animated gesticulating of foreigners can seem undignified and even comical to them. Also, a smile doesn't necessarily mean happiness. Chinese people may also smile when they're embarrassed or worried.

For more on body language, see **romance**, page 142.

| | |
|---|---|
| **I'm sorry, it's against my beliefs.** | 不好意思，这是违背我的信仰的。<br>Bùhǎo yìsi, zhèshì wéibèi wǒde xìnyǎng de. |
| **I'm sorry, it's against my religion.** | 不好意思，这是违背我的宗教的。<br>Bùhǎo yìsi, zhèshì wéibèi wǒde zōngjiào de. |
| **This is different.** | 这有点与众不同。<br>Zhè yǒudiǎn yǔzhòng bùtóng. |
| **This is fun.** | 这有点好玩。<br>Zhè yǒudiǎn hǎowán. |
| **This is interesting.** | 这有点意思。<br>Zhè yǒudiǎn yìsi. |

# Sports

## KEY PHRASES

| | | |
|---|---|---|
| **What sport do you play?** | 你喜欢玩什么体育项目？ | Nǐ xǐhuān wán shénme tǐyù xiàngmù? |
| **What's your favourite team?** | 你最喜欢的球队是谁？ | Nǐ zuì xǐhuān de qiúduì shì shéi? |
| **What's the score?** | 几比几？ | Jǐbǐjǐ? |

## SPORTING INTERESTS

In Mandarin any sport can be 'played' using the verb wán 玩, but generally this has light-hearted connotations, as in 'to have a kick of the ball', expressing such a playful interest in sport.

| | |
|---|---|
| Q **What sport do you play?** | 你喜欢玩什么体育项目？<br>Nǐ xǐhuān wán shénme tǐyù xiàngmù? |
| A **I play/do ...** | 我喜欢玩……<br>Wǒ xǐhuān wán ... |

To say that you really play a sport, you need to use an appropriate verb such as 'hit' (dǎ 打) or 'kick' (tī 踢). If you follow a sport, use the verb 'follow' (kàn 看).

| | |
|---|---|
| **I play (football/soccer).** | 我喜欢踢（足球）。<br>Wǒ xǐhuān tī (zúqiú). |
| **I follow (rugby).** | 我喜欢看（英式橄榄球）。<br>Wǒ xǐhuān kàn (yīngshì gǎnlǎnqiú). |

| | |
|---|---|
| **I play ...** | 我喜欢打……<br>Wǒ xǐhuān dǎ ... |
| **I follow ...** | 我喜欢看……<br>Wǒ xǐhuān kàn ... |

| | | |
|---|---|---|
| **badminton** | 羽毛球 | yǔmáoqiú |
| **basketball** | 篮球 | lánqiú |
| **handball** | 手球 | shǒuqiú |
| **hockey** | 曲棍球 | qūgùnqiú |
| **table tennis** | 乒乓球 | pīngpāng qiú |
| **tennis** | 网球 | wǎngqiú |
| **(beach) volleyball** | (沙滩)排球 | (shātān) páiqiú |
| **water polo** | 水球 | shuǐqiú |

The verb 'do' (gǎo 搞) can be used when you're not sure whether you should hit, kick or train harder (as in cycling or athletics).

| | |
|---|---|
| **I do ...** | 我喜欢搞……<br>Wǒ xǐhuān gǎo ... |
| **I follow ...** | 我喜欢看……<br>Wǒ xǐhuān kàn ... |

| | | |
|---|---|---|
| **archery** | 射箭 | shèjiàn |
| **fencing** | 剑术 | jiànshù |
| **long-distance running** | 长跑 | chángpǎo |
| **rowing** | 划船 | huáchuán |
| **sailing** | 帆船 | fānchuán |
| **scuba diving** | 潜水 | qiánshuǐ |
| **shooting** | 射击 | shèjī |
| **swimming** | 游泳 | yóuyǒng |
| **track & field** | 田径 | tiánjìng |
| **weightlifting** | 举重 | jǔzhòng |

Some sports (such as gymnastics and martial arts) are identified not by hits or kicks but by the rigorous 'repetitive training' required of the practitioner, expressed by the verb liàn 练.

| | |
|---|---|
| **I play/do ...** | 我喜欢练……<br>Wó xǐhuān liàn ... |
| **I follow ...** | 我喜欢看……<br>Wó xǐhuān kàn ... |

| | | |
|---|---|---|
| **gymnastics** | 体操 | tǐcāo |
| **judo** | 柔道 | róudào |
| **karate** | 空手道 | kōngshǒudào |
| **martial arts (Chinese kung fu)** | 武术 (中国功夫) | wǔshù (Zhōngguó gōngfu) |
| **tae kwon do** | 跆拳道 | táiquándào |
| **t'ai chi** | 太极拳 | tàijíquán |

| | |
|---|---|
| **I like to cycle.** | 我喜欢骑自行车。<br>Wǒ xǐhuān qí zìxíngchē. |
| **I like to run.** | 我喜欢跑步。<br>Wǒ xǐhuān pǎobù. |
| **I like to walk.** | 我喜欢散步。<br>Wǒ xǐhuān sànbù. |
| **Who's your favourite sportsperson?** | 你最喜欢的球星是谁？<br>Nǐ zuì xǐhuān de qiúxīng shì shéi? |
| **Who's your favourite team?** | 你最喜欢的球队是谁？<br>Nǐ zuì xǐhuān de qiúduì shì shéi? |
| Q **Do you like to play (table tennis)?** | 你喜欢打 (乒乓球) 吗？<br>Nǐ xǐhuān dǎ (pīngpāngqiú) ma? |
| A **Yes, very much.** | 很喜欢。<br>Hěn xǐhuān. |

| | |
|---|---|
| (A) **Not really.** | 不太喜欢。<br>Bùtài xǐhuān. |
| (A) **I like watching it.** | 我喜欢看。<br>Wǒ xǐhuān kàn. |
| (Q) **What's the score?** | 几比几？<br>Jǐbǐjǐ? |
| (A) **draw/even** | 打平<br>dǎ píng |
| (A) **love/zero** | 零<br>líng |
| (A) **match point** | 赛点<br>sàidiǎn |

## GOING TO A GAME

| | |
|---|---|
| **Would you like to go to a game with me?** | 你想跟我去看球赛吗？<br>Nǐ xiǎng gēn wǒ qù kàn qiúsài ma? |
| **Who are you supporting?** | 你支持哪个队？<br>Nǐ zhīchí nǎge duì? |
| **Who's playing?** | 谁在打？<br>Shéi zài dǎ? |
| **Who's winning?** | 谁占上风？<br>Shéi zhànshàngfēng? |

### LISTEN FOR

| | | |
|---|---|---|
| 进门！ | Jìnmén! | What a goal! |
| 好球！ | Hǎoqiú! | What a hit! |
| 踢得好！ | Tīde hǎo! | What a kick! |
| 传得好！ | Chuánde hǎo! | What a pass! |
| 真精彩！ | Zhēn jīngcǎi! | What a performance! |

| | |
|---|---|
| **Come on!** | 加油！<br>Jiāyóu! |
| **That was a bad game!** | 比赛打得真差劲！<br>Bǐsài dǎde zhēn chàjìn! |
| **That was a great game!** | 比赛打得真精彩！<br>Bǐsài dǎde zhēn jīngcǎi! |

## PLAYING SPORT

| | |
|---|---|
| Q **Do you want to play?** | 你想玩吗？<br>Nǐ xiǎng wán ma? |
| A **I have an injury.** | 我受伤了。<br>Wǒ shòushāng le. |
| Q **Can I join in?** | 我可以跟你们一起玩吗？<br>Wǒ kěyǐ gēn nǐmen yīqǐ wán ma? |
| A **Great.** | 好。<br>Hǎo. |
| **Your/My point.** | 你/我得分。<br>Nǐ/Wǒ dé fēn. |
| **Kick/Pass it to me!** | 踢/传给我！<br>Tī/Chuán gěi wǒ! |
| **You're a good player.** | 你打得很好。<br>Nǐ dǎde hěnhǎo. |
| **Thanks, I enjoyed the game.** | 多谢你，我打得很开心。<br>Duōxiè nǐ, wǒ dǎ de hěn kāixīn. |
| **Do I have to be a member to attend?** | 只对会员开放吗？<br>Zhǐ duì huìyuán kāifàng ma? |
| **Is there a women-only session?** | 有女子班吗？<br>Yǒu nǚzǐ bān ma? |
| **Where are the changing rooms?** | 更衣室在哪儿？<br>Gēngyīshì zài nǎr? |

**Where's the nearest ...?** 最近的……在哪里？
Zuìjìnde ... zài nǎli?

| | | |
|---|---|---|
| **golf course** | 高尔夫球场 | gāo'ěrfū qiúchǎng |
| **gym** | 健身房 | jiànshēn fáng |
| **swimming pool** | 游泳池 | yóuyǒng chí |
| **tennis court** | 网球场 | wǎngqiú chǎng |

**What's the charge per ...?** 每……要花多少钱？
Měi ... yàohuā duōshǎo qián?

| | | |
|---|---|---|
| **day** | 天 | tiān |
| **game** | 场 | chǎng |
| **hour** | 小时 | xiǎoshí |
| **visit** | 次 | cì |

真精彩！
Zhēn jīngcǎi!
***What a performance!***

| | |
|---|---|
| **Can I hire a ...?** | 我可以租一……吗？<br>Wǒ kěyǐzūyī ... ma? |

| | | |
|---|---|---|
| **ball** | 个球 | ge qiú |
| **bicycle** | 辆自行车 | liàng zìxíngchē |
| **court** | 个场地 | ge chǎngdì |
| **racquet** | 副拍子 | fù pāizi |

## TABLE TENNIS

| | |
|---|---|
| **I'd like to play table tennis.** | 我想打乒乓球。<br>Wǒ xiǎng dǎ pīngpāng qiú. |
| **Do you know where I can find a table-tennis table?** | 哪里有乒乓球桌?<br>Nǎli yǒu pīngpāng qiú zhuō? |
| **Can I book a table?** | 我可以预订一个乒乓球桌吗?<br>Wǒ kěyǐ yùdìng yīge pīngpāng qiú zhuō ma? |
| **bat** | 拍子<br>pāizi |
| **net** | 网<br>wǎng |
| **serve** | 发球<br>fāqiú |
| **table** | 球桌<br>qiúzhuō |
| **table-tennis ball** | 乒乓球<br>pīngpāng qiú |

### CULTURE TIP: CHINESE MARTIAL ARTS

In Mandarin, the many styles of martial arts are collectively known as wǔshù (Zhōngguó gōngfu) 武术(中国功夫). Each style embodies its own particular spirit and philosophy (drawing on Confucianism, Taoism, Buddhism and Zen). Here are a few styles that travellers to China may see:

| | | |
|---|---|---|
| **Bagua Zhang (Eight-Trigram Boxing)** | 八卦掌 | Bāguà zhǎng |

The characteristics of this martial art style, in which practitioners wheel around in circles kicking and landing palm strikes, are the skills of subterfuge, evasion, speed and unpredictability.

| | | |
|---|---|---|
| **Shaolin Boxing** | 少林拳 | Shàolín quán |

Originating at the Shaolin monastery and still practised there today, this major martial art form draws on Zen Buddhist beliefs and bases its forms on five animals: dragon, snake, tiger, leopard and crane.

| | | |
|---|---|---|
| **Taijiquan** | 太极拳 | Tàijíquán |

Known in the West as t'ai chi, this graceful centuries-old Chinese system promotes flexibility, circulation, strength, balance, meditation and relaxation. Based on Taoist beliefs, it's traditionally practised as a form of self-defence without the use of force.

| | | |
|---|---|---|
| **Xingyi Quan (Body-Mind Boxing)** | 形意拳 | Xíngyì quán |

Often mentioned in the same breath as *taijiquan*, this martial art is more dynamic and powerful. The movements of it – perhaps the oldest form of martial art still practised in China – are performed in a relaxed state but quickly and directly.

# Outdoors

## KEY PHRASES

| | | |
|---|---|---|
| **Where can I buy supplies?** | 在哪里能买到预备品？ | Zài nǎli néng mǎidào yùbèipǐn? |
| **Do we need a guide?** | 需要向导吗？ | Xūyào xiàngdǎo ma? |
| **Is it safe?** | 安全吗？ | Ānquán ma? |
| **I'm lost.** | 我迷路了。 | Wǒ mílù le. |
| **What's the weather like?** | 天气怎么样？ | Tiānqì zěnmeyàng? |

## HIKING

| | |
|---|---|
| **Where can I buy supplies?** | 在哪里能买到预备品？<br>Zài nǎli néng mǎidào yùbèipǐn? |
| **Where can I find someone who knows this area?** | 在哪里能找路熟的人？<br>Zài nǎli néng zhǎo lùshú de rén? |
| **Where can I get a map?** | 在哪里能买地图？<br>Zài nǎli néng mǎi dìtú? |
| **Do we need to take bedding?** | 需要带上被褥吗？<br>Xūyào dàishàng bèirù ma? |
| **Do we need to take food?** | 需要带上食品吗？<br>Xūyào dàishàng shípǐn ma? |
| **Do we need to take water?** | 需要带上饮用水吗？<br>Xūyào dàishàng yǐnyòngshuǐ ma? |
| **How high is the climb?** | 山有多高？<br>Shān yǒu duō gāo? |

| | |
|---|---|
| **How long is the trail?** | 步行有多远?<br>Bùxíng yǒu duō yuǎn? |
| **Do we need a guide?** | 需要向导吗?<br>Xūyào xiàngdǎo ma? |
| **Are there guided treks?** | 有徒步旅行团吗?<br>Yǒu túbù lǚxíng tuán ma? |
| **Is it safe?** | 安全吗?<br>Ānquán ma? |
| **Is the track easy to follow?** | 路好找吗?<br>Lù hǎozhǎo ma? |
| **Is the track open?** | 路开通了吗?<br>Lù kāitōng le ma? |
| **Is the track scenic?** | 路边风景好吗?<br>Lù biān fēngjǐng hǎo ma? |
| **Which is the easiest route?** | 哪条路最容易?<br>Nǎtiáo lù zuì róngyì? |
| **Which is the most interesting route?** | 哪条路最有意思?<br>Nǎtiáo lù zuì yǒu yìsi? |
| **Which is the shortest route?** | 哪条路最短?<br>Nǎtiáo lù zuì duǎn? |
| **Is there somewhere to spend the night?** | 有地方住吗?<br>Yǒu dìfāng zhù ma? |
| **When does it get dark?** | 天什么时候变黑?<br>Tiān shénme shíhòu biànhēi? |
| **Where's the nearest village?** | 最近的村子在哪里?<br>Zuìjìn de cūnzi zài nǎli? |
| **Where have you come from?** | 你从哪边过来的?<br>Nǐ cóng nǎbiān guòlái de? |
| **How long did it take?** | 走了有多久?<br>Zǒule yǒu duōjiǔ? |
| **Does this path go to ...?** | 这条路到……吗?<br>Zhètiáo lù dào ... ma? |

| | |
|---|---|
| **Can I go through here?** | 我能从这里穿过吗？<br>Wǒ néng cóng zhèlǐ chuānguò ma? |
| **Is the water OK to drink?** | 这水能喝吗？<br>Zhè shuǐ nénghē ma? |
| **I'm lost.** | 我迷路了。<br>Wǒ mílù le. |

## AT THE BEACH

| | |
|---|---|
| **Where's the best beach?** | 最好的海滩在哪里？<br>Zuìhǎo de shātān zài nǎli? |
| **Where's the nearest beach?** | 最近的海滩在哪里？<br>Zuìjìn de shātān zài nǎli? |
| **Where's the public beach?** | 公共的海滩在哪里？<br>Gōnggòng de shātān zài nǎli? |
| **Is it safe to swim here?** | 这里游泳安全吗？<br>Zhèlǐ yóuyǒng ānquán ma? |
| **What time is high/low tide?** | 涨/退潮是几点钟？<br>Zhǎng/Tuì cháo shì jǐdiǎnzhōng? |
| **Do we have to pay?** | 要买票吗？<br>Yào mǎipiào ma? |

## WEATHER

| | |
|---|---|
| Q **What's the weather like?** | 天气怎么样？<br>Tiānqì zěnmeyàng? |
| Q **What will the weather be like tomorrow?** | 明天天气会怎么样？<br>Míngtiān tiānqì huì zěnmeyàng? |

SOCIAL OUTDOORS

**It's ...** 天气…… Tiānqì ...

| | | |
|---|---|---|
| **cloudy** | 多云 | duō yún |
| **cold** | 冷 | lěng |
| **fine** | 晴 | qíng |
| **freezing** | 很冷 | hěnlěng |
| **hot** | 热 | rè |
| **raining** | 下雨 | xiàyǔ |
| **snowing** | 下雪 | xiàxuě |
| **sunny** | 晴朗 | qínglǎng |
| **warm** | 暖和 | nuǎnhuo |
| **windy** | 刮风 | guāfēng |

**Where can I buy a rain jacket?** 在哪里能买到雨衣？ Zài nǎli néng mǎidào yǔyī?

**Where can I buy an umbrella?** 在哪里能买到雨伞？ Zài nǎli néng mǎidào yǔsǎn?

**dry season** 旱季 hànjì

**monsoon season** 季风季节 jìfēng jìjié

**wet season** 雨季 yǔjì

# FLORA & FAUNA

**What ... is that?** 那个……是什么？ Nàge ... shì shénme?

| | | |
|---|---|---|
| **animal** | 动物 | dòngwù |
| **flower** | 花 | huā |
| **plant** | 植物 | zhíwù |
| **tree** | 树 | shù |

## LISTEN FOR

| | | |
|---|---|---|
| 大熊猫 | dà xióng māo | giant panda |
| 荷花 | héhuā | lotus |
| 牡丹 | mǔdān | peony |
| 丹顶鹤 | dāndǐng hè | red-necked crane |
| 小熊猫 | xiǎo xióng māo | red panda |
| 东北虎 | dōngběi hǔ | Siberian tiger |

**Is it ...?** 是……的吗？
Shì ... de ma?

| | | |
|---|---|---|
| **common** | 常见 | chángjiàn |
| **dangerous** | 危险 | wēixiǎn |
| **endangered** | 濒危 | bīnwēi |
| **protected** | 受保护 | shòu bǎohù |

**What's it used for?** 它用来做什么？
Tā yònglái zuò shénme?

**Can you eat the fruit?** 果子能吃吗?
Guǒzi néngchī ma?

# SAFE TRAVEL

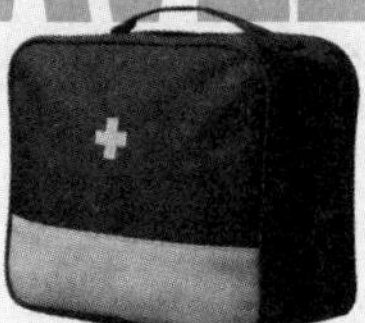


| | |
|---|---|
| EMERGENCIES | 162 |
| POLICE | 164 |
| HEALTH | 166 |

# Emergencies

## KEY PHRASES

| | | |
|---|---|---|
| **Help!** | 救命！ | Jiùmìng! |
| **It's an emergency.** | 有急事。 | Yǒu jíshì. |
| **Where are the toilets?** | 厕所在哪儿？ | Cèsuǒ zài nǎr? |

| | |
|---|---|
| **Help!** | 救命！<br>Jiùmìng! |
| **Stop!** | 站住！<br>Zhànzhù! |
| **Go away!** | 走开！<br>Zǒukāi! |
| **Thief!** | 小偷！<br>Xiǎotōu! |
| **Fire!** | 着火啦！<br>Zháohuǒ la! |
| **Watch out!** | 小心！<br>Xiǎoxīn! |
| **It's an emergency.** | 有急事。<br>Yǒu jíshì. |
| **Call a doctor!** | 请叫医生来！<br>Qǐng jiào yīshēng lái! |
| **Call an ambulance!** | 请叫一辆急救车！<br>Qǐng jiào yīliàng jíjiù chē! |
| **I'm ill.** | 我生病了。<br>Wǒ shēngbìng le. |

### LOOK FOR

| | | |
|---|---|---|
| 急诊科 | Jízhěn Kē | Emergency Department |
| 医院 | Yīyuàn | Hospital |
| 警察 | Jǐngchá | Police |
| 派出所 | Pàichūsuǒ | Police Station |

**My friend/child is ill.**
我的朋友/孩子生病了。
Wǒde péngyou/háizi shēngbìng le.

**He/She is having a/an ...**
他/她……
Tā ...

| | | |
|---|---|---|
| **allergic reaction** | 过敏症发作 | guòmǐnzhèng fāzuò |
| **asthma attack** | 哮喘发病 | xiàochuǎn fābìng |
| **baby** | 在生孩子 | zài shēng háizi |
| **epileptic fit** | 癫痫病发作 | diānxiánbìng fāzuò |
| **heart attack** | 心脏病发作 | xīnzàngbìng fāzuò |

**I'm lost.**
我迷路了。
Wǒ mílù le.

**Could you please help?**
你能帮我吗？
Nǐ néng bāngwǒ ma?

**Can I use your phone?**
我能借用你的电话吗？
Wǒ néng jièyòng nǐde diànhuà ma?

**Where are the toilets?**
厕所在哪儿？
Cèsuǒ zài nǎr?

# Police

## KEY PHRASES

| | | |
|---|---|---|
| **Where's the police station?** | 派出所在哪里? | Pàichūsuǒ zài nǎli? |
| **I want to contact my embassy/ consulate.** | 我要联系我的大使馆/领事馆。 | Wǒ yào liánxì wǒde dàshǐguǎn/ lǐngshìguǎn. |
| **I've lost my bags.** | 我的行李丢了。 | Wǒde xíngli diū le. |

In China, it's the Public Security Bureau or PSB (gōng'ānjú 公安局) that's responsible for introducing and enforcing regulations concerning foreigners. Turn to them for mediation in disputes with hotels, restaurants or taxi drivers.

| | |
|---|---|
| **Where's the police station?** | 派出所在哪里?<br>Pàichūsuǒ zài nǎli? |
| **Please telephone 110.** | 请打110。<br>Qǐng dǎ yāo yāo líng. |
| **I want to report an offence.** | 我要报案。<br>Wǒ yào bào'àn. |
| **It was him/her.** | 是他/她做的。<br>Shì tā zuòde. |
| **I've been (assaulted).** | 我被(侵犯)了。<br>Wǒ bèi (qīnfàn)le. |
| **I've been (robbed).** | 我被(抢劫)了。<br>Wǒ bèi (qiǎngjié)le. |
| **He/She has been (raped).** | 他/她被(强奸)了。<br>Tā bèi (qiángjiān)le. |

| | |
|---|---|
| **I've lost my ...** | 我的……丢了。<br>Wǒde ... diū le. |

| | | |
|---|---|---|
| **bags** | 行李 | xíngli |
| **jewellery** | 首饰 | shǒushì |
| **money** | 钱 | qián |
| **papers** | 文件 | wénjiàn |
| **passport** | 护照 | hùzhào |

| | |
|---|---|
| **What am I accused of?** | 我被指控犯了什么罪?<br>Wǒ bèi zhǐkòng fànle shénme zuì? |
| **I didn't do it.** | 不是我做的。<br>Bùshì wǒ zuòde. |
| **I want to contact my embassy/consulate.** | 我要联系我的大使馆/领事馆。<br>Wǒ yào liánxì wǒde dàshǐguǎn/lǐngshìguǎn. |
| **Can I have a lawyer who speaks English?** | 我想找一个会说英文的律师。<br>Wǒ xiǎng zhǎo yīge huìshuō Yīngwén de lǜshī. |
| **This drug is for personal use.** | 这个药品是私用的。<br>Zhège yàopǐn shì sīyòngde. |
| **I have a prescription for this drug.** | 这个药我有处方。<br>Zhège yào wǒ yǒu chǔfāng. |

## LISTEN FOR

| | |
|---|---|
| 你被指控犯了破坏秩序。 | Nǐ bèi zhǐkòng fànle pòhuài zhìxù.<br>You're charged with disturbing the peace. |
| 他/她被指控犯了随带禁物。 | Tā bèi zhǐkòng fànle suídài jìnwù.<br>He/She is charged with possession of illegal substances. |
| 他/她被指控犯了盗窃。 | Tā bèi zhǐkòng fànle dàoqiè.<br>He/She is charged with theft. |

# Health

## KEY PHRASES

| | | |
|---|---|---|
| **Where's the nearest hospital?** | 最近的医院在哪儿？ | Zuìjìnde yīyuàn zài nǎr? |
| **I'm sick.** | 我病了。 | Wǒ bìng le. |
| **I need a doctor (who speaks English).** | 我要看（会说英文的）医生。 | Wǒ yào kàn (huìshuō Yīngwénde) yīshēng. |
| **I'm on medication for ...** | 我有……的处方药。 | Wǒ yǒu ... de chǔfāngyào. |
| **I'm allergic to ...** | 我对……过敏。 | Wǒ duì ... guòmǐn. |

## DOCTOR

**Where's the nearest ...?** 最近的……在哪儿？ Zuìjìnde ... zài nǎr?

| | | |
|---|---|---|
| **(night) pharmacist** | （昼夜）药房 | (zhòuyè) yàofáng |
| **dentist** | 牙医 | yáyī |
| **doctor** | 医生 | yīshēng |
| **emergency department** | 急诊科 | jízhěn kē |
| **hospital** | 医院 | yīyuàn |
| **optometrist** | 眼科 | yǎnkē |

**I need a doctor (who speaks English).** 我要看（会说英文的）医生。 Wǒ yào kàn (huìshuō Yīngwénde) yīshēng.

### LISTEN FOR

| | |
|---|---|
| 哪儿疼呢？ | Nǎr téng ne?<br>Where does it hurt? |
| 发烧吗？ | Fāshāo ma?<br>Do you have a temperature? |
| 这个情况持续了多久？ | Zhège qíngkuàng chíxùle duōjiǔ?<br>How long have you been like this? |
| 以前有过这样的情况吗？ | Yǐqián yǒuguò zhèyàngde qíngkuàng ma?<br>Have you had this before? |
| 你喝酒吗？ | Nǐ hējiǔ ma?<br>Do you drink? |
| 你抽烟吗？ | Nǐ chōuyān ma?<br>Do you smoke? |
| 你吸毒吗？ | Nǐ xīdú ma?<br>Do you take drugs? |
| 你有过敏症吗？ | Nǐ yǒu guòmǐnzhèng ma?<br>Are you allergic to anything? |
| 你有处方药吗？ | Nǐ yǒu chǔfāngyào ma?<br>Are you on medication? |

| | |
|---|---|
| **Could I see a female doctor?** | 最好要看一位女医生。<br>Zuìhǎo yàokàn yīwèi nǚyīshēng. |
| **Could the doctor come here?** | 医生能到这儿来吗？<br>Yīshēng néng dào zhèr lái ma? |
| **Is there an after-hours emergency number?** | 有晚上急诊电话号码吗？<br>Yǒu wǎnshàng jízhěn diànhuà hàomǎ ma? |
| **I've run out of my medication.** | 我用完了我的处方药。<br>Wǒ yòngwánle wǒde chǔfāngyào. |
| **This is my usual medicine.** | 我平时服这个药。<br>Wǒ píngshí fú zhège yào. |

| | |
|---|---|
| **What's the correct dosage?** | 剂量是多少？<br>Jìliàng shì duōshǎo? |
| **I don't want a blood transfusion.** | 我不要输血。<br>Wǒ bùyào shūxuè. |
| **Please use a new syringe.** | 请用一个新针头。<br>Qǐng yòngyīge xīn zhēntóu. |
| **I've been vaccinated against ...** | 我打过……的免疫针。<br>Wǒ dǎguò ... de miǎnyì zhēn. |

| | | |
|---|---|---|
| **hepatitis A/B/C** | 甲/乙/丙肝炎 | jiǎ/yǐ/bǐng gānyán |
| **rabies** | 狂犬病 | kuángquǎnbìng |
| **tetanus** | 破伤风 | pòshāngfēng |
| **typhoid** | 伤寒 | shānghán |

| | |
|---|---|
| **I need new contact lenses.** | 我要买新的隐形眼镜。<br>Wǒ yàomǎi xīnde yǐnxíng yǎnjìng. |
| **I need new glasses.** | 我要买新的眼镜。<br>Wǒ yàomǎi xīnde yǎnjìng. |
| **Can I have a receipt for my insurance?** | 能给我保险发票吗?<br>Néng gěi wǒ bǎoxiǎn fāpiào ma? |

## SYMPTOMS & CONDITIONS

| | |
|---|---|
| **I'm sick.** | 我病了。<br>Wǒ bìng le. |
| **My friend is sick.** | 我的朋友病了。<br>Wǒde péngyou bìng le. |
| **My child is sick.** | 我的孩子病了。<br>Wǒde háizi bìng le. |
| **It hurts here.** | 这里痛。<br>Zhèlǐ tòng. |
| **I'm dehydrated.** | 我脱水了。<br>Wǒ tuōshuǐ le. |

LISTEN FOR

| | |
|---|---|
| 你需要住院。 | Nǐ xūyào zhùyuàn.<br>You need to be admitted to hospital. |
| 你回国要做检查。 | Nǐ huíguó hòu yàozuò jiǎnchá.<br>You should have it checked when you go home. |

**I feel ...** 我感到…… Wǒ gǎndào ...

| | | |
|---|---|---|
| **dizzy** | 头晕 | tóuyūn |
| **hot and cold** | 忽冷忽热 | hūlěng hūrè |
| **nauseous** | 恶心 | ěxīn |
| **shivery** | 全身发抖 | quánshēn fādǒu |

| | |
|---|---|
| **I've been (injured).** | 我(受伤)了。<br>Wǒ (shòushāng)le. |
| **He/She has been (vomiting).** | 他/她(常呕吐)了。<br>Tā (cháng ǒutù)le. |
| **I'm on medication for ...** | 我有……的处方药。<br>Wǒ yǒu ... de chǔfāngyào. |
| **I have ...** | 我有……<br>Wǒ yǒu ... |
| **I've recently had ...** | 我最近有……<br>Wǒ zuìjìn yǒu ... |

## WOMEN'S HEALTH

| | |
|---|---|
| **(I think) I'm pregnant.** | 我(好像)怀孕了。<br>Wǒ (hǎoxiàng) huáiyùn le. |
| **I'm on the pill.** | 我用避孕药。<br>Wǒ yòng bìyùn yào. |

### LISTEN FOR

| | |
|---|---|
| 你有性生活吗？ | Nǐ yǒu xìngshēnghuó ma? Are you sexually active? |
| 你有过非安全性交吗？ | Nǐ yǒuguò fēi ānquán xìngjiāo ma? Have you had unprotected sex? |
| 你用避孕措施吗？ | Nǐ yòng bìyùn cuòshī ma? Are you using contraception? |
| 你的月经还来吗？ | Nǐde yuèjīng háilái ma? Are you menstruating? |
| 上次月经是什么时候？ | Shàngcì yuèjīng shì shénme shíhòu? When did you last have your period? |
| 你怀孕了吗？ | Nǐ huáiyùn le ma? Are you pregnant? |
| 你怀孕了。 | Nǐ huáiyùn le. You're pregnant. |

| | |
|---|---|
| **I haven't had my period for (six) weeks.** | 我（六）个星期没来月经了。 Wǒ (liù)ge xīngqī méi lái yuèjīng le. |
| **I need contraception.** | 我要买避孕品。 Wǒ yàomǎi bìyùn pǐn. |
| **I need the morning-after pill.** | 我要买事后避孕药。 Wǒ yàomǎi shìhòu bìyùn yào. |
| **I need a pregnancy test.** | 我要做一个怀孕测试。 Wǒ yàozuò yīge huáiyùn cèshì. |
| **I've noticed a lump here.** | 我发现这儿长了一个疙瘩。 Wǒ fāxiàn zhèr zhǎngle yīge gēda. |

## ALLERGIES

| | |
|---|---|
| **I have a skin allergy.** | 我皮肤过敏。 Wǒ pífū guòmǐn. |

| | | |
|---|---|---|
| **I'm allergic to ...** | 我对……过敏。<br>Wǒ duì ... guòmǐn. | |
| **anti-inflammatories** | 抗炎药 | kàngyányào |
| **codeine** | 可待因 | kědàiyīn |
| **penicillin** | 青霉素 | qīngméisù |
| **sulphur-based drugs** | 硫基药物 | liújī yàowù |

## ALTERNATIVE TREATMENTS

Herbal medicine (zhōngyào 中药) and acupuncture (zhēnjiǔ 针灸) are the most common medical systems in China.

| | | |
|---|---|---|
| **I don't use (Western medicine).** | 我不吃(西药)。<br>Wǒ bùchī (Xīyào). | |
| **Can I see someone who practises ...?** | 哪里能看……大夫?<br>Nǎli néngkàn ... dàifu? | |
| **acupuncture** | 针灸 | zhēnjiǔ |
| **Chinese herbal medicine** | 中药 | zhōngyào |
| **Chinese medicine** | 中医 | zhōngyī |
| **meridian massage** | 经络按摩 | jīngluò ànmó |

### LOOK FOR

| | | |
|---|---|---|
| 不许吸烟 | Bùxǔ xīyān | No Smoking |
| 不许吐痰 | Bùxǔ tǔtán | No Spitting |

# PARTS OF THE BODY

| | |
|---|---|
| **My ... hurts.** | 我的……疼。<br>Wǒde ... téng. |
| **I can't move my ...** | 我的……不能动。<br>Wǒde ... bùnéng dòng. |
| **I have a cramp in my ...** | 我的……抽筋了。<br>Wǒde ... chōujīn le. |
| **My ... is swollen.** | 我的……发肿了。<br>Wǒde ... fāzhǒng le. |

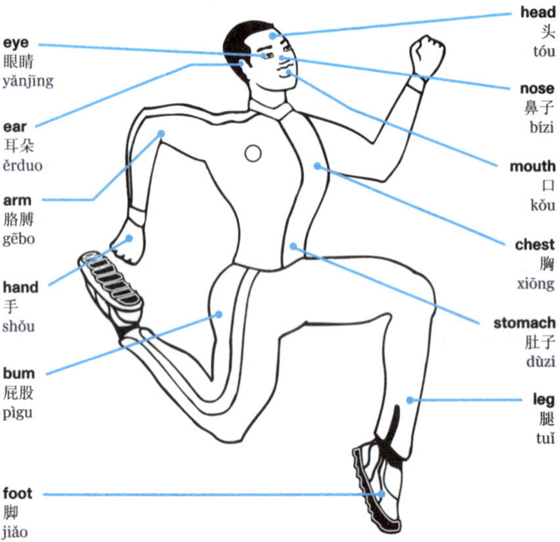

### LISTEN FOR

| | |
|---|---|
| 必须用完。 | Bìxū yòngwán.<br>You must complete the course. |
| 以前吃过吗？ | Yǐqián chīguò ma?<br>Have you taken this before? |
| 一天两次（与饭一起吃）。 | Yītiān liǎngcì (yú fàn yīqǐ chī).<br>Twice a day (with food). |

# CHEMIST/PHARMACIST

| | |
|---|---|
| **I need something for ...** | 我要……的药。<br>Wǒ yào ... de yào. |
| **Do I need a prescription for ...?** | ……需要处方吗？<br>... xūyào chǔfāng ma? |
| **I have a prescription.** | 我有处方。<br>Wǒ yǒu chǔfāng. |
| **My prescription is ...** | 我的处方是……<br>Wǒ de chǔfāng shì ... |
| **How many times a day?** | 每天吃几次？<br>Měitiān chī jǐcì? |
| **Will it make me drowsy?** | 吃后犯困吗？<br>Chīhòu fànkùn ma? |

# DENTIST

| | |
|---|---|
| **I have a toothache.** | 我有牙疼。<br>Wǒ yǒu yáténg. |
| **I have a broken tooth.** | 我有崩牙。<br>Wǒ yǒu bēngyá. |
| **I have a cavity.** | 我有牙洞。<br>Wǒ yǒu yádòng. |

### LISTEN FOR

| | | |
|---|---|---|
| 张开口。 | Zhāngkāi kǒu. | Open wide. |
| 咬一下。 | Yǎoyīxià. | Bite down on this. |
| 漱口！ | Shùkǒu! | Rinse! |

| | |
|---|---|
| **I've lost a filling.** | 我的牙齿填充物掉了。<br>Wǒ de yáchǐ tiánchōngwù diàole. |
| **My dentures are broken.** | 我的假牙坏了。<br>Wǒde jiǎyá huàile. |
| **My gums hurt.** | 我齿龈好痛。<br>Wǒ chǐyín hǎotòng. |
| **I need an anaesthetic.** | 我需要麻醉药。<br>Wǒ xūyào mázuì yào. |
| **I need a filling.** | 我需要补牙。<br>Wǒ xūyào bǔyá. |

# FOOD

| | |
|---|---|
| EATING OUT | 176 |
| SELF-CATERING | 192 |
| VEGETARIAN & SPECIAL MEALS | 196 |

# Eating Out

## KEY PHRASES

| | | |
|---|---|---|
| **Can you recommend a restaurant?** | 你可以推荐一个饭馆吗？ | Nǐ kěyǐ tuījiàn yīge fànguǎn ma? |
| **I'd like a table for (five).** | 我要一张（五个人的）桌子。 | Wǒ yào yīzhāng (wǔge rén de) zhuōzi. |
| **I'd like a menu (in English).** | 我要（英文）菜单。 | Wǒ yào (Yīngwén) càidān. |
| **I'll have (a beer).** | 我来一个（啤酒）。 | Wǒ lái yīge (píjiǔ). |
| **Bill, please!** | 买单！ | Mǎidān! |

## BASICS

Depending on the region, dinner is often the main meal of the day and may include a selection of stirfried dishes, soup, rice, and beer. Lunch can range from a simplified version of that to a bowl of noodles. All meals are served hot – hot food is believed to be better for digestion.

| | |
|---|---|
| **breakfast** | 早饭<br>zǎofàn |
| **lunch** | 午饭<br>wǔfàn |
| **dinner** | 晚饭<br>wǎnfàn |
| **snack** | 小吃<br>xiǎochī |

| | |
|---|---|
| **to eat** | 吃<br>chī |
| **to drink** | 喝<br>hē |
| **I'm starving!** | 我饿坏了！<br>Wǒ è huài le! |

## FINDING A PLACE TO EAT

| | |
|---|---|
| **Can you recommend a ...?** | 你可以推荐一个……吗？<br>Nǐ kěyǐ tuījiàn yīge ... ma? |

| | | |
|---|---|---|
| **bar** | 酒吧 | jiǔbā |
| **cafe** | 咖啡店 | kāfēidiàn |
| **noodle house** | 面馆 | miànguǎn |
| **restaurant** | 饭馆 | fànguǎn |
| **snack shop** | 小吃店 | xiǎochī diàn |
| **(wonton) stall** | (馄饨)摊 | (húntun) tān |
| **street vendor** | 街头小吃 | jiētóu xiǎochī |
| **teahouse** | 茶馆 | cháguǎn |

| | |
|---|---|
| **Where would you go for (a) ...?** | ……该到哪里去？<br>... gāi dàonǎli qù? |

| | | |
|---|---|---|
| **banquet** | 办宴席 | bàn yànxí |
| **celebration** | 举行庆祝会 | jǔxíng qìngzhù huì |
| **cheap meal** | 吃得便宜一点的 | chīde piányi yīdiǎn de |
| **local specialities** | 地方小吃 | dìfāng xiǎochī |
| **yum cha** | 饮茶 | yǐnchá |

LISTEN FOR

| | | |
|---|---|---|
| 关门了。 | Guānmén le. | We're closed. |
| 客满了。 | Kè mǎn le. | We're full. |
| 请等一下。 | Qǐng děng yīxià. | One moment. |
| 坐哪里？ | Zuò nǎli? | Where would you like to sit? |

| | |
|---|---|
| **I'd like to reserve a table for (two) people.** | 我想预订一张（两个）人的桌子。<br>Wǒ xiǎng yùdìng yīzhāng (liǎngge) rén de zhuōzi. |
| **I'd like to reserve a table for (eight) o'clock.** | 我想预订一张（八）点钟的桌子。<br>Wǒ xiǎng yùdìng yīzhāng (bā) diǎn zhōng de zhuōzi. |
| **Are you still serving food?** | 你们还营业吗？<br>Nǐmen hái yíngyè ma? |
| **How long is the wait?** | 吃饭要等多久？<br>Chīfàn yàoděng duōjiǔ? |

## AT THE RESTAURANT

The Chinese have a word, rènào 热闹 (literally 'hot and noisy', ie 'bustling'), which typifies the atmosphere of their restaurants. When the Chinese eat out, they like to have raucous, lip-smacking fun. The style of whispering couples sipping expensive wine by candle-light is not their thing.

| | |
|---|---|
| **What would you recommend for the main meal?** | 有什么主菜可以推荐的?<br>Yǒu shénme zhǔcài kěyǐ tuījiàn de? |
| **What would you recommend for dessert?** | 有什么甜点可以推荐的?<br>Yǒu shénme tiándiǎn kěyǐ tuījiàn de? |
| **What would you recommend for drinks?** | 有什么饮料可以推荐的?<br>Yǒu shénme yǐnliào kěyǐ tuījiàn de? |

| | |
|---|---|
| **What's in that dish?** | 这道菜用什么东西做的?<br>Zhèdào cài yòng shénme dōngxi zuòde? |
| **I'll have that.** | 来一个吧。<br>Lái yīge ba. |
| **I'd like a/the ...** | 我要……<br>Wǒ yào ... |

| | | |
|---|---|---|
| **drink list** | 酒水单 | jiǔshuǐ dān |
| **half portion** | 半份 | bànfèn |
| **menu in English** | 英文菜单 | Yīngwén càidān |
| **nonsmoking table** | 不吸烟的桌子 | bùxīyān de zhuōzi |
| **smoking table** | 吸烟的桌子 | xīyān de zhuōzi |
| **table for (five)** | 一张(五个人的)桌子 | yīzhāng (wǔge rén de) zhuōzi |

| | | |
|---|---|---|
| **For two, please.** | 两个人,谢谢。 | Liǎngge rén, xièxie. |

| | |
|---|---|
| **Can I see the menu, please?** | 能不能给我看一下菜单?<br>Néng bù néng gěiwǒ kànyīxià càidān? |

| | | |
|---|---|---|
| **Menu, please.** | 菜单,谢谢。 | Càidān, xièxie. |

| | |
|---|---|
| **Is it self-serve?** | 这里是自助的吗?<br>Zhèlǐ shì zìzhù de ma? |
| **Are these complimentary?** | 这是赠送的吗?<br>Zhè shì zèngsòng de ma? |
| **I'd like the beef noodle soup.** | 我想吃牛肉面。<br>Wǒ xiǎng chī niúròu miàn. |
| **I'd like a local speciality.** | 我想吃一个地方特色菜。<br>Wǒ xiǎng chī yīge dìfāng tèsè cài. |
| **I'd like a meal fit for a king.** | 我想吃山珍海味。<br>Wǒ xiǎng chī shānzhēn hǎiwèi. |

LISTEN FOR

| | | |
|---|---|---|
| 想点什么？ | Xiǎng diǎn shénme? | What can I get for you? |
| 你喜欢……吗？ | Nǐ xǐhuān ... ma? | Do you like ...? |
| 我建议…… | Wǒ jiànyì ... | I suggest the ... |
| 上菜了！ | Shàng cài le! | Here you go! |

## REQUESTS

**Please bring a ...** 请拿一……来。 Qǐng ná yī ... lái.

| | | |
|---|---|---|
| **cloth** | 块抹布 | kuài mǒbù |
| **glass** | 个杯子 | ge bēizi |
| **knife and fork** | 副刀叉 | fù dāochā |
| **napkin** | 块餐巾 | kuài cānjīn |
| **wineglass** | 个葡萄酒杯 | ge pútáo jiǔbēi |

**I'd like it with ...** 多放一点…… Duōfàng yīdiǎn ...

**I'd like it without ...** 不要放…… Bùyàofàng ...

| | | |
|---|---|---|
| **chili** | 辣椒 | làjiāo |
| **garlic** | 大蒜 | dàsuàn |
| **nuts** | 果仁 | guǒrén |
| **oil** | 油 | yóu |
| **MSG** | 味精 | wèijīng |

For phrases relating to allergies and food choices, see **vegetarian & special meals**, page 196.

# Eating Out

CAN I SEE THE MENU, PLEASE?
能不能给我看一下菜单?
Néng bù néng gěiwǒ kàngyīxià càidān?

WHAT WOULD YOU RECOMMEND FOR ...?
有什么……可以推荐的?
Yǒu shénme ... kěyǐ tuījiàn de?

THE MAIN MEAL
主菜
zhǔcài

DESSERT
甜点
tiándiǎn

DRINKS
饮料
yǐnliào

CAN YOU BRING ME SOME ..., PLEASE?
请拿些……来。
Qǐng ná xiē ... lái.

PLEASE BRING THE BILL.
请给我账单。
Qǐng gěiwǒ zhàngdān.

| I (don't) want it ... | 我(不)要……的。<br>Wǒ (bù)yào ... de. |
|---|---|

| | | |
|---|---|---|
| **barbecued** | 烧烤 | shāokǎo |
| **boiled** | 煮 | zhǔ |
| **braised** | 煎 | jiān |
| **deep-fried** | 油炸 | yóuzhá |
| **grilled** | 铁板烤 | tiěbǎn kǎo |
| **medium** | 半生半熟 | bànshēng bànshú |
| **rare** | 半生 | bànshēng |
| **reheated** | 重热 | chóngrè |
| **roasted** | 烤 | kǎo |
| **steamed** | 蒸 | zhēng |
| **stir-fried** | 炒 | chǎo |
| **well done** | 熟 | shú |

| Do you have ...? | 有没有……?<br>Yǒuméiyǒu ...? |
|---|---|

| | | |
|---|---|---|
| **chili sauce** | 辣椒酱 | làjiāo jiàng |
| **dipping sauce** | 蘸酱 | zhàngjiàng |
| **garlic** | 大蒜 | dàsuàn |
| **soy sauce** | 酱油 | jiàngyóu |
| **vinegar** | 醋 | cù |

For additional items, see the **menu decoder**, page 199.

## COMPLIMENTS & COMPLAINTS

| I love this dish. | 这道菜真香。<br>Zhè dào cài zhēnxiāng. |
|---|---|
| **I love the local cuisine.** | 这个地方的菜真好吃。<br>Zhège dìfāng de cài zhēn hǎochī. |

| | |
|---|---|
| **That was delicious!** | 真好吃！<br>Zhēn hǎochī! |
| **I'm full.** | 吃饱了。<br>Chībǎo le. |
| **This dish is (too) cold.** | 这个菜(太)凉了。<br>Zhège cài (tài) liáng le. |
| **This dish is (too) spicy.** | 这个菜(太)辣了。<br>Zhège cài (tài) là le. |
| **This dish is superb.** | 这个菜好极了。<br>Zhège cài hǎojí le. |



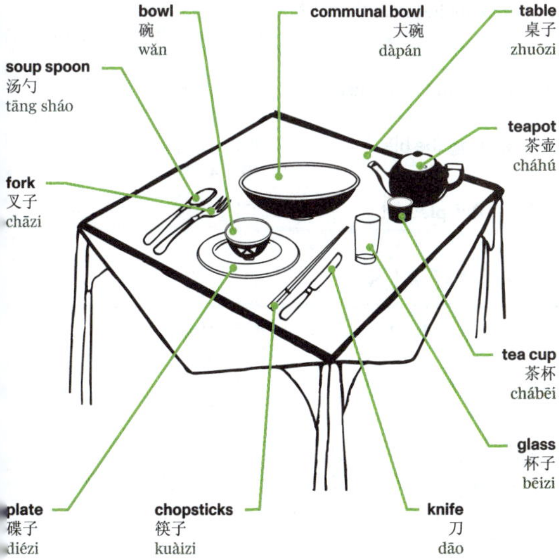

### CULTURE TIP: BILL-PAYING ETIQUETTE

A favourite Chinese sport is fighting over the bill in restaurants. It's considered polite to offer to pay the bill once or even twice, even if you're clearly the guest. A protest along the following lines may be made loudly, to show sincerity, even when it's a bluff:

| | |
|---|---|
| 你请客，我买单。 | Nǐ qǐngkè, wǒ mǎidān.<br>You were tonight's host, but I'll pay the bill. |

## PAYING THE BILL

| | |
|---|---|
| **Is service included in the bill?** | 帐单中包括服务费吗？<br>Zhàngdān zhōng bāokuò fúwù fèi ma? |
| **There's a mistake in the bill.** | 帐单上有问题。<br>Zhàngdān shàng yǒu wèntí. |
| **Please bring the bill.** | 请给我账单。<br>Qǐng gěiwǒ zhàngdān. |

| | | |
|---|---|---|
| **Bill, please!** | 买单！ | Mǎidān! |

## LIGHT MEALS

| | |
|---|---|
| **What's that called?** | 那个叫什么？<br>Nàge jiào shénme? |
| **I'd like ..., please.** | 请给我……<br>Qǐng gěi wǒ ... |

| | | |
|---|---|---|
| **one slice** | 一块 | yīkuài |
| **a piece** | 一份 | yīfèn |
| **a sandwich** | 一个三明治 | yīge sānmíngzhì |
| **that one** | 那一个 | nàyīge |

## LOOK FOR

| | | |
|---|---|---|
| 凉菜 | liángcài | appetisers (cold) |
| 主菜 | zhǔ cài | main courses (usually meat dishes) |
| 海鲜 | hǎixiān | seafood dishes |
| 汤类 | tānglèi | soups |
| 蔬菜 | shūcài | vegetable dishes (may contain meat) |
| 主食 | zhǔshí | staples |
| 甜品 | tiánpǐn | desserts |
| 啤酒 | píjiǔ | beer |
| 果汁 | guǒzhī | fruit juice |
| 汽水 | qìshuǐ | soft drinks |
| 起泡酒 | qǐpàojiǔ | sparkling wines |
| 白酒 | báijiǔ | spirits |
| 白兰地 | báilándì | brandy |
| 加饭酒 | jiāfànjiǔ | digestifs |

For more words you might see on a menu, see the **menu decoder**, page 199.

# NONALCOHOLIC DRINKS

**... water** ……水 ... shuǐ

| | | |
|---|---|---|
| **boiled** | 开 | kāi |
| **cold** | 凉开 | liáng kāi |
| **sparkling mineral** | 矿泉汽 | kuàngquán qì |
| **still mineral** | 矿泉 | kuàngquán |

### CULTURE TIP: SHARING MEALS

Meals in Chinese restaurants typically come in communal plates (dàpán 大盘) rather than individual servings, and diners eat directly from them. This style of eating contributes to the fun, social atmosphere of dining in China.

| | |
|---|---|
| **fresh drinking yogurt** | 酸奶<br>suānnǎi |
| **(orange) juice** | (橙)汁<br>(chéng) zhī |
| **lychee juice** | 荔枝汁<br>lìzhī zhī |
| **soft drink** | 汽水<br>qìshuǐ |
| **sour plum drink** | 酸梅汤<br>suānméitāng |
| **cup of coffee with (milk)** | 一杯咖啡加(牛奶)<br>yībēi kāfēi jiā (niúnǎi) |
| **cup of tea without (sugar)** | 一杯茶不加(糖)<br>yībēi chá bù jiā (táng) |
| **... coffee** | ……咖啡<br>... kāfēi |

| | | |
|---|---|---|
| **black** | 黑 | hēi |
| **decaffeinated** | 低咖啡因 | dī kāfēiyīn |
| **espresso** | 浓缩 | nóngsuō |
| **iced** | 冰 | bīng |
| **strong** | 特浓 | tènóng |
| **weak** | 淡 | dàn |
| **white** | 白 | bái |

# ALCOHOLIC DRINKS

Keep an eye out for people tapping their fingers on the tablecloth as their glass is filled. It indicates appreciation of the service rendered.

| | |
|---|---|
| **beer** | 啤酒<br>píjiǔ |
| **brandy** | 白兰地<br>báilándì |
| **Champagne** | 香槟<br>xiāngbīn |
| **Chinese spirit** | 白酒<br>báijiǔ |
| **cocktail** | 鸡尾酒<br>jīwěi jiǔ |
| **craft beer** | 精酿啤酒<br>jīngniàng píjiǔ |
| **yellow wine** | 黄酒<br>huángjiǔ |

### CULTURE TIP: TEA

Generally speaking, the Chinese are tea rather than coffee drinkers. Though the major cities have a vibrant coffee culture, coffee can be hard to find outside the major cities. The good news is that China has many delicious teas, just as you might expect.

| | | |
|---|---|---|
| 红茶 | hóngchá | black tea |
| 菊花茶 | júhuāchá | chrysanthemum tea |
| 绿茶 | lǜchá | green tea |
| 花茶 | huāchá | floral tea |
| 乌龙茶 | wūlóngchá | oolong tea |

## CULTURE TIP: STREET FOOD

China's bustling towns and cities teem with street vendors (jiētóu xiǎochī 街头小吃) selling delicious snacks (xiǎochī 小吃) to eat on the go. Choose from this array of popular treats:

| | | |
|---|---|---|
| 凉粉 | liángfěn | cold clear bean-flour noodles |
| 玉米棒 | yùmǐ bàng | corn on the cob |
| 饺子 | jiǎozi | dumpling (boiled) |
| 锅贴 | guōtie | potstickers (panfried dumplings) |
| 包子 | bāozi | bun (steamed) |
| 煎饼 | jiānbǐng | egg and spring-onion pancake |
| 烧饼 | shāobǐng | flat bread topped with sesame seeds |
| 肉饼 | ròubǐng | meat-filled thin-crust pancake |
| 馅饼 | xiànbǐng | thick, round, stuffed flat bread |
| 烧卖 | shāomài | steamed dumpling with pork, prawn, mushroom and bamboo-shoot filling |
| 粽子 | zòngzi | sticky rice wrapped in bamboo leaves |
| 馄饨 | húntun | wonton soup |

**a shot of ...** 一小杯/一个shot…… yīxiǎobēi/yīgè shot ...

| | | |
|---|---|---|
| **gin** | 金酒 | jīnjiǔ |
| **rum** | 朗姆酒 | lǎngmǔjiǔ |
| **tequila** | 龙舌兰酒 | lóngshélán jiǔ |
| **vodka** | 伏特加 | fútèjiā |
| **whisky** | 威士忌 | wēishìjì |

| | |
|---|---|
| **a bottle/glass of ... wine** | 一瓶/一杯……葡萄酒<br>yīpíng/yībēi ... pútáo jiǔ |

| | | |
|---|---|---|
| **dessert** | 甜 | tián |
| **red** | 红 | hóng |
| **sparkling** | 起泡酒 | qǐpàojiǔ |
| **white** | 白 | bái |

| | |
|---|---|
| **a glass of beer** | 一杯啤酒<br>yī bēi píjiǔ |
| **a large bottle of beer** | 一大瓶啤酒<br>yī dàpíng píjiǔ |
| **a small bottle of beer** | 一小瓶啤酒<br>yī xiǎopíng píjiǔ |

# IN THE BAR

| | |
|---|---|
| **Excuse me!** | 劳驾！<br>Láojià! |
| Q **What would you like to drink?** | 你想喝什么？<br>Nǐ xiǎng hē shénme? |
| A **I'll have ...** | 我来一个……<br>Wǒ lái yīge ... |
| **Same again, please.** | 请再来一个。<br>Qǐng zài lái yīge. |
| **No ice, thanks.** | 不要加冰块。<br>Bùyào jiā bīngkuài. |

## LISTEN FOR

| | |
|---|---|
| 你喝了什么？ | Nǐ hē le shénme?<br>What are you having? |
| 你喝多了。 | Nǐ hē duō le.<br>I think you've had enough. |

## ✔ CULTURE TIP: CHINESE CUISINE

Chinese cuisine can be divided into four main schools. The character of these regional cuisines is encapsulated by the saying 'The East is sour, the West is spicy, the South is sweet and the North is salty.' (dōng suān, xī là, nán tián, běi xián 东酸, 西辣, 南甜, 北咸).

A number of provincial cooking styles are recognised, too, including the ones given below.

| | | |
|---|---|---|
| 皖菜 | Wǎncài | Anhui cuisine |
| 浙菜 | Zhècài | Eastern (Shanghai) cuisine |
| 闽菜 | Mǐncài | Hokkien cuisine |
| 湘菜 | Xiāngcài | Hunan cuisine |
| 苏菜 | Sūcài | Jiangsu cuisine |
| 鲁菜 | Lǔcài | Northern (Shandong) cuisine |
| 川菜 | Chuāncài | Western (Sichuan) cuisine |
| 粤菜 | Yuècài | Southern (Cantonese) cuisine |

| | |
|---|---|
| **What are you drinking?** | 喝什么？<br>Hē shénme? |
| **I'll buy you one.** | 我请客。<br>Wǒ qǐng kè. |
| **How much is that?** | 总共多少钱？<br>Zǒnggòng duōshǎo qián? |
| **Do you serve meals here?** | 你们提供饭菜吗？<br>Nǐmen tígōng fàncài ma? |

## DRINKING UP

| | |
|---|---|
| **Cheers!** | 干杯！<br>Gānbēi! |
| **This is hitting the spot.** | 太顺口了。<br>Tài shùnkǒu le. |

| | |
|---|---|
| **I feel fantastic!** | 感觉真爽!<br>Gănjué zhēnshuăng! |
| **I think I've had one too many.** | 我是不是喝多了。<br>Wŏ shìbùshì hēduō le. |
| **I'm feeling drunk.** | 我有点醉。<br>Wŏ yŏudiăn zuì. |
| **I feel nauseous.** | 我想吐。<br>Wŏ xiăng tŭ. |
| **Where's the toilet?** | 哪里有厕所?<br>Năli yŏu cèsuŏ? |
| **I'm tired, I'd better go home.** | 我困了，该回家了。<br>Wŏ kùn le, gāi huíjiā le. |
| **Can you call a taxi for me?** | 你能帮我叫个车吗?<br>Nĭ néng bāngwŏ jiào ge chē ma? |

# Self-Catering

## KEY PHRASES

| | | |
|---|---|---|
| **What's the local speciality?** | 有什么地方特产？ | Yǒu shénme dìfāng tèchǎn? |
| **Where can I find the ... section?** | 哪里有卖……？ | Nǎli yǒu mài ...? |
| **I'd like ...** | 我要…… | Wǒyào ... |

## BUYING FOOD

| | |
|---|---|
| **What's the local speciality?** | 有什么地方特产？<br>Yǒu shénme dìfāng tèchǎn? |
| **What's that?** | 那是什么？<br>Nà shì shénme? |
| **Can I taste it?** | 能尝一下吗？<br>Néng chángyīxià ma? |
| **Can I have a bag, please?** | 我买一包吧？<br>Wǒ mǎi yībāo ba. |
| **How much?** | 多少钱？<br>Duōshǎo qián? |
| **How much is (half a kilo of apples)?** | (一斤苹果)多少钱？<br>(Yījīn píngguǒ) duōshǎo qián? |
| **Do you have anything cheaper?** | 你有便宜一点的吗？<br>Nǐ yǒu piányi yīdiǎn de ma? |
| **Do you have other kinds?** | 你有别的吗？<br>Nǐ yǒu biéde ma? |

## LISTEN FOR

| | |
|---|---|
| 你想要什么？ | Nǐ xiǎng yào shénme?<br>What would you like? |
| 想点什么呢？ | Xiǎng diǎn shénme ne?<br>What can I get for you? |
| 没有。 | Méiyǒu le.<br>No, we don't have any. |
| 还要别的吗？ | Háiyào biéde ma?<br>Would you like anything else? |
| 总共(五块)钱。 | Zǒnggòng (wǔ kuài) qián.<br>That's (five kuai). |

**I'd like ...** 我要……
Wǒyào ...

| | | |
|---|---|---|
| **half a dozen** | 半打 | bàndá |
| **a dozen** | 一打 | yīdá |
| **a bottle** | 一瓶 | yīpíng |
| **a jar** | 一罐 | yīguàn |
| **a litre** | 一公升 | yīgōngshēng |
| **a packet** | 一盒 | yīhé |
| **a piece** | 一块 | yīkuài |
| **(three) pieces** | (三)块 | (sān) kuài |
| **a slice** | 一份 | yīfèn |
| **(six) slices** | (六)份 | (liù) fèn |
| **a tin** | 一罐 | yīguàn |
| **some ...** | 一些…… | yīxiē ... |
| **that one** | 那个 | nàge |
| **this one** | 这个 | zhège |

| | |
|---|---|
| **Less.** | 少一点。<br>Shǎo yīdiǎn. |
| **A bit more.** | 多一点。<br>Duō yīdiǎn. |
| **Enough!** | 够了，够了！<br>Gòule, gòule! |
| **Where can I find the ... section?** | 哪里有卖……？<br>Nǎli yǒu mài ...? |

| | | |
|---|---|---|
| **dairy** | 奶制品 | nǎizhìpǐn |
| **frozen goods** | 冰冻食品 | bīngdòng shípǐn |
| **fruit and vegetable** | 水果和蔬菜 | shuǐguǒ hé shūcài |
| **meat** | 肉 | ròu |
| **poultry** | 鸡 | jī |
| **seafood** | 海鲜 | hǎixiān |

## COOKING

| | |
|---|---|
| **Could I please borrow a/an ...?** | 我能借一……吗？<br>Wǒ néng jiè yī ... ma? |
| **I need a/an ...** | 我想要一……<br>Wǒ xiǎngyào yī ... |

| | | |
|---|---|---|
| **bottle opener** | 个开瓶器 | ge kāipíng qì |
| **can opener** | 个开罐器 | ge kāiguàn qì |
| **corkscrew** | 个螺旋开瓶器 | ge luóxuán kāipíng qì |
| **frying pan** | 口煎锅 | kǒu jiānguō |
| **meat cleaver** | 把菜刀 | bǎ càidāo |
| **rice cooker** | 个电饭锅 | ge diànfànguō |
| **saucepan** | 口小锅 | kǒu xiǎoguō |
| **steamer** | 个蒸笼 | ge zhēnglóng |
| **toaster** | 个烤面包机 | ge kǎomiànbāo jī |
| **wok** | 口锅 | kǒu guō |

能尝一下吗？
Néng chángyīxià ma?
***Can I taste it?***

| | |
|---|---|
| **cooked** | 熟<br>shú |
| **cured** | 腌制<br>yānzhì |
| **dried** | 干<br>gān |
| **fresh** | 鲜<br>xiān |
| **frozen** | 冰冻<br>bīngdòng |
| **raw** | 生<br>shēng |
| **smoked** | 熏<br>xūn |

# Vegetarian & Special Meals

## KEY PHRASES

| | | |
|---|---|---|
| **Do you have vegetarian food?** | 有没有素食食品？ | Yǒuméiyǒu sùshí shípín? |
| **Could you prepare a meal without ...?** | 能不能做一个不放……的菜？ | Néngbùnéng zuòyīge bùfàng ... de cài? |
| **I'm allergic to ...** | 我对……过敏。 | Wǒ duì ... guòmǐn. |

## SPECIAL DIETS & ALLERGIES

**I'm allergic to ...** 我对……过敏。 Wǒ duì ... guòmǐn.

| | | |
|---|---|---|
| **butter** | 黄油 | huángyóu |
| **chili** | 辣椒 | làjiāo |
| **dairy produce** | 奶制品 | nǎizhìpǐn |
| **eggs** | 鸡蛋 | jīdàn |
| **gelatine** | 明胶 | míngjiāo |
| **gluten** | 面筋 | miànjīn |
| **honey** | 蜂蜜 | fēngmì |
| **MSG** | 味精 | wèijīng |
| **nuts** | 果仁 | guǒrén |
| **peanuts** | 花生 | huāshēng |
| **seafood** | 海鲜 | hǎixiān |
| **shellfish** | 贝类海鲜 | bèilèi hǎixiān |

| | |
|---|---|
| **I'm on a special diet.** | 我在节食。<br>Wǒ zài jiéshí. |
| **I don't eat (pork).** | 我不吃(猪肉)。<br>Wǒ bùchī (zhūròu). |

To explain your dietary restrictions with reference to religious beliefs, see **beliefs & culture**, page 145.

## ORDERING FOOD

| | |
|---|---|
| **Do you have halal food?** | 有没有清真食品？<br>Yǒuméiyǒu qīngzhēn shípín? |
| **Do you have kosher food?** | 有没有犹太食品？<br>Yǒuméiyǒu yóutài shípín? |
| **Do you have vegetarian food?** | 有没有素食食品？<br>Yǒuméiyǒu sùshí shípín? |
| **Is there a (vegetarian) restaurant near here?** | 附近有没有(素食)饭馆？<br>Fùjìn yǒuméiyǒu (sùshí) fànguǎn? |
| **Is it cooked with (meat stock)?** | 是用(肉汤)做的吗？<br>Shì yòng (ròutāng) zuòde ma? |
| **Could you prepare a meal without ...?** | 能不能做一个不放……的菜？<br>Néngbùnéng zuòyīge bùfàng ... de cài? |

| | | |
|---|---|---|
| **eggs** | 鸡蛋 | jīdàn |
| **fish** | 鱼 | yú |
| **fish stock** | 鱼汤 | yútāng |
| **MSG** | 味精 | wèijīng |
| **poultry** | 家禽 | jiāqín |
| **red meat** | 牛羊肉 | niúyángròu |

**Is this ...?** 这个是……的吗？
Zhège shì ... de ma?

| | | |
|---|---|---|
| **free of animal produce** | 没有动物成份 | méiyǒu dòngwù chéngfèn |
| **free-range** | 自由放养 | zìyóu fàngyǎng |
| **genetically modified** | 转基因 | zhuǎn jīyīn |
| **gluten-free** | 无筋面粉 | wújīn miànfěn |
| **halal** | 清真 | qīngzhēn |
| **kosher** | 犹太 | yóutài |
| **low fat** | 低脂肪 | dī zhīfáng |
| **low sugar** | 低糖 | dītáng |
| **organic** | 有机 | yǒujī |
| **salt-free** | 不加盐 | bùjiā yán |

# MENU Decoder

## 饭食词表

These Chinese dishes and ingredients are listed in alphabetical order according to their pronunciation so you can easily understand what's on offer and ask for what takes your fancy when eating out in China. The following abbreviations identify the cuisine to which individual dishes belong:

**NC** – Northern Cuisine, **SC** – Southern Cuisine,
**EC** – Eastern Cuisine, **WC** – Western Cuisine

## B

**bābǎo fàn** 八宝饭 'eight treasure rice' – sweet rice dish traditionally eaten at Chinese New Year containing colourful sugary fruits, nuts & seeds
**bābǎo làjiàng** 八宝辣酱 (EC) 'eight treasure hot sauce' – made from pressed tofu & chili
**bái hújiāo** 白胡椒 white pepper
**bái jièmo** 白芥末 white mustard
**bái mǐfàn** 白米饭 rice – the staple & imbued with an almost spiritual significance to the Chinese people
**bái pútáo jiǔ** 白葡萄酒 white wine
**báicài** 白菜 Chinese white cabbage
**báicù** 白醋 white rice vinegar
**báijiǔ** 白酒 a strong, clear distilled spirit made from sorghum, rice or millet
**báilándì** 白兰地 brandy
**báimǐ** 白米 plain rice
**báizhuóxiā** 白灼虾 (SC) fresh whole prawns that are scalded & served with a simple soy-sauce dip
**bājiǎo** 八角 star anise
**bājiǎo fěn** 八角粉 powder made from ground star anise
**bàn shēng** 半生 rare
**bànban jī** 拌拌鸡 (WC) '*bang-bang* chicken' – cold dish featuring cooked shredded chicken, cucumber & cellophane (bean thread) noodles with a sesame-paste, sesame-oil, garlic, ginger & chili-sauce dressing
**bàngzi** 蚌子 clam • mussel
**bànshēng bànshú** 半生半熟 medium
**bào** 爆 'exploded' – stir-fried in hot oil
**bàochǎo miàn** 爆炒面 (WC) 'hot-wok noodles' – pan-fried crispy egg noodles often served with meat & vegetables
**bàoyú** 鲍鱼 abalone
**bāozǎi fàn** 煲仔饭 'clay-pot rice' – braised rice cooked in a clay pot with Chinese sausage, salted fish, vegetables & mushrooms
**bāozi** 包子 steamed dumpling
**básī píngguǒ** 拔丝苹果 apple pieces dipped in batter then deep-fried & coated in toffee

**Běijīng kǎoyā** 北京烤鸭 (NC) Peking duck – slices of spice-imbued roast duck often served with pancakes, shallots & plum sauce
**biǎndòu** 扁豆 green bean
**biànlì diàn** 便利店 convenience store
**bīngdòng** 冰冻 frozen
**bǐnggān** 饼干 Western-style biscuit
**bīngkuài** 冰块 ice cubes
**bīngqílín** 冰淇淋 bīngqílín cream
**bōcài** 菠菜 spinach
**bòhé** 薄荷 mint
**bōló** 菠萝 pineapple
**bùdīng** 布丁 (SC) Western-style pudding

## C

**càidān** 菜单 menu
**càihuā** 菜花 cauliflower
**càishì** 菜市 fresh-food market
**càitān** 菜摊 greengrocer
**càixīn** 菜心 Chinese flowering cabbage – sometimes known as 'choi sum' or 'choy sum' in English
**càiyóu** 菜油 vegetable oil
**cānguǎn** 餐馆 restaurant
**cǎoméi** 草莓 strawberry
**chá** 茶 tea
**chángfěn** 肠粉 (SC) steamed rice-noodle roll stuffed with shrimp, pork or beef & served with soy sauce & sesame oil
**chǎo** 炒 stir-fried
**chǎo shānsù** 炒三素 (SC) vegetarian stir-fried dish of mushrooms, lotus root, ginkgo nuts & fresh vegetables
**chǎofàn** 炒饭 fried rice
**chǎofěn** 炒粉 fried rice noodles
**chǎomiàn** 炒面 fried rice noodles
**Cháozhōu lúshuǐ é** 潮州卤水鹅 (SC) goose stewed in a rich sauce & served with a garlic & vinegar dip
**Cháozhōu yīmiàn** 潮州伊面 (SC) thin egg noodles pan-fried until crunchy & served with chives, sugar & vinegar
**Cháozhōu yútāng** 潮州鱼汤 (SC) soup made from sliced fish (usually pomfret), squid, celery, mushrooms & rice cooked in chicken stock & sprinkled with dried fish pieces
**Cháozhōucài** 潮州菜 Chaozhou cuisine
**chāshāo** 叉烧 (SC) honey-glazed barbecued pork
**chāshāobāo** 叉烧包 (SC) steamed barbecued pork bun
**cháyè dàn** 茶叶蛋 'tea egg' – marbled hard-boiled egg flavoured with black tea & star anise
**chéncù** 陈醋 dark vinegar
**chéng zhī** 橙汁 orange juice
**chéngjiàng** 橙酱 marmalade
**chéngzi** 橙子 orange
**chénpí** 陈皮 (SC) mandarin or tangerine peel used as a flavouring
**Chóngqìng huǒguō** 重庆火锅 (WC) 'Chongqing hotpot' – cook-it-yourself meal requiring diners to dip various meats & vegetables into a pot of boiling spicy stock
**chóngrè** 重热 reheated
**chòu dòufu** 臭豆腐 (EC) 'stinky tofu' – tofu fermented in cabbage juice with a pungent result
**Chuāncài** 川菜 Western (Sichuan) cuisine – renowned for its use of the red chili & fiery peppercorns; pork, poultry, legumes & soybeans are the main staples
**chūnjuǎn** 春卷 (NC) 'spring roll' – deep-fried pancake stuffed with a mixture that can include vegetables, chicken, pork, prawns, mushrooms, sprouts & noodles
**cōngbào yángròu** 葱爆羊肉 (NC) hot-wok lamb with shallots
**cōngyóubǐng** 葱油饼 (NC) 'onion cakes' – pastries filled with spring onion
**cù** 醋 vinegar
**cuì** 脆 crisp
**cuìpí** 脆皮 pork crackling or crisp-skinned

## D

**dà cài** 大菜 main course
**dà cōng** 大葱 leek
**dàn** 蛋 egg
**dànbái** 蛋白 egg white
**dàndàn miàn** 担担面 (WC) '*dan-dan* noodles' – thin wheat noodles served with pork, scallions & a red-hot chili-oil, soy-sauce, sesame-paste, garlic, ginger & Sichuan roasted-peppercorn sauce
**dàngāo** 蛋糕 cake
**dàngāo diàn** 蛋糕店 cake shop
**dànhuáng** 蛋黄 egg yolk
**dànmiàn** 蛋面 (SC) egg noodles – sold dried or fresh
**dàntà** 蛋挞 (SC) baked puff pastry with an egg custard filling
**dàntāng** 蛋汤 (SC) 'egg drop soup' – soup based on chicken broth into which raw eggs are whisked & cooked
**dàsuàn** 大蒜 garlic
**dàxiā** 大虾 prawn
**dàzháxiè** 大闸蟹 (SC) 'hairy crab' – so called for the hair-like growths on their legs & underbellies, these crabs are a Shanghainese delicacy
**diǎnxīn** 点心 (SC) dim sum – an umbrella term for the vast array of steamed & fried dumplings & small delicacies served at a *yǐnchá*
**dìguā** 地瓜 sweet potato
**dīng** 丁 cubed beef, chicken or pork
**dīngxiāng** 丁香 clove
**dōngcài** 冬菜 (NC) Tianjin pickled cabbage
**dōngguā** 冬瓜 winter melon – type of melon with thick white flesh used in soups & other dishes
**dòufěn** 豆粉 bean noodles
**dòufu** 豆腐 tofu (soybean curd)
**dòufu nǎo** 豆腐脑 (NC) salty bean-curd soup
**dòufu pí** 豆腐皮 dried bean curd
**dòufu tāng** 豆腐汤 (WC) casserole of bean curd with bamboo shoots, ham, scallions, Chinese cabbage, ginger & shrimps
**dòujiāng** 豆浆 fresh soy milk
**dòujiǎo** 豆角 chopped green beans
**dòumiáo** 豆苗 pea shoots
**dòunǎi fěn** 豆奶粉 powdered soy milk
**dòushā bāo** 豆沙包 sweet steamed red-bean-paste bun
**dòuyá** 豆芽 bean sprout
**dòuzi** 豆子 bean
**dùn** 炖 stewed

## E

**é** 鹅 goose
**èlí** 鳄梨 avocado

## F

**fāngbiàn miàn** 方便面 instant noodles
**fànguǎn** 饭馆 restaurant
**fānqié chǎo jīdàn** 番茄炒鸡蛋 stir-fried tomato & egg
**fānqié jiàng** 番茄酱 ketchup • tomato sauce
**fèi** 肺 lung
**féicháng** 肥肠 large intestines of pig
**fēicháng kělè** 非常可乐 'extreme cola' – Chinese version of Coca-Cola
**féiròu** 肥肉 fatty meat
**fēngmì** 蜂蜜 honey
**fèngzhuǎ (jījiǎo)** 凤爪（鸡脚） 'phoenix claws' – chicken feet
**fěnsī** 粉丝 vermicelli
**fóshǒu** 佛手 (EC) Buddha's hand – fragant citrus fruit also known as the fingered citron
**fǔrǔ** 腐乳 fermented tofu cubes, dried, steamed then bottled with wine & possessing a curiously Camembert-like taste & texture
**fútèjiā** 伏特加 vodka
**fǔzhú** 腐竹 dried yellow soy-milk sticks

## G

**gān** 干 dried
**gān** 肝 liver
**gānbiǎn** 干煸 'dry-fried' – fried with a minimum of liquids which are then boiled away to leave the food coated in sauce
**gānbiǎn niúròu** 干煸牛肉 (WC) shredded beef, deep-fried then tossed with chilies
**gānbiǎn sìjì dòu** (WC) 干煸四季豆 deep-fried snake beans stir-fried with garlic, ginger & shrimps & served with soy sauce, wine, vinegar & sesame oil
**gǎnlǎn yóu** 橄榄油 olive oil
**gānzhè** 甘蔗 sugar cane
**gēzi** 鸽子 pigeon
**gōngbào jīdīng** 宫爆鸡丁 (NC) marinated chicken cubes stir-fried with chilies & peanuts & seasoned with a sweet bean sauce
**gōngfu chá** 功夫茶 (SC) gongfu tea – very strong short black tea
**gǒuqǐzi** 枸杞子 box thorn – similar in texture & nutritional value to spinach
**guā** 瓜 melon • vegetable marrow
**guāzi** 瓜子 melon seeds
**guìpí** 桂皮 cinnamon bark
**guǒgān** 果干 dried fruit
**guǒjiàng** 果酱 jam
**guǒrén** 果仁 nuts
**guōtiē** 锅贴 fried dumpling
**guǒzhī** 果汁 juice
**gǔsuí** 骨髓 bone marrow

## H

**hǎidài** 海带 kelp
**hǎishēn** 海参 sea cucumber
**hǎixiān** 海鲜 seafood
**hǎizhé** 海蜇 jellyfish – sold in sheets & packed in salt & served shredded
**hànbǎobao** 汉堡包 hamburger
**háoyóu** 蚝油 (SC) oyster sauce
**háoyóu jièlán** 蚝油芥兰 (SC) dish of jièlán (also known as 'gai laan', Chinese broccoli or Chinese kale) with oyster sauce
**háozi** 蚝子 oyster
**héfàn** 盒饭 generic term for a take-away box
**héfěn** 河粉 thin round or flat slippery rice noodles
**hélán dòu** 荷兰豆 snow pea
**hétáo** 核桃 walnut
**hóng pútáo jiǔ** 红葡萄酒 red wine
**hóngchá** 红茶 black tea
**hóngcù** 红醋 red rice vinegar
**hóngdòu** 红豆 red mung bean
**hóngshāo** 红烧 (WC) 'red-stewed' – braised in soy sauce with rock sugar and spices
**hóngshāo páigǔ** 红烧排骨 (WC) red-stewed pork spare ribs
**hóngshāo ròu** 红烧肉 (WC) red-stewed pork
**huāchá** 花茶 floral tea
**Huáiyáng cài** 淮扬菜 East Coast cuisine – relatively vegetarian-friendly cuisine that makes use of a wide variety of condiments & fresh ingredients; also home of the red stew (meat braised in dark soy sauce, sugar & spices)
**huángdòu** 黄豆 soy bean
**huángguā** 黄瓜 cucumber
**huángjiàng** 黄酱 (NC) black-bean dipping sauce
**huángjiǔ** 黄酒 'yellow wine' – rice wine similar in taste to sherry & best served warm
**huángshàn** 黄鳝 paddy eel
**huángyóu** 黄油 butter
**huāshēng** 花生 peanut
**huāshēng jiàng** 花生酱 peanut butter
**huāshēng yóu** 花生油 peanut oil
**huíguō ròu** 回锅肉 (NC) twice-cooked pork – simmered pork belly that is sliced and stirfried with spices and aromatics.
**hújiāo fěn** 胡椒粉 pepper (condiment)

**húluóbo** 胡萝卜 carrot
**húntun** 馄饨 wonton soup – dumplings stuffed with pork & shrimp served in broth
**húntūn miàn** 馄饨面 wonton with noodles in broth
**huǒjī** 火鸡 turkey
**huǒtuǐ** 火腿 ham

## J

**jiān** 煎 pan-fried
**jiānbǐng** 煎饼 egg & spring onion pancake
**jiānbǐng** 煎饼 (SC) fortune cookies
**jiāng** 姜 ginger
**jiàngyóu** 酱油 soy sauce
**jiàngzhī páigǔ** 酱汁排骨 (EC) barbecued pork ribs – a speciality of the city of Wuxi
**jiāobái** 茭白 (EC) wild-rice root
**jiàohuā jī** 叫花鸡 (EC) 'beggar's chicken' – whole, deboned chicken stuffed with pork, vegetables, mushrooms, ginger & other seasonings wrapped in lotus leaves & wet clay or pastry & baked for several hours
**jiàomǔ** 酵母 yeast
**jiǎozi** 饺子 boiled dumpling
**jiǎyú** 甲鱼 tortoise
**jīchì** 鸡翅 chicken wing
**jīdàn** 鸡蛋 chicken egg
**jièlán** 芥兰 'gai laan' (also known in English as Chinese broccoli or Chinese kale)
**jiētóu xiǎochī** 街头小吃 street food
**jīnqiāng yú** 金枪鱼 tuna
**jīnsīmiàn** 金丝面 (WC, NC) gold-thread noodles – hair-thin noodles in broth
**jīnzhēngū** 金针菇 golden needle mushroom (also known as enoki mushroom)
**jīròu** 鸡肉 chicken
**jītāng** 鸡汤 chicken stock
**jītuǐ** 鸡腿 drumstick
**jiǔbā** 酒吧 bar
**jiǔcài** 韭菜 Chinese chives
**jiǔlèi** 酒类 alcoholic drinks
**jīwěi jiǔ** 鸡尾酒 cocktail
**júhuā** 菊花 chrysanthemum – flowering plant with a taste similar to lettuce used as an accompaniment to dishes
**júhuāchá** 菊花茶 chrysanthemum tea
**júzi** 橘子 mandarin

## K

**kāfēi** 咖啡 coffee
**kāfēiwū** 咖啡屋 cafe
**kāishuǐ** 开水 boiled water
**kāixīnguǒ** 开心果 pistachio
**kǎo** 烤 roasted
**kǎo miànbāo** 烤面包 toast
**kǎo yángròu chuàn** 烤羊肉串 (WC) chargrilled lamb kebab – a Uighur speciality
**Kǒushuǐ Jī** 口水鸡 (WC) Mouth-watering chicken – steamed chicken dressed with peanuts and a fiery sauce
**kuàngquánshuǐ** 矿泉水 mineral water
**kǔguā** 苦瓜 bitter melon – resembles a knobbly cucumber & has a strong bitter taste

## L

**là** 辣 hot chili
**làjiāo** 辣椒 chili pepper
**làjiāo jiàng** 辣椒酱 chili sauce
**Lánzhōu lāmiàn** 兰州拉面 (WC) Lanzhou hand-pulled beef noodles
**làzi jīdīng** 辣子鸡丁 (WC) tender braised chili chicken
**lí** 梨 pear
**liáng kāishuǐ** 凉开水 chilled boiled water
**liángcài** 凉菜 appetiser
**liángfěn** 凉粉 cold bean-flour noodles

**lián'ǒu** 莲藕 lotus root – the tuber stem of the water lily which can be stuffed with rice & steamed, stir-fried or used in soups & stews
**liúlián** 榴莲 (SC) durian – spiky fruit prized by the Southern Chinese as the 'king of fruits', with a repellent smelly-sock aroma & a dense creamy flesh
**lǐyú** 鲤鱼 carp
**lìzhī** 荔枝 lychee
**lìzi** 栗子 chestnut
**lóngxiā** 龙虾 rock lobster
**Lǔcài** 鲁菜 Northern (Shandong) cuisine – typical ingredients are wheat pancakes, spring onions & fermented bean paste
**lǜchá** 绿茶 green tea
**lǜdòu** 绿豆 green mung bean
**luóbo** 萝卜 radish
**luóbo gāo** 萝卜糕 (SC) radish cake featuring grated radish dressed with dried shrimp, mushrooms, and Chinese sausage; eaten steamed or pan-fried
**luóhàn zhāi** 罗汉斋 (SC) vegetarian stew (with many variations) which usually includes wood-ear fungus & lily bud stems
**lǘròu** 驴肉 donkey

# M

**máhuā** 麻花 (NC) Tianjin Muslim-style bread twist
**málà tàng** 麻辣烫 (WC) 'numbingly hot soup' – the standard cooking broth that goes with Chóngqìng huǒguō with liberal doses of mouth-scorching Sichuan pepper & chili oil
**mángguǒ** 芒果 mango
**mántou** 馒头 steamed bun
**mányú** 鳗鱼 river eel
**máodòu** 毛豆 fresh soy beans
**máotái jiǔ** 茅台酒 a strong, clear distilled spirit made from fermented sorghum
**mápó dòufu** 麻婆豆腐 (WC, NC) '*ma-po* bean curd' – fresh bean curd marinated in spices then deep-fried in chili oil & garnished with shredded pork & fiery peppercorns
**mǎyǐ shàngshù** 蚂蚁上树 (WC, NC) 'ants climbing a tree' – cellophane noodles with braised minced pork seasoned with soy sauce & served sprinkled with chopped spring onions
**méicài kòuròu** 梅菜扣肉 (SC) double-cooked steamed pork with pickled salted cabbage
**méizi** 梅子 plum
**miànbāo** 面包 bread
**miànfěn** 面粉 flour
**miànguǎn** 面馆 noodle house
**miànjīn qiú** 面筋球 meaty-textured gluten ball made from dough that is washed so only gluten remains – used in vegetarian dishes
**miàntiáo** 面条 noodles
**mǐfěn** 米粉 rice noodles
**míhóutáo** 猕猴桃 kiwi fruit
**Mǐncài** 闽菜 Hokkien cuisine
**mógū** 蘑菇 mushroom
**mòlì huāchá** 茉莉花茶 jasmine tea
**mùguā** 木瓜 papaya • pawpaw
**mùxūròu** 木须肉 (NC) stir-fried pork with wood-ear fungus

# N

**nǎilào** 奶酪 cheese
**nǎizhìpǐn** 奶制品 dairy
**nánguā** 南瓜 pumpkin
**niángāo** 年糕 Chinese New Year sweets • rice cake
**níngméng** 柠檬 lemon
**níngméng jī** 柠檬鸡 (SC) lemon chicken
**niúròu** 牛肉 beef
**niúròu tāng** 牛肉汤 beef stock
**nuòmǐ** 糯米 glutinous rice (also known as sticky rice or sweet rice)

## O

**Ōushì zǎocān** 欧式早餐 continental breakfast

## P

**páigǔ** 排骨 spare ribs
**péigēn** 培根 bacon
**piàn** 片 slice
**pídàn shòuròu zhōu** 皮蛋瘦肉粥 (SC) preserved duck egg & pork congee
**píjiǔ** 啤酒 beer
**píngguǒ** 苹果 apple
**pǔ'ěr chá** 普洱茶 *pu-erh* tea – black tea that has gone through a complex fermentation process, rendering it smooth and earthy
**pútáo** 葡萄 grapes
**pútáo jiǔ** 葡萄酒 wine
**pútáogān** 葡萄干 raisins

## Q

**qiǎokèlì** 巧克力 chocolate
**qiézi** 茄子 aubergine • eggplant
**qíncài** 芹菜 celery
**qīngcài** 青菜 green leafy vegetables
**qīngjiāo** 青椒 bell pepper
**qīngtāng** 清汤 broth
**qīngzhēn** 清真 halal
**qīngzhēng dàzháxiè** 清蒸大闸蟹 (EC) steamed hairy crab served with a vinegary dip
**qìshuǐ** 汽水 soft drink • soda
**quánjiāfú** 全家福 (EC) 'family happiness seafood spectacular' – seafood braised with mushrooms & pig tendon
**quánmài miànbāo** 全麦面包 wholemeal bread

## R

**rénshēn** 人参 ginseng – prized as a tonic & aphrodisiac
**rèqiǎokèlì** 热巧克力 hot chocolate
**ròu** 肉 meat (pork unless specified)
**ròubǐng** 肉饼 large pork pie
**ròudiàn** 肉店 butcher's shop
**ròujiāmó** 肉夹馍 (NC) finely chopped braised pork & coriander stuffed into a pocket of flat bread
**ròupái** 肉排 steak (beef)
**ròuxiàn** 肉馅 mince

## S

**sānmíngzhì** 三明治 sandwich
**sānwén yú** 三文鱼 salmon
**shādiē** 沙嗲 (SC) satay – sauce made with spices, shallots and peanuts originally from Southeast Asia but popular in Guangdong
**shāguō dòufu** 砂锅豆腐 (EC) bean curd in a clay pot with dried bamboo & vermicelli
**shālā** 沙拉 salad
**shānméi** 山梅 raspberry
**shāobǐng** 烧饼 flat bread topped with sesame seeds
**shāomài** 烧卖 thin wrappers filled with ground pork, prawn and bamboo shoot then steamed
**shāokǎo** 烧烤 barbecued
**shāowèi** 烧味 (SC) Siu mei – an umbrella term for barbecued meats popular in Guangdong and Hong Kong
**shātáng** 砂糖 sugar
**shēng** 生 raw
**shēngcài** 生菜 lettuce
**shéròu** 蛇肉 snake
**shìzi** 柿子 persimmon
**shòuròu** 瘦肉 lean meat
**shú** 熟 cooked • well done
**shuàn yángròu** 涮羊肉 (NC) 'Mongolian lamb hotpot' – sliced meat is dipped into a flame-heated hotpot of hot broth brought to the table & cabbage & noodles are later added to make a soup
**shūcài** 蔬菜 vegetable dishes – not usually vegetarian but featuring a specific vegetable

**shuǐguǒ** 水果 fruit
**shuǐjīng yáoròu** 水晶肴肉 (EC) pig's trotter jelly
**shuǐzhǔ dàn** 水煮蛋 boiled egg
**shuǐzhǔ zhūzá** 水煮猪杂 (WC) stewed pig intestines in a fiery blend of chili powder, chili paste & fresh mountain chilies
**sìjì páigǔ** 四季排骨 (SC) spareribs braised with green beans
**sōngrén** 松仁 pine nut
**suān** 酸 sour
**suānlà** 酸辣 'sour & hot' – usually a soupy style of cooking with plenty of Chinese vinegar & chili oil
**suānlà tāng** 酸辣汤 'hot & sour soup' – warming Sichuanese winter soup that traditionally included solidified chicken blood & is made with pepper, chilies & vinegar
**suānméi** 酸梅 dried sour plum
**suānméi tāng** 酸梅汤 sour plum drink
**suànmiáo** 蒜苗 garlic chives
**suānnǎi** 酸奶 fresh drinking yogurt
**suànní** 蒜泥 'garlic slush' – cooked with a liberal dose of pureed garlic & oil
**Sūcài** 苏菜 Jiangsu cuisine
**sǔn** 笋 bamboo shoot

## T

**táng hétao** 糖核桃 candied walnut
**tángchǎo lìzi** 糖炒栗子 hot roasted chestnut – the ideal winter hand warmer
**tángcù** 糖醋 'sweet & sour' – piquant sauce composed of sugar & vinegar used as a condiment or for dipping
**tángcù lǐyú** 糖醋鲤鱼 (EC) sweet & sour fish
**tángcù páigǔ** 糖醋排骨 (EC) sweet & sour pork ribs
**tángguǒ** 糖果 candy
**tánghúlu** 糖葫芦 (NC) toffeed crab-apple stick
**tānglèi** 汤类 soup
**táozi** 桃子 peach
**tián** 甜 sweet
**tiánbǐng** 甜饼 cookie • sweet biscuit
**tiáncài** 甜菜 beetroot • beet
**tiánjī** 田鸡 'field chicken', ie frog
**tiánpǐn** 甜品 dessert
**tiáowèipǐn** 调味品 flavour enhancer
**tiěbǎn kǎo** 铁板烤 grilled on a hotplate
**tǔdòu** 土豆 potato
**tùròu** 兔肉 rabbit

## W

**Wǎncài** 皖菜 Anhui cuisine
**wāndòu** 豌豆 pea
**wǎnfàn** 晚饭 dinner
**wèidao** 味道 flavour • taste
**wèijīng** 味精 MSG
**wèishìjì** 威士忌 whisky
**wōwotóu** 窝窝头 (NC) steamed yellow corn bun
**wǔfàn** 午饭 lunch
**wúhuā guǒ** 无花果 fig
**wūlóngchá** 乌龙茶 oolong tea – delicious dark tea that is partially fermented before drying

## X

**xī húlu** 西葫芦 courgette • zucchini
**xī yòuzi** 西柚子 grapefruit
**xiājiǎo** 虾饺 (SC) bonnet-shaped prawn dumpling with translucent dough
**xiāmi** 虾米 dried shrimp
**xiān** 鲜 fresh
**xián** 咸 cured • salty • savoury
**xiàn bǐng** 馅饼 stuffed flatbread
**Xī'ān húlu jī** 西安葫芦鸡 (WC) Xi'an casseroled griddled chicken
**xiánbǐnggān** 咸饼干 cracker
**xiáncài** 咸菜 pickled vegetables
**xiāngbīn** 香槟 champagne
**Xiāngcài** 湘菜 Hunan cuisine
**xiāngcǎo** 香草 vanilla

**xiāngcháng** 香肠 pork sausage
**xiāngjiāo** 香蕉 banana
**xiāngliào** 香料 culinary herbs • spices
**xiányā** 咸鸭 salty preserved duck
**xiányú** 咸鱼 (SC) salted fish
**xiǎo báicài** 小白菜 bok choy (cabbage-like vegetable)
**xiǎo cōng** 小葱 shallot • spring onion
**xiǎochī** 小吃 snack
**xiǎochī diàn** 小吃店 snack shop
**xiǎomǐ** 小米 millet – the Chinese staple until it was supplanted by rice during the Han dynasty
**xiārén guōba** 虾仁锅巴 (EC) crisped rice with shrimp
**xiāzi** 虾子 prawn • shrimp
**xīduō** 西多 (SC) Cantonese French toast – peanut butter sandwiched between two slices of white bread before deep-frying
**xīguā** 西瓜 watermelon
**xīhóngshì** 西红柿 tomato
**xīlánhuā** 西兰花 broccoli
**xìngrén** 杏仁 almond
**xìngtáo** 杏桃 apricot
**xuè dòufu** 血豆腐 bean curd soaked in pig's blood, often made into a soup
**xūn** 熏 smoked

# Y

**yā** 鸭 duck
**yābǐng** 鸭饼 (SC) salted, boned & pressed duck immersed in peanut oil then steamed
**yán** 盐 salt
**yáng cōng** 洋葱 onion
**yángròu** 羊肉 lamb
**yángròu zhuāfàn** 羊肉抓饭 (WC) pilaf – cumin-flavoured rice cooked with carrot & lamb; a Uighur speciality
**Yángzhōu chǎofàn** 扬州炒饭 (EC) Yangzhou fried rice – there are many variations of this dish but it may include shrimp & pieces of chicken or pork
**Yángzhōu shīzi tóu** 扬州狮子头 (EC) 'lion's head meatballs' – oversized pork meatballs cooked with bok choy in a clay pot
**yánjú jī** 盐焗鸡 (SC) 'salt-baked chicken' – chicken stuffed with ginger, garlic & green onions & baked with rock salt
**yànmài piàn** 燕麦片 oats
**yāoguǒ** 腰果 cashew nut
**yāozi** 腰子 kidney
**yèxiāo** 夜宵 practice of eating snacks in the late evening – popular items include eggs, bean curd & vegetables boiled in stock & presented on a stick
**yēzi** 椰子 coconut
**yìdàlì miàn** 意大利面 'Italian noodles' – pasta
**yīmiàn** 伊面 (SC) deep-fried egg noodles
**yǐnchá** 饮茶 yum cha – a meal of snack-like portions taken from mid-morning to late afternoon
**yīngtáo** 樱桃 cherry
**yǐnliào** 饮料 drink
**yóucài** 油菜 mustard greens – term covers a diverse range of greens which are often used in salads when young or pickled
**yóuchǎo miàn** 油炒面 (NC) oily fried noodles
**yóutiáo** 油条 fried dough stick – a popular breakfast item
**yóuyú** 鱿鱼 calamari • squid
**yóuzhá** 油炸 deep-fried
**yòuzi** 柚子 grapefruit • pomelo
**yú** 鱼 fish
**yuánliào** 原料 ingredient
**Yuècài** 粤菜 Southern (Cantonese) cuisine – this style has the most varied range of ingredients & the most elaborate methods of preparation of any Chinese cuisine
**yúgān** 鱼干 dried fish
**yùmǐ** 玉米 corn

**yùmǐ bàng** 玉米棒 corn cob
**yútān** 鱼摊 fish shop
**yùtou** 芋头 (EC) yam
**yúxiāng** 鱼香 'fragrant fish' – eggplant or tofu braised with preserved chillis and an assortment of aromatics and condiments; it is supposed to evoke a traditional braised fish dish in Sichuan where this cooking method originated, but without actually containing any fish

## Z

**zǎo** 枣 date
**zǎofàn** 早饭 breakfast
**zhá ānchun** 炸鹌鹑 fried quail
**Zhècài** 浙菜 Eastern (Shanghai) cuisine – the dishes of this region are generally richer and sweeter than other Chinese cuisines; preserved vegetables & pickles, & salted meats are common ingredients
**zhēng** 蒸 steamed
**zhēnzi** 榛子 hazelnut
**zhīma jiàng** 芝麻酱 sesame paste
**zhōu** 粥 porridge
**zhǒuzi** 肘子 hock (fatty pork elbow)
**zhǔ** 煮 boiled
**zhūròu** 猪肉 pork
**zhǔshí** 主食 staples
**zhūyóu** 猪油 pork lard

# DICTIONARY

## English to Mandarin

英文 – 普通话

The symbols ⓝ, ⓐ and ⓥ (noun, adjective and verb) have been added for clarity where this is not clear from the English word itself. Where necessary, sg (singular), pl (plural), inf (informal) and pol (polite) forms are also indicated.



### A

**abalone** 鲍鱼 bàoyú
**aboard** 在……上 zài ... shàng
**abortion** 堕胎 duòtāi
**about** 关于 guānyú
**above** 以上 yǐshàng
**abroad** 国外 guówài
**accident** 事故 shìgù
**accommodation** 住宿 zhùsù
**(bank) account** 帳戶 zhànghù
**across** 对面 duìmiàn
**actor** 演员 yǎnyuán
**acupuncture** 针灸 zhēnjiǔ
**adaptor** 双边插座 shuāngbiān chāzuò
**addiction** 瘾 yǐn
**address** ⓝ 地址 dìzhǐ
**administration** 行政部门 xíngzhèng bùmén
**admission price** 门票费 ménpiàofèi
**admit (let in)** 允许 yǔnxǔ
**adult** ⓝ 大人 dàrén
**advertisement** 广告 guǎnggào
**advice** 建议 jiànyì
**aeroplane** 飞机 fēijī
**Africa** 非洲 Fēizhōu
**after** 以后 yǐhòu
**(this) afternoon** (今天) 下午 (jīntiān) xiàwǔ
**aftershave** 须后水 xūhòu shuǐ
**again** 再一次 zài yīcì
**age** ⓝ 年龄 niánlíng
**(three days) ago** (三天) 前 (sāntiān) qián
**agree** 同意 tóngyì
**agriculture** 农业 nóngyè
**ahead** 前面 qiánmiàn
**AIDS** 艾滋病 àizībìng
**air** ⓝ 空气 kōngqì
**Air Quality Index (AQI)** 空气质量指数 Kōngqì Zhìliàng Zhǐshù
**air-conditioned** 有空调的 yǒu kōngtiáo de
**air-conditioning** 空调 kōngtiáo
**airline** 航空公司 hángkōng gōngsī
**airmail** 航空邮件 hángkōng yóujiàn
**airplane** 飞机 fēijī
**airport** 飞机场 fēijī chǎng
**airport tax** 机场税 jīchǎng shuì
**aisle (on plane)** 走廊 zǒuláng
**alarm clock** 闹钟 nàozhōng
**alcohol** 酒精 jiǔjīng
**all** 所有的 suǒyǒu de
**allergic** 过敏 guòmǐn
**alleyway** 胡同 hútòng
**almond** 杏仁 xìngrén
**almost** 差一点 chà yīdiǎn

**alone** 独自一个人 dúzì yīge rén
**already** 已经 yǐjīng
**also** 也 yě
**altitude** 海拔 hǎibá
**always (continuously)** 一直 yīzhí
**always (repeatedly)** 总是 zǒngshì
**ambassador** 大使 dàshǐ
**ambulance** 急救车 jíjiù chē
**American football** 美式橄榄球 Měishì gǎnlǎnqiú
**anaemia** 贫血 pínxuè
**ancestors** 祖先 zǔxiān
**ancestral home** 老家 lǎojiā
**ancient** 古代 gǔdài
**and** 和 hé
**angry** 生气 shēngqì
**animal** 动物 dòngwù
**ankle** 脚踝 jiǎohuái
**another** 再一个 zài yīge
**answer** 答复 dáfù
**ant** 蚂蚁 mǎyǐ
**antibiotics** 抗生素 kàngshēngsù
**antihistamines** 抗组胺药 kàngzǔ'ān yào
**antique** ⓝ 古董 gǔdǒng
**antique market** 古董市场 gǔdǒng shìchǎng
**antiseptic** ⓝ 消毒剂 xiāodú jì
**any** 任何 rènhé
**apartment (downmarket)** 楼房 lóufáng
**apartment (upmarket)** 公寓 gōngyù
**appendix (body part)** 阑尾 lánwěi
**apple** 苹果 píngguǒ
**appointment (to meet someone)** 约会 yuēhuì
**apricot** 杏桃 xìngtáo
**April** 四月 sìyuè
**archaeology** 考古学 kǎogǔxué
**architect** 建筑师 jiànzhùshī
**architecture** 建筑学 jiànzhùxué
**argue** 吵架 chǎojià
**arm** 胳膊 gēbo
**arrest** 逮捕 dàibǔ
**arrivals (inbound)** 入境 rùjìng
**arrive** 到达 dàodá
**art** ⓝ 艺术 yìshù
**art gallery** 艺术馆 yìshùguǎn
**artisan** 工匠 gōngjiàng
**artist** 艺术家 yìshùjiā
**ashtray** 烟灰缸 yānhuīgāng
**Asia** 亚洲 Yàzhōu
**ask (a question)** 问 wèn
**ask (for something)** 请求 qǐngqiú
**aspirin** 阿斯匹林 āsīpǐlín
**asthma** 哮喘 xiàochuǎn
**at** 在 zài
**athletics** 田径 tiánjìng
**August** 八月 bāyuè
**aunt** 阿姨 āyí
**Australia** 澳大利亚 Àodàlìyà
**Australian Rules Football** 澳式橄榄球 Àoshì gǎnlǎnqiú
**automated teller machine (ATM)** 自动取款机 zìdòng qǔkuǎn jī
**autumn** 秋天 qiūtiān
**avenue** 大街 dàjiē
**awful** 可恶 kěwù

# B

**B&W (film)** 黑白（胶片）hēibái (jiāopiàn)
**baby** ⓝ 小娃娃 xiǎo wáwa
**baby food** 婴儿食品 yīng'ér shípǐn
**baby formula** 婴儿奶粉 yīngér nǎifěn
**babysitter** 临时保姆 línshí bǎomǔ
**back (body)** 背 bèi
**back (position)** 后面 hòumian
**backpack** 背包 bèibāo
**bacon** 培根 péigēn
**bad** 坏 huài
**bag** 包 bāo
**baggage** 行李 xínglǐ
**baggage allowance** 行李额 xínglǐ é
**baggage claim** 行李领取处 xínglǐ lǐngqǔ chù
**balance (account)** ⓝ 余额 yú'é
**balcony** 阳台 yángtái
**ball** 球 qiú
**ballet** 芭蕾舞 bālěi wǔ
**bamboo shoots** 笋 sǔn
**banana** 香蕉 xiāngjiāo
**band (music)** 乐队 yuè duì
**bandage** ⓝ 绷带 bēngdài
**Band-Aid** 创口贴 chuāngkǒu tiē

**bank (money)** 银行 yínháng
**bank account** 银行账户 yínháng zhànghù
**banknote** 纸币 zhǐbì
**baptism** 洗礼 xǐlǐ
**bar** 酒吧 jiǔbā
**barbecued** 烧烤 shāokǎo
**barbershop** 理发店 lǐfā diàn
**baseball** 棒球 bàngqiú
**basin** 水盆 shuǐpén
**basket** 篮子 lánzi
**basketball** 篮球 lánqiú
**bath** ⓝ 浴缸 yùgāng
**bathing suit** 游泳衣 yóuyǒngyī
**bathroom** 浴室 yùshì
**battery** 电池 diànchí
**be (I want to be ...)** 当 dāng
**beach** ⓝ 沙滩 shātān
**beach volleyball** 沙滩排球 shātān páiqiú
**bean** 豆子 dòuzi
**bean noodles** 豆粉 dòufěn
**bean sprout** 豆芽 dòuyá
**beautiful** 美丽 měilì
**beauty salon** 美容院 měiróng yuàn
**because** 因为 yīnwèi
**bed** 床 chuáng
**bed linen** 床单 chuángdān
**bedding** 被褥 bèirù
**bedroom** 卧室 wòshì
**bee** 蜜蜂 mìfēng
**beef** 牛肉 niúròu
**beer** 啤酒 píjiǔ
**beer (craft)** 精酿啤酒 jīngniàng píjiǔ
**before** 以前 yǐqián
**beggar** 乞丐 qǐgài
**behind** 背面 bèimiàn
**Beijing** 北京 Běijīng
**Belgium** 比利时 Bǐlìshí
**below** 下面 xiàmian
**beside** 旁边 pángbiān
**best** 最好的 zuìhǎo de
**bet** ⓝ 赌博 dǔbó
**better** 更好 gènghǎo
**between** 中间 zhōngjiān
**Bible** 圣经 shèngjīng
**bicycle** ⓝ 自行车 zìxíngchē
**big** 大 dà
**bigger** 更大 gèngdà
**biggest** 最大 zuìdà
**bike** ⓝ 自行车 zìxíngchē
**bike chain** 车链 chēliàn
**bike lock** 车锁 chēsuǒ
**bike path** 自行车道 zìxíng chēdào
**bike shop** 修车店 xiūchē diàn
**bill (restaurant etc)** ⓝ 帐单 zhàngdān
**binoculars** 望远镜 wàngyuǎnjìng
**bird** 鸟 niǎo
**birth certificate** 出生证 chūshēngzhèng
**birthday** 生日 shēngrì
**biscuit** 饼干 bǐnggān
**bite (dog)** ⓝ 咬 yǎo
**bite (insect)** ⓝ 叮 dīng
**bitter** 苦 kǔ
**bitter melon** 苦瓜 kǔguā
**black** 黑色 hēisè
**bladder** 膀胱 pángguāng
**blanket** 毛毯 máotǎn
**blind (unable to see)** 眼瞎 yǎnxiā
**blister** ⓝ 起泡 qǐpào
**blocked (toilet)** 堵塞 dǔsè
**blogger** 博主 bózhǔ
**blood** 血液 xuèyè
**blood group** 血型 xuèxíng
**blood pressure** 血压 xuèyā
**blood test** 验血 yànxuè
**blue** 蓝色 lánsè
**board (a plane, ship etc)** 登 dēng
**boarding pass** 登机牌 dēngjī pái
**boat** 船 chuán
**body** 身体 shēntǐ
**boil** ⓥ 煮 zhǔ
**bok choy** 小白菜 xiǎo báicài
**bone** ⓝ 骨头 gǔtou
**book** ⓝ 书 shū
**book (make a booking)** ⓥ 订 dìng
**book shop** 书店 shūdiàn
**booked out** 订满 dìngmǎn
**boots** 靴子 xuēzi
**border** ⓝ 边界 biānjiè
**bored** 闷 mèn

A-Z

B – C ENGLISH – MANDARIN

**boring** 无聊 wúliáo
**borrow** 借 jiè
**botanic garden** 植物园 zhíwù yuán
**both** 两个都 liǎnggèdōu
**bottle** 瓶子 píngzǐ
**bottle opener** 开瓶器 kāipíng qì
**bottom (body part)** 屁股 pìgǔ
**bottom (position)** 底 dǐ
**bowl** ⓝ 碗 wǎn
**box (big)** ⓝ 箱子 xiāngzǐ
**boxer shorts** 平角裤 píngjiǎokù
**boxing** 拳击 quánjī
**boy** 男孩子 nán háizǐ
**boyfriend** 男朋友 nánpéngyǒu
**(the) Boys (Beijing slang)** 哥们儿 gēménr
**bra** 胸罩 xiōngzhào
**brakes** 车闸 chēzhá
**brandy** 白兰地 báilándì
**brave** 勇敢 yǒnggǎn
**bread** 面包 miànbāo
**break** ⓥ 折断 zhéduàn
**break down** ⓥ 崩溃 bēngkuì
**breakfast** 早饭 zǎofàn
**breast (body part)** 乳房 rǔfáng
**breathe** 呼吸 hūxī
**bribe** ⓝ 行贿 xínghuì
**bridge** 桥 qiáo
**briefs** 内裤 nèikù
**brilliant (clever)** 聪明 cōngming
**bring** 带 dài
**broccoli** 西兰花 xīlánhuā
**broken** 坏了 huài le
**broken down (car)** 抛锚 pāomáo
**bronze medal** 铜牌 tóngpái
**brother** 兄弟 xiōngdì
**brother (elder)** 哥哥 gēge
**brother (younger)** 弟弟 dìdì
**brown** 咖啡色 kāfēi sè
**bruise** ⓝ 瘀青 yūqīng
**brush (calligraphy)** ⓝ 毛笔 máobǐ
**bucket** 水桶 shuǐtǒng
**Buddha** 大佛 dàfó
**Buddhism** 佛教 fójiào
**Buddhist** 佛教徒 fójiào tú
**budget** ⓝ 预算 yùsuàn
**buffet** 自助餐 zìzhùcān
**bug** ⓝ 虫子 chóngzi
**build** 建 jiàn
**builder** 建筑工人 jiànzhùgōngrén
**building** 楼 lóu
**bumbag** 腰包 yāobāo
**bun (steamed)** 包子 bāozi
**burn** ⓝ 烧伤 shāoshāng
**burnt** 烧焦 shāojiāo
**bus (city)** 大巴 dàbā
**bus (intercity)** 长途车 chángtú chē
**bus station (intercity)** 长途车站 chángtú chēzhàn
**bus stop** 车站 chēzhàn
**business** ⓝ 生意 shēngyì
**business class** 商务舱 shāngwù cāng
**business trip** 出差 chūchāi
**businessman** 商人 shāngrén
**businesswoman** 商人 shāngrén
**busy (occupied)** 忙碌 mánglù
**busy (state of mind)** 有事 yǒushì
**but** 但是 dànshì
**butcher** ⓝ 屠夫 túfū
**butcher's shop** 肉店 ròudiàn
**butter** ⓝ 黄油 huángyóu
**butterfly** 蝴蝶 húdié
**button** ⓝ 纽扣 niǔkòu
**buy** ⓥ 买 mǎi

# C

**cabbage** 白菜 báicài
**cafe** 咖啡店 kāfēi diàn
**cake** 蛋糕 dàngāo
**cake shop** 蛋糕店 dàngāo diàn
**calendar** 日历 rìlì
**call** ⓥ 叫 jiào
**calligraphy** 书法 shūfǎ
**camera** 照相机 zhàoxiàng jī
**camera equipment shop** 摄影器材店 shèyǐng qìcái diàn
**camp** ⓥ 野营 yěyíng
**can (be able)** 能 néng
**can (have permission)** 可以 kěyǐ
**can (tin)** 罐头 guàntou
**can opener** 开罐器 kāiguàn qì

Canada 加拿大 Jiānádà
cancel 取消 qǔxiāo
cancer (illness) 癌症 áizhèng
candle 蜡烛 làzhú
candy 糖果 tángguǒ
cantaloupe 哈密瓜 hāmì guā
Cantonese (language) ⓝ 广东话 Guǎngdōng huà
capitalism 资本主义 zīběn zhǔyì
capsicum 青椒 qīngjiāo
car 车 chē
car hire 车租赁 chē zūlìn
car park 停车场 tíngchē chǎng
car registration 车号 chēhào
carbon emission 碳排放 tàn páifàng
carbon reduction 碳减排 tàn jiǎnpái
cardiac arrest 心脏病 xīnzàng bìng
cards (playing) 扑克牌 pūkè pái
care (for someone) ⓥ 关心 guānxīn
careful! 小心！xiǎoxīn!
carp (fish) 鲤鱼 lǐyú
carpenter 木匠 mùjiàng
carrot 胡萝卜 húluóbo
carry (on the back) 背 bēi
cash ⓝ 现金 xiànjīn
cash (a cheque) ⓥ 兑现 duìxiàn
cash register 收银台 shōuyín tái
cashier 收银员 shōuyín yuán
casino 赌场 dǔchǎng
casual work 临时工作 línshí gōngzuò
cat 猫 māo
cathedral 大教堂 dàjiàotáng
Catholic 天主教 Tiānzhǔjiào
cave 山洞 shāndòng
celebration 庆祝会 qìngzhù huì
cemetery ⓝ 坟地 féndì
cent 分 fēn
centimetre 厘米 límǐ
centre 中心 zhōngxīn
ceramics 陶瓷 táocí
certificate 证书 zhèngshū
chain ⓝ 链子 liànzi
chair 椅子 yǐzi
Champagne 香槟 xiāngbīn
chance 机会 jīhuì
change 换 huàn
change (coins) 零钱 língqián
change (money) ⓥ 换钱 huànqián
changing room 更衣室 gēngyīshì
charming 有魅力 yǒu mèilì
chat ⓥ 聊天 liáotiān
chat up 调情 tiáoqíng
cheap 实惠 shíhuì
cheat ⓝ 骗子 piànzi
check ⓥ 确认 quèrèn
check (bill) 账单 zhàngdān
check-in (desk) 登记台 dēngjì tái
checkpoint 检查站 jiǎnchá zhàn
cheese 奶酪 nǎilào
chef 厨师 chúshī
cheque (banking) 支票 zhīpiào
cherry 樱桃 yīngtáo
chess (Chinese) 象棋 xiàngqí
chess (Western) 国际象棋 guójì xiàngqí
chest (body) 胸 xiōng
chestnut 栗子 lìzi
chewing gum 口香糖 kǒuxiāngtáng
chi 气 qì
chicken 鸡 jī
chicken pox 水痘 shuǐdòu
child 孩子 háizi
child seat 婴儿座 yīng'érzuò
childminding 幼儿园 yòu'éryuán
children 孩子们 háizimén
chili 辣椒 làjiāo
chili sauce 辣椒酱 làjiāo jiàng
China 中国 Zhōngguó
Chinese (language) 中文 Zhōngwén
Chinese flowering cabbage 包菜 bāocài
Chinese medicine 中药 Zhōngyào
Chinese medicine doctor 中医 Zhōngyī
chocolate 巧克力 qiǎokèlì
cholera 霍乱 huòluàn
choose 选择 xuǎnzé
chopping board 菜板 càibǎn
chopsticks 筷子 kuàizi
Christian 基督教徒 Jīdū jiàotú
Christmas 圣诞节 shèngdànjié

**Christmas Day** 圣诞日 shèngdànrì
**Christmas Eve** 平安夜 píng'ān yè
**chrysanthemum** 菊花 júhuā
**chrysanthemum tea** 菊花茶 júhuāchá
**church** 教堂 jiàotáng
**cigarette** 香烟 xiāngyān
**cigarette lighter** 打火机 dǎhuǒjī
**cinema** 电影院 diànyǐngyuàn
**cinnamon bark** 桂皮 guìpí
**circus** 马戏团 mǎxì tuán
**citizenship** 公民 gōngmín
**city** 城市 chéngshì
**city centre** 市中心 shìzhōngxīn
**city walk** 城市漫步 chéngshì mànbù
**civil rights** 公民权 gōngmín quán
**clams** 蚌 bàng
**class (category)** 类 lèi
**class system** 等级制度 děngjí zhìdù
**classical** 古典 gǔdiǎn
**clean** ⓐ 干净 gānjìng
**clean** ⓥ 打扫 dǎsǎo
**cleaning** 清洁 qīngjié
**client** 客户 kèhù
**cliff** 悬崖 xuányá
**climate (weather)** 气候 qìhòu
**climb (mountain)** 爬山 páshān
**cloakroom** 寄存处 jìcúnchù
**clock** 时钟 shízhōng
**close (shut)** 关闭 guānbì
**close (nearby)** 附近 fùjìn
**closed** 关门 guānmén
**clothing** 衣服 yīfu
**clothing store** 服装店 fúzhuāngdiàn
**cloud** 云 yún
**cloudy** 多云 duōyún
**club (dance club, lounge, bar)** 夜店 yèdiàn
**clutch (car)** 换档踏板 huàndǎng tàbǎn
**coach (bus)** 大巴 dàbā
**coach (sports)** 教练 jiàoliàn
**coast** 海边 hǎibiān
**coat** 大衣 dàyī
**cockroach** 蟑螂 zhāngláng
**cocktail** 鸡尾酒 jīwěi jiǔ
**cocoa** 可可粉 kěkě fěn
**coffee** 咖啡 kāfēi
**coins** 硬币 yìngbì
**(have a) cold** 伤风 shāngfēng
**cold** 冷 lěng
**cold medicine** 感冒药 gǎnmào yào
**colleague** 同事 tóngshì
**collect (objects)** 收集 shōují
**college (university)** 大学 dàxué
**colour** 颜色 yánsè
**comb** 梳子 shūzi
**come** 来 lái
**comedy** 喜剧 xǐjù
**comfortable** 舒服 shūfu
**commission** 代理费 dàilǐ fèi
**common people** 老百姓 lǎobǎixìng
**communication** 沟通 gōutōng
**communications (profession)** 交通 jiāotōng
**communism** 共产主义 gòngchǎn zhǔyì
**communist (party member)** 党员 dǎngyuán
**communist (party official)** 干部 gànbù
**companion (friend)** 同伴 tóngbàn
**company (business)** 公司 gōngsī
**compass** 指南针 zhǐnán zhēn
**competition** 竞赛 jìngsài
**complain** 抱怨 bàoyuàn
**complaint** 投诉 tóusù
**complimentary (tickets)** 赠（票） zèng (piào)
**computer** 电脑 diànnǎo
**computer game** 电子游戏 diànzǐ yóuxì
**comrade** 同志 tóngzhì
**concert** 音乐会 yīnyuè huì
**concussion** 脑震荡 nǎozhèndàng
**conditioner (hair)** 护发素 hùfā sù
**condom** 避孕套 bìyùntào
**conference** 会议 huìyì
**confession** 坦白 tǎnbái
**confirm (a booking)** 确认（预订） quèrèn (yùdìng)
**congratulations** 恭喜 gōngxǐ

**conjunctivitis** 结膜炎 jiémó yán
**connection** 连接 liánjiē
**conservative** 保守 bǎoshǒu
**constipation** 便秘 biànmì
**consulate** 领事馆 lǐngshìguǎn
**contact lens solution** 隐形眼镜药水 yǐnxíng yǎnjìng yàoshuǐ
**contact lenses** 隐形眼镜 yǐnxíng yǎnjìng
**contraceptives** 避孕用品 bìyùn yòngpǐn
**contract** 合同 hétóng
**convenience store** 便利店 biànlì diàn
**cook** ⓝ 厨子 chúzi
**cook** ⓥ 炒菜 chǎocài
**cooking** 做菜 zuòcài
**cool (temperature)** 凉快 liángkuài
**coordinates** 坐标 zuòbiāo
**corkscrew** 螺旋开瓶器 luóxuán kāipíng qì
**corn** 玉米 yùmǐ
**corner** 角 jiǎo
**corrupt** 贪污 tānwū
**cost (price)** 价格 jiàgé
**cotton** 棉花 miánhuā
**cough** 咳嗽 késòu
**count** 计算 jìsuàn
**counter (at hotel)** 柜台 guìtái
**country (nation)** 国家 guójiā
**countryside** 乡下 xiāngxià
**coupon** 优惠券 yōuhuì juàn
**court (legal)** 法庭 fǎtíng
**court (tennis)** (网球)场 (wǎngqiú) chǎng
**cover charge** 入场费 rùchǎng fèi
**cow** 牛 niú
**crafts** 手艺 shǒuyì
**crash (of cars)** 撞车 zhuàngchē
**crazy** 疯了 fēngle
**credit** 信用 xìnyòng
**credit card** 信用卡 xìnyòng kǎ
**crop (field)** 农田 nóngtián
**cross (religious)** 十字架 shízìjià
**crowded** 拥挤 yōngjǐ
**cucumber** 黄瓜 huángguā
**cup** 杯子 bēizǐ
**cupboard** 柜子 guìzi
**cupping (traditional therapy)** 拔罐 báguàn
**currency exchange** 货币兑换 huòbì duìhuàn
**current (electricity)** (电)流 (diàn) liú
**current affairs** 时事 shíshì
**curry** 咖喱 gālí
**custom** 风俗 fēngsú
**customs (immigration)** 海关 hǎiguān
**cut** ⓥ 切 qiē
**cut (wound)** ⓝ 伤口 shāngkǒu
**cutlery** 刀叉 dāochā
**CV** 简历 jiǎnlì
**cycle** 骑自行车 qí zìxíngchē
**cyclist** 自行车骑手zìxíngchē qíshǒu
**cystitis** 膀胱炎 pángguāng yán

# D

**dad** 爸爸 bàba
**daily** 日常 rìcháng
**dam** 大坝 dàbà
**dance** 跳舞 tiàowǔ
**dance (art form)** 舞蹈 wǔdǎo
**dangerous** 危险 wēxiǎn
**dark** 黑暗 hēiàn
**dark (of colour)** 深色 shēnsè
**date (a person)** 谈朋友 tán péngyou
**date (appointment)** 约会 yuēhuì
**date (day)** 日期 rìqī
**date (fruit)** 枣 zǎo
**date of birth** 出生日 chūshēngrì
**daughter** 女儿 nǚ'ér
**dawn** 日出 rìchū
**day** 白天 báitiān
**day after tomorrow** 后天 hòutiān
**day before yesterday** 前天 qiántiān
**dead** 死了 sǐle
**deaf** 耳聋 ěrlóng
**deal (cards)** 发牌 fā (pái)
**December** 十二月 shí'èr yuè
**decide** 决定 juédìng
**deep** 深 shēn
**deforestation** 森林砍伐 sēnlín kǎnfá

**degrees (temperature)** 度 dù
**delay** 延迟 yánchí
**deliver** 递送 dìsòng
**democracy** 民主主义 mínzhǔ zhǔyì
**demonstration (protest)** 游行 yóuxíng
**Denmark** 丹麦 Dānmài
**dentist** 牙医 yáyī
**depart (leave)** 离开 líkāi
**department store** 百货商店 bǎihuò shāngdiàn
**departure** 出发 chūfā
**departure gate** 登机口 dēngjī kǒu
**deposit (bank)** 存钱 cúnqián
**deposit (surety)** 押金 yājīn
**descendant** 后裔 hòuyì
**desert** 沙漠 shāmò
**design** 设计 shèjì
**dessert** 甜点 tiándiǎn
**destination** 目的地 mùdì dì
**details** 细节 xìjié
**diabetes** 糖尿病 tángniàobìng
**diameter** 直径 zhíjìng
**diaper** 尿裤 niàokù
**diaphragm (anatomical)** 横膈膜 héng gémó
**diaphragm (contraceptive)** 避孕药 bìyùn yào
**diarrhoea** 拉肚子 lādùzi
**diary** 日记 rìjì
**dice** 骰子 tóuzi
**dictionary** 词典 cídiǎn
**die** 去世 qùshì
**diet** 减肥 jiǎnféi
**different** 不同 bùtóng
**difficult** 困难 kùnnán
**dim sum** 点心 diǎnxīn
**dining car** 餐车 cānchē
**dinner** 晚饭 wǎnfàn
**dipping sauce** 蘸料 zhànliào
**direct** 直接 zhíjiē
**direction** 方向 fāngxiàng
**director (business)** 董事 dǒngshì
**director (film)** 导演 dǎoyǎn
**dirty** 脏 zāng
**disabled** 残疾 cánjí
**discharge (from hospital)** 出院 chūyuàn
**discount** 折扣 zhékòu
**discrimination** 歧视 qíshì
**disease** 疾病 jíbìng
**dish (food item)** 盘 pán
**diving (underwater)** 潜水 qiánshuǐ
**diving (scuba)** 水肺潜水 shuǐfèi qiánshuǐ
**diving equipment** 潜水设备 qiánshuǐ shèbèi
**divorced** 离婚 líhūn
**dizzy** 头晕 tóuyūn
**do** 做 zuò
**doctor** 医生 yīshēng
**document (electronic)** 文件 wénjiàn
**documentary** 纪录片 jìlù piàn
**dog** 狗 gǒu
**doll** 洋娃娃 yángwáwa
**(American) dollar** (美) 元 (měi) yuán
**donate** 捐赠 juānzèng
**door** 门 mén
**dormitory** 宿舍 sùshè
**double** 双 shuāng
**double bed** 双人床 shuāngrén chuáng
**double room** 双人间 shuāngrén jiān
**down** 下面 xiàmiàn
**downhill** 下坡 xiàpō
**dozen** 打 dá
**drama** 戏剧 xìjù
**dream** ⓝ 梦 mèng
**dress** ⓝ 连衣裙 liányīqún
**dried** 干 gān
**dried fruit** 干果 gānguǒ
**drink** 喝 hē
**drink (alcoholic)** 酒 jiǔ
**drink (nonalcoholic)** 饮料 yǐnliào
**drive** 开车 kāichē
**driver's licence** 驾照 jiàzhào
**drug addiction** 毒瘾 dúyǐn
**drug dealer** 毒贩 dúfàn
**drug trafficking** 贩毒 fàndú
**drug user** 吸毒者 xīdúzhě
**drugs (medication)** 药品 yàopǐn
**drum (instrument)** 鼓 gǔ

drunk 醉 zuì
dry (arid) ⓐ 干旱 gānhàn
(blow) dry (吹)干 (chuī) gān
dryer (for clothes) 烘干机 hōnggān jī
dryer 烘干机 hōnggān jī
duck 鸭子 yāzi
dummy (pacifier) 奶嘴 nǎizuǐ
dumpling (boiled) 饺子 jiǎozi
dumpling (glutinous rice) 粽子 zòngzi
dumpling (potstickers) 锅贴 guōtiē
durian 榴莲 liúlián
duvet 被子 bèizi
dysentery 痢疾 lìjí

# E

e-cigarettes 电子烟 diànzǐ yān
each 每个 měigè
ear 耳朵 ěrduǒ
early 早 zǎo
earn (money) 挣(钱) zhèng (qián)
earplugs 耳塞子 ěrsāizi
earrings 耳环 ěrhuán
Earth 地球 dìqiú
earthquake 地震 dìzhèn
east 东方 dōngfāng
Easter 复活节 Fùhuójié
easy 容易 róngyì
eat 吃饭 chīfàn
economy 经济 jīngjì
economy class 经济舱 jīngji cāng
eczema 湿疹 shīzhěn
editor 编辑 biānjí
education 教育 jiàoyù
egg (chicken) 鸡蛋 jīdàn
eggplant 茄子 qiézi
election 选举 xuǎnjǔ
electric vehicle 电动汽车 diàndòng qìchē
electrical store 电子用品店 diànzǐ yòngpǐn diàn
electricity 电 diàn
elevator 电梯 diàntī
email 电邮 diànyóu
embarrassed (slightly) 不好意思 bùhǎo yìsi
embarrassed (very) 尴尬 gāngà
embassy 大使馆 dàshǐguǎn
emergency 紧急情况 jǐnjí qíngkuàng
emotional 情绪化的 qíngxùhuà de
emperor 皇帝 huángdì
employee 职员 zhíyuán
employer 老板 lǎobǎn
empress 皇后 huánghòu
empty 空 kōng
end 结束 jiéshù
endangered species 濒危动物 bīnwēi dòngwù
engaged (betrothed) 订婚 dìnghūn
engaged (occupied) 有事 yǒushì
engagement (betrothal) 婚约 hūnyuē
engine 发动机 fādòngjī
engineer 工程师 gōngchéng shī
engineering 工程学 gōngchéng xué
England 英国 Yīngguó
English 英文 Yīngwén
English teacher 英文老师 Yīngwén lǎoshī
enjoy (oneself) 玩得开心 wánde kāixīn
enough 足够 zúgòu
enter (venue) 入场 rùchǎng
entertainment guide 娱乐指南 yúlè zhǐnán
entry 入口 rùkǒu
envelope 信封 xìnfēng
environment 环境 huánjìng
environmental protection 环保 huánbǎo
epilepsy 癫痫 diānxián
equal opportunity 平等待遇 píngděng dàiyù
equality 平等 píngděng
equipment 设备 shèbèi
escalator 自动扶梯 zìdòng fútī
estate agency 房地产公司 fángdìchǎn gōngsī
euro 欧元 ōuyuán
Europe 欧洲 Ōuzhōu
euthanasia 安乐死 ānlè sǐ
evening 晚上 wǎnshàng
every 每次 měicì
everyone 每个人 měige rén

**everything** 一切 yīqiè
**exactly** 确切 quèqiè
**example** 举例 jǔlì
**excellent** 好极了 hǎojíle
**excess (baggage)** 超重(行李) chāozhòng (xíngli)
**exchange** ⓝ 交换 jiāohuàn
**exchange** ⓥ 换 huàn
**exchange rate** 兑换率 duìhuàn lǜ
**excluded** 不包括 bù bāokuò
**exhaust (car)** 废气 fèiqì
**exhibition** 展览 zhǎnlǎn
**exit** 出口 chūkǒu
**expensive** 贵 guì
**experience** 经验 jīngyàn
**exploitation** 剥削 bōxuē
**express** 快速 kuàisù
**express (mail)** 快递(信) kuàidì (xìn)
**express mail (by)** (寄)特快 jì tèkuài
**extension (visa)** (签证)延期 (qiānzhèng) yánqī
**eye(s)** 眼睛 yǎnjīng
**eye drops** 眼药水 yǎnyàoshuǐ

# F

**fabric** 布料 bùliào
**face** 脸 liǎn
**face cloth** 毛巾 máojīn
**factory** 工厂 gōngchǎng
**factory worker** 工人 gōngrén
**fall (autumn)** 秋天 qiūtiān
**fall (down)** 掉下 diàoxia
**family** 家庭 jiātíng
**family name** 姓 xìng
**famous** 出名 chūmíng
**fan (hand held)** 扇子 shànzi
**fan (machine)** 电风扇 diànfēngshàn
**fan (sport etc)** 球迷 qiú mí
**fans (supporters)** 粉丝 fěnsī
**far** 远 yuǎn
**fare** 票价 piàojià
**farm** 农地 nóngdì
**farmer (peasant)** 农民 nóngmín
**fashion** 时髦 shímáo
**fast** 快 kuài
**fat** 胖 pàng
**father** 父亲 fùqīn
**father-in-law** 岳父 yuèfù
**faucet** 水龙头 shuǐlóngtóu
**fault (someone's)** 责任 zérèn
**faulty** 有毛病 yǒu máobìng
**February** 二月 èryuè
**feed (baby, animals)** 喂 wèi
**feel (touch)** 触摸 chùmō
**feeling (physical)** 情感 qínggǎn
**feelings** 感情 gǎnqíng
**female** 女性 nǚxìng
**fen (measure)** 分 fēn
**fence** 篱笆 líba
**fencing (sport)** 剑术 jiànshù
**fengshui** 风水 fēngshuǐ
**ferry** 渡船 dùchuán
**festival** 节日 jiérì
**fever** 发烧 fāshāo
**few** 一些 yīxiē
**fiancé** 未婚夫 wèihūnfū
**fiancée** 未婚妻 wèihūnqī
**fiction (novel)** 虚构(小说) xūgòu (xiǎoshuō)
**fight** ⓥ 打架 dǎjià
**fill** 填满 tiánmǎn
**fillet** 鱼片 yúpiàn
**film (cinema)** 电影 diànyǐng
**film (for camera)** 胶卷 jiāojuǎn
**film speed** 感光度 gǎnguāngdù
**filtered** 过滤 guòlǜ
**find** 找到 zhǎodào
**fine** ⓐ 蛮好 mánhǎo
**fine (penalty)** 罚款 fákuǎn
**finger** 手指 shǒuzhǐ
**finished (over)** 结束 jiéshù
**finish (complete)** ⓥ 完成 wánchéng
**Finland** 芬兰 Fēnlán
**fire** 火 huǒ
**firewood** 柴火 cháihuo
**first** 第一 dìyī
**first class** 头等舱 tóuděng cāng
**first-aid kit** 急救装备 jíjiù zhuāngbèi
**first name** 名字 míngzì
**fish** ⓝ 鱼 yú
**ecosystem** 生态系统 shēngtài xìtǒng

**fishing** 钓鱼 diàoyú
**flag (country)** 国旗 guóqí
**flannel** 擦布 cābù
**flashlight (torch)** 手电筒 shǒudiàntǒng
**flat** ⓐ 贬 biǎn
**flea** 跳蚤 tiàozǎo
**flight** 航班 hángbān
**flood** 洪水 hóngshuǐ
**floor (ground)** 地板 dìbǎn
**floor (storey)** 层 céng
**floral tea** 花茶 huāchá
**florist** 花店 huādiàn
**flour (wheat)** 面粉 miànfěn
**flower** 花 huā
**flu** 感冒 gǎnmào
**fly** 飞 fēi
**foggy** 有雾 yǒuwù
**folk music** 民谣 mínyáo
**follow** 跟随 gēnsuí
**food** ⓝ 食品 shípǐn
**food supplies** 预备食品 yùbèi shípǐn
**foot** 脚 jiǎo
**football (soccer)** 足球 zúqiú
**foot massage** 足底按摩 zúdǐ ànmó
**foreign goods** 进口货 jìnkǒu huò
**foreigner** 外国人 wàiguó rén
**forest** 森林 sēnlín
**forever** 永远 yǒngyuǎn
**forget** 忘掉 wàngdiào
**forgive** 原谅 yuànliàng
**fork** 叉子 chāzi
**fortune teller** 相士 xiàngshì
**foul** 犯规 fànguī
**foyer** 大堂 dàtáng
**fragile** 脆弱 cuìruò
**France** 法国 Fǎguó
**free (available)** 有空 yǒukòng
**free (gratis)** 免费 miǎnfèi
**free (not bound)** 自由 zìyóu
**freelance work** 自由职业 zìyóu zhíyè
**freeze** 冻结 dòngjié
**fresh** 新鲜 xīnxiān
**Friday** 礼拜五 lǐbài wǔ
**fridge** 冰箱 bīngxiāng
**fried (deep-fried)** 油炸 yóuzhá
**fried rice** 炒饭 chǎofàn
**friend** 朋友 péngyǒu
**from** 从 cóng
**frost** 霜 shuāng
**frozen** 冰冻 bīngdòng
**fruit** 水果 shuǐguǒ
**fry (stir-fry)** 炒 chǎo
**full** 满 mǎn
**full-time** 专职的 zhuānzhíde
**fun** 好玩 hǎowán
**funeral** 葬礼 zànglǐ
**funny** 搞笑 gǎoxiào
**furniture** 家具 jiājù
**future** 将来 jiānglái

## G

**game (football)** 球赛 qiú sài
**garage** 车库 chēkù
**garbage** 垃圾 lājī
**garbage can** 垃圾箱 lājī xiāng
**garden** 花园 huāyuán
**gardening** 园艺 yuányì
**garlic** 大蒜 dàsuàn
**gas (for cooking)** 煤气 méiqì
**gas (petrol)** 汽油 qìyóu
**gastroenteritis** 肠胃炎 chángwèiyán
**gate (airport)** 登机口 dēngjīkǒu
**gate (general)** 门 mén
**gauze** 纱布 shābù
**gay** 同志 tóngzhì
**gay (bar)** 同志（吧）tóngzhì (bā)
**gender** 性别 xìngbié
**gender-inclusive** 性别友善 xìngbié yǒushàn
**Germany** 德国 Déguó
**get (fetch)** 接来 jiēlái
**get off (a train etc)** 下（车）xià (chē)
**giardiasis** 鞭毛虫病 biānmáochóngbìng
**gift** 礼物 lǐwù
**gig** 节目 jiémù
**gin** 金酒 jīnjiǔ
**ginger** 姜 jiāng
**ginseng** 人参 rénshēn

**girl** 女孩子 nǚháizi
**girlfriend** 女朋友 nǚpéngyou
**give** 送 sòng
**given name** 名字 míngzi
**glandular fever** 腺热 xiànrè
**glass (drinking)** 玻璃杯 bōli bēi
**glass (material)** 玻璃 bōli
**glasses (spectacles)** 眼镜 yǎnjìng
**glove** 手套 shǒutào
**glue** 胶水 jiāoshuǐ
**go** 去 qù
**go out** 出去 chūqù
**go shopping** 逛街 guàngjiē
**goal (aim)** 目的 mùdì
**(score a) goal** 进门 jìnmén
**goalkeeper** 守门员 shǒuményuán
**goat** 山羊 shānyáng
**god** 神 shén
**goggles (swimming)** 游泳镜 yóuyǒng jìng
**gold** 黄金 huángjīn
**gold medal** 金牌 jīnpái
**golf ball** 高尔夫球 gāo'ěrfū qiú
**golf course** 高尔夫场 gāo'ěrfū chǎng
**good** 好 hǎo
**goodbye** 再见 zàijiàn
**goose** 鹅 é
**government** 政府 zhèngfǔ
**gram** 克 kè
**granddaughter** 孙女 sūnnǚ
**grandfather (maternal)** 外公 wàigōng
**grandfather (paternal)** 爷爷 yéye
**grandmother (maternal)** 外婆 wàipó
**grandmother (paternal)** 奶奶 nǎinai
**grandson** 孙子 sūnzi
**grapes** 葡萄 pútáo
**grass** 草 cǎo
**grasslands** 草原 cǎoyuán
**grateful** 感谢 gǎnxiè
**grave** 坟墓 fénmù
**gray** 灰色 huīsè
**great (fantastic)** 棒 bàng
**Great Wall** 长城 Chángchéng
**green** 绿色 lǜsè
**green beans** 扁豆 biǎndòu
**green tea** 绿茶 lǜchá
**greengrocer** 菜摊 càitān
**grey** 灰色 huīsè
**groceries** 食品杂货 shípǐn záhuò
**groundnut (peanut)** 花生 huāshēng
**grow** 长大 zhǎngdà
**guaranteed** 有保证 yǒu bǎozhèng
**guess** 猜 cāi
**guest** 客人 kèrén
**guesthouse** 宾馆 bīnguǎn
**guide (audio)** 语音导览 yǔyīn dǎolǎn
**guide (person)** 导游 dǎoyóu
**guide dog** 导盲犬 dǎománg quǎn
**guidebook** 旅行指南 lǚxíngzhǐnán
**guided tour** 有导游的旅游 yǒu dǎoyóu de lǚyóu
**guilty** 有罪 yǒuzuì
**guitar** 吉他 jítā
**gum (teeth)** 齿龈 chǐyín
**gun** 手枪 shǒuqiāng
**gut blockers (for diarrhoea)** 止泻药 zhǐxiè yào
**gym (place)** 健身房 jiànshēn fáng
**gymnastics** 体操 tǐcāo
**gynaecologist** 妇科医生 fùkē yīshēng

## H

**hair** 头发 tóufa
**hair salon** 发廊 fàláng
**hairbrush** 梳子 shūzi
**haircut** 理发 lǐfà
**hairdresser** 理发师 lǐfà shī
**halal** 清真 qīngzhēn
**half** 半个 bànge
**ham** 火腿 huǒ tuǐ
**hammer** 锤子 chuízi
**hammock** 吊床 diàochuáng
**hand** 手 shǒu
**handbag** 手袋 shǒudài
**handball** 手球 shǒuqiú
**handicrafts** 手艺 shǒuyì
**handlebars** 车把 chēbǎ
**handmade** 手工的 shǒugōng de
**handsome** 英俊 yīngjùn
**happy** 快乐 kuàilè
**harassment** 骚扰 sāorǎo

harbour 港口 gǎngkǒu
hard (difficult) 困难 kùnnán
hard (not soft) 很硬 hén yìng
hard seat 硬座 yìngzuò
hard sleeper 硬卧 yìngwò
hardboiled egg 水煮蛋 shuǐzhǔ dàn
hardware store 五金店 wǔjīn diàn
hat 帽子 màozi
have 有 yǒu
hay fever 花粉热 huāfěn rè
he/him 他 tā
head 头 tóu
head massage 头部按摩 tóubù ànmó
headache 头疼 tóuténg
headlights 车灯 chēdēng
health 健康 jiànkāng
hear 听到 tīngdào
hearing aid 助听器 zhùtīng qì
heart 心脏 xīnzàng
heart attack 心脏病发作 xīnzàngbìng fāzuò
heart condition 心脏病 xīnzàngbìng
heat 热气 rèqì
heated 有暖气 yǒu nuǎnqì
heater (water) 热水器 rèshuǐqì
heating 暖气 nuǎnqì
heavy 重 zhòng
hello (general greeting) 你好 nǐhǎo
hello (Beijing) pol 您好 nínhǎo
hello (answering telephone) 喂 wèi.
helmet 头盔 tóukuī
help 帮助 bāngzhù
Help! (others) 救人！Jiùrén!
Help! (self) 救命！Jiùmìng!
hepatitis 肝炎 gānyán
her 她的 tāde
herb (culinary) 香料 xiāngliào
herb (medicinal) 药材 yàocái
herbalist 中医 zhōng yī
here 这里 zhèlǐ
heterosexual (straight) 异性恋 yìxìngliàn
high 高 gāo
high school 中学 zhōngxué
high-speed rail 高铁 gāotiě
high-speed rail station 高铁站 gāotiě zhàn
highchair 高凳 gāodèng
highway 高速公路gāosù gōnglù
hike ⓥ 爬山 páshān
hiking trip 徒步旅行 túbù lǚxíng
hiking boots 登山鞋 dēngshān xié
hiking route 徒步路线 túbù lùxiàn
hill 山丘 shānqiū
Hindu 印度教徒 Yìndùjiào tú
Hinduism 印度教 Yìndùjiào
hire 租赁 zūlìn
his 他的 tāde
historical (site) 古迹 gǔjì
history 历史 lìshǐ
hitchhike 搭便车 dā biànchē
HIV 艾滋病毒 àizī bìngdú
hockey 曲棍球 qūgùn qiú
holiday 度假 dùjià
holidays 假期 jiàqī
home 家 jiā
homeless 无家可归 wújiā kěguī
homosexual 同性恋 tóngxìng liàn
honey 蜂蜜 fēngmì
honeymoon 蜜月 mìyuè
Hong Kong 香港 Xiānggǎng
horoscope (Western) 星座 xīngzuò
horse 马 mǎ
horse riding 骑马 qímǎ
hospital 医院 yīyuàn
hospitality 好客 hàokè
hot 热 rè
hot spring 温泉 wēnquán
hot water 热水 rèshuǐ
hotel 酒店 jiǔdiàn
hour 小时 xiǎoshí
house 房子 fángzi
housework 家务 jiāwù
how 怎么 zěnme
how much 多少 duōshǎo
hug 抱住 bàozhù
huge 巨大 jùdà
human resources 人事 rénshì
human rights 人权 rénquán
humanities & arts 文科 wénkē

**humankind** 人类 rénlèi
**humid** 潮湿 cháoshī
**hundred** 百 bǎi
**hungry (to be)** 饿 è
**hunting** 打猎 dǎliè
**Hurry up!** 快点！Kuàidiǎn!
**hurt** 疼 téng
**husband** 丈夫 zhàngfū

## I

**I** 我 wǒ
**ice** 冰 bīng
**ice axe** 冰槌 bīngchuí
**ice cream** 冰淇淋 bīngqílín
**ice hockey** 冰球 bīngqiú
**ice skating** 溜冰 liūbīng
**identification** 证件 zhèngjiàn
**identification card (ID)** 身份证 shēnfēn zhèng
**idiot** 白痴 báichī
**if** 如果 rúguǒ
**ill** 生病 shēngbìng
**imagination** 幻想 huànxiǎng
**immigration** 移民 yímín
**important** 重要 zhòngyào
**impossible** 不可能 bù kěnéng
**in** 在……里面 zài ... lǐmian
**in front of ...** 在……前面 zài ... qiánmian
**included** 包括 bāokuò
**income tax** 所得税 suǒdé shuì
**India** 印度 Yìndù
**indicator** 指标 zhǐbiāo
**indigestion** 消化不良 xiāohuà bùliáng
**indoor** 室内 shìnèi
**industry** 行业 hángyè
**infection** 感染 gǎnrǎn
**inflammation** 发炎 fāyán
**influencer** 网红 wǎnghóng
**influenza** 感冒 gǎnmào
**inform** 通知 tōngzhī
**information** 信息 xìnxī
**ingredient** 原料 yuánliào
**inhaler** 吸入器 xīrù qì
**inject** 注射 zhùshè
**injection** 打针 dǎzhēn
**injured/injury** 受伤 shòushāng
**inner tube** 内胎 nèitāi
**innocent** 无辜 wúgū
**inside** 里面 lǐmian
**instruction manual** 说明书 shuōmíng shū
**instructor** 培训员 péixùn yuán
**insurance** 保险 bǎoxiǎn
**interesting** 有趣 yǒuqù
**intermission** 中场休息 zhōngchǎng xiūxi
**international** 国际 guójì
**internet** 网络 wǎngluò
**interpreter** 翻译 fānyì
**interview** 采访 cǎifǎng
**invitation** 邀请 yāoqǐng
**invite** 请客 qǐngkè
**iodine** 碘水 diǎnshuǐ
**Ireland** 爱尔兰 Ài'ěrlán
**iron (for clothes)** 熨斗 yùndǒu
**island** 岛 dǎo
**Israel** 以色列 Yǐsèliè
**it** 它 tā
**IT** 信息技术 xìnxī jìshù
**Italy** 意大利 Yìdàlì
**itch** 痒 yǎng
**itinerary** 日程表 rìchéng biǎo
**IUD** 宫内节育器 gōngnèi jiéyù qì

## J

**jacket** 外套 wàitào
**jail** 监狱 jiānyù
**jam** 果酱 guǒjiàng
**January** 一月 yīyuè
**Japan** 日本 Rìběn
**jasmine tea** 茉莉花茶 mòlìhuā chá
**jaw** 下巴 xiàbā
**jealous** 嫉妒 jìdù
**jeans** 牛仔裤 niúzǎi kù
**jeep** 吉普车 jípǔ chē
**jellyfish (food)** 海蜇 hǎizhé
**jet lag** 时差反应 shíchā fǎnyìng
**jewellery** 首饰 shǒushì
**Jewish** 犹太 Yóutài

**jin (measure)** 斤 jīn
**job** 工作 gōngzuò
**jogging** 慢跑 mànpǎo
**joke** ⓝ 开玩笑 kāi wánxiào
**journalist** 记者 jìzhě
**journey** 旅程 lǚchéng
**judge** 法官 fǎguān
**juice** 果汁 guǒzhī
**July** 七月 qīyuè
**jump** 跳 tiào
**jumper (sweater)** 毛衣 máoyī
**June** 六月 liùyuè

## K

**kelp** 海带 hǎidài
**ketchup** 番茄酱 fānqié jiàng
**key** 钥匙 yàoshi
**keyboard** 键盘 jiànpán
**kick** ⓥ 踢 tī
**kidney** 肾 shèn
**kilogram** 公斤 gōngjīn
**kilometre** 公里 gōnglǐ
**kind (nice)** 善良 shànliáng
**kindergarten** 幼儿园 yòu'éryuán
**king** 国王 guówáng
**kiosk** 小卖部 xiǎo màibù
**kiss** ⓝ 亲吻 qīnwěn
**kiss** ⓥ 亲 qīn
**kitchen** 厨房 chúfáng
**kiwi fruit** 猕猴桃 míhóu táo
**knee** 膝盖 xīgài
**knife** 刀 dāo
**know** 知道 zhīdào
**Korea (North)** 朝鲜 Cháoxiǎn
**Korea (South)** 韩国 Hánguó
**Korean (language)** 朝鲜话 Cháoxiǎn huà
**kosher (food)** 洁食 jiéshí
**kuai (currency)** 块 kuài

## L

**Labour Day** 劳动节 láodòngjié
**labourer** 劳工 láogōng
**labyrinth** 迷宫 mígōng
**lace** 蕾丝 lěisī
**lake** 湖 hú
**lamb** 羊肉 yángròu
**land** 土地 tǔdì
**landlady/landlord** 房东 fángdōng
**landmark** 地标 dìbiāo
**landslide** 滑坡 huápō
**language** 语言 yǔyán
**laptop** 手提电脑 shǒutí diànnǎo
**large** 很大 hěndà
**last (final)** 最后的 zuìhòude
**last (previous)** 前一个 qián yīgè
**last (week)** 上个(星期) shàngge (xīngqī)
**late** 迟到 chídào
**later** 以后 yǐhòu
**laugh** ⓥ 笑 xiào
**launderette** 洗衣店 xǐyīdiàn
**laundry (to do)** 洗衣服 xǐ yīfu
**law (study, professsion)** 法律 fǎlǜ
**lawyer** 律师 lǜshī
**laxative** 止泻药 zhǐxiè yào
**lazy** 懒惰 lǎnduò
**leader** 领导 lǐngdǎo
**leaf** 叶子 yèzi
**leafy vegetables** 青菜 qīngcài
**learn** 学习 xuéxí
**leather** 皮革 pígé
**lecturer** 讲师 jiǎngshī
**left (direction)** 左边 zuǒbiān
**left luggage** 行李寄存 xíngli jìcún
**left-luggage office** 寄存处 jìcún chù
**left-wing** 左派 zuǒpài
**leg** 腿 tuǐ
**legal (lawful)** 合法 héfǎ
**leggings** 长袜 chángwà
**legislation** 法规 fǎguī
**legume** 豆类 dòulèi
**leisure** 消遣 xiāoqiǎn
**lemon** 柠檬 níngméng
**lemonade** 柠檬汁 níngméng zhī
**lens** 透镜 tòujìng
**lentil** 小扁豆 xiǎobiǎndòu
**lesbian** 女同志 nǚ tóngzhì
**less** 少 shǎo
**letter (mail)** 信 xìn

**lettuce** 生菜 shēngcài
**liar** 骗子 piànzi
**library** 图书馆 túshū guǎn
**lice** 头虱 tóushī
**licence** 执照 zhízhào
**licence plate number** 车号 chēhào
**lie (not stand)** 躺下 tǎngxià
**life** 生命 shēngmìng
**life jacket** 救生衣 jiùshēng yī
**lift (elevator)** 电梯 diàntī
**light** 光 guāng
**light (not heavy)** 轻 qīng
**light (of colour)** 浅色 qiǎnsè
**light bulb** 灯泡 dēngpào
**light meter** 测光表 cèguāng biǎo
**lighter (cigarette)** 打火机 dǎhuǒ jī
**like ...** 同……一样 tóng ... yīyàng
**lime (chemical)** 石灰 shíhuī
**linen (material)** 亚麻布 yàmá bù
**linen (sheets etc)** 床单 chuángdān
**lip balm** 润唇膏 rùn chúngāo
**lips** 嘴唇 zuǐchún
**lipstick** 口红 kǒuhóng
**listen (to)** 听 tīng
**litre** 公升 gōngshēng
**little** 小 xiǎo
**(a) little** 一点 yīdiǎn
**live (inhabit)** 住 zhù
**liver** 肝 gān
**livestream** 直播 zhíbō
**lizard (gecko)** 壁虎 bìhǔ
**local** 地方 dìfāng
**lock** ⓝ 锁 suǒ
**lock** ⓥ 锁上 suǒshàng
**locked (door etc)** 锁上了 suǒshàng le
**lollies** 糖果 tángguǒ
**long** 长 cháng
**look** 看 kàn
**look after** 照顾 zhàogù
**look for** 找 zhǎo
**lookout** 了望台 liàowàng tái
**loose** 很松 hěnsōng
**loose change** 零钱 língqián
**lose** 丢 diū
**lost (one's way)** 迷路 mílù
**lost property** 遗失物 yíshī wù
**(a) lot** 好多 hǎoduō
**loud** 吵 chǎo
**love** ⓝ 爱情 àiqíng
**love** ⓥ 爱 ài
**lover** 爱人 àirén
**low** 低 dī
**lubricant** 润滑剂 rùnhuájì
**luck** 运气 yùnqì
**lucky** 幸运 xìngyùn
**luggage** 行李 xíngli
**luggage lockers** 行李寄存柜 xíngli jìcúnguì
**luggage tag** 行李牌 xíngli pái
**lump (small, on skin)** 疙瘩 gēda
**lunch** 午饭 wǔfàn
**lung** 肺 fèi
**luxury** 奢侈 shēchǐ
**lychee** 荔枝 lìzhī

# M

**machine** 机器 jīqì
**magazine** 杂志 zázhì
**mahjong** 麻将 májiàng
**mail (letters)** 来信 láixìn
**mail (postal system)** 邮政 yóuzhèng
**mailbox** 信箱 xìnxiāng
**main** 主要 zhǔyào
**main road** 干道 gàndào
**make** 制作 zhìzuò
**make love** 做爱 zuò'ài
**makeup (cosmetics)** 化妆品 huàzhuāng pǐn
**malaria** 疟疾 nüèji
**mammogram** 乳腺钼靶检查 rǔxiàn mùbǎ jiǎnchá
**man (male person)** 男人 nánrén
**manager** 经理 jīnglǐ
**mandarin** 橘子 júzi
**Mandarin** 普通话 pǔtōnghuà
**mandatory** 强制性 qiángzhìxìng
**mango** 芒果 mángguǒ
**manual worker** 手工 shǒugōng
**many** 好多 hǎoduō
**maotai (sorghum and wheat spirit)** 茅台酒 máotái jiǔ

**map** 地图 dìtú
**March** 三月 sānyuè
**marital status** 婚姻状况 hūnyīn zhuàngkuàng
**market** 市场 shìchǎng
**marriage** 婚姻 hūnyīn
**married** 已婚 yǐ hūn
**marry** 结婚 jiéhūn
**martial arts (Chinese kung fu)** 武术(中国功夫) wǔshù (Zhōngguó gōngfu)
**mass (Catholic)** 弥撒 mísā
**massage** 按摩 ànmó
**masseur/masseuse** 按摩师 ànmó shī
**mat** 地毯 dìtǎn
**match (sports)** 比赛 bǐsài
**matches (for lighting)** 火柴 huǒchái
**mattress** 垫子 diànzi
**May** 五月 wǔyuè
**maybe** 可能 kěnéng
**mayor** 市长 shìzhǎng
**me** 我 wǒ
**meal** 一顿饭 yīdùn fàn
**measles** 麻疹 mázhěn
**meat** 肉 ròu
**mechanic** 机修工 jīxiūgōng
**social media** 社媒 shèméi
**media** 媒体 méitǐ
**medicine (study, profession)** 医学 yīxué
**medicine (medication)** 医药 yīyào
**meditation** 静坐 jìngzuò
**meet** 见面 jiànmiàn
**melon** 瓜 guā
**member** 成员 chéngyuán
**menstruation** 月经 yuèjīng
**menu** 菜单 càidān
**message** 信息 xìnxī
**metal** 金属 jīnshǔ
**metre** 米 mǐ
**meter (taxi)** 表 biǎo
**metro (train)** 地铁 dìtiě
**metro station** 地铁站 dìtiě zhàn
**microwave (oven)** 微波炉 wēibō lú
**midday/noon** 中午 zhōngwǔ
**midnight** 午夜 wǔyè
**migraine** 偏头疼 piān tóuténg
**military** 军事 jūnshì
**military service** 兵役 bīngyì
**milk** 牛奶 niúnǎi
**millet** 小米 xiǎomǐ
**millimetre** 毫米 háomǐ
**million** 百万 bǎiwàn
**mince (stuffing)** 肉馅 ròuxiàn
**mineral water** 矿泉水 kuàngquán shuǐ
**minute** 分钟 fēnzhōng
**mirror** 镜子 jìngzi
**miscarriage** 流产 liúchǎn
**miss (feel absence of)** 想念 xiǎngniàn
**mistake** 过失 guòshī
**mix** 调拌 tiáobàn
**mobile phone** 手机 shǒujī
**modern** 现代 xiàndài
**moisturiser** 护肤膏 hùfū gāo
**monastery (Buddhist)** 佛寺 fósì
**Monday** 星期一 xīngqī yī
**money** 钱 qián
**Mongolia** 蒙古 Ménggǔ
**monk** 和尚 héshang
**month** 月 yuè
**monument** 纪念碑 jìniàn bēi
**moon** 月亮 yuèliang
**more** 多 duō
**morning (after breakfast)** 早上 zǎoshàng
**morning (before lunch)** 上午 shàngwǔ
**morning sickness** 晨吐症 chéntùzhèng
**mosque** 清真寺 qīngzhēn sì
**mosquito** 蚊子 wénzi
**mosquito coil** 蚊香 wénxiāng
**mosquito net** 蚊帐 wénzhàng
**mosquito repellent** 驱蚊剂 qūwén jì
**mother** 母亲 mǔqin
**mother-in-law** 岳母 yuèmǔ
**motorbike** 摩托车 mótuō chē
**motorboat** 摩托艇 mótuō tǐng
**motorway (tollway)** 收费公路 shōufèi gōnglù
**mountain** 山 shān
**mountain bike** 山地车 shāndì chē

**mountain climbing** 爬山 páshān
**mountain path** 山路 shānlù
**mountain range** 山脉 shānmài
**mouse** 耗子 hàozi
**mouth** 口 kǒu
**movie** 电影 diànyǐng
**Mr** 先生 xiānsheng
**Ms** 女士 nǚshì
**Miss** 小姐 xiǎojiě
**MSG** 味精 wèijīng
**mud** 泥巴 níba
**mum** 妈妈 māma
**mumps** 麻疹 mázhěn
**mung beans (red)** 红豆 hóngdòu
**murder** ⓝ 杀人犯 shārén fàn
**murder** ⓥ 谋杀 móushā
**muscle** 瘦肉 shòuròu
**museum** 博物馆 bówù guǎn
**mushroom** 蘑菇 mógū
**music** 音乐 yīnyuè
**vinyl (records)** 黑胶唱片 hēijiāo chàngpiàn
**musician** 音乐家 yīnyuè jiā
**Muslim** 穆斯林 Mùsīlín
**mussel** 青口/海红 qīngkǒu/hǎihóng
**mustard** 芥末 jièmo
**mustard greens** 油菜 yóucài
**mute** 哑巴 yǎba
**my** 我的 wǒde

# N

**nail clippers** 指甲刀 zhǐjiadāo
**name** 名字 míngzi
**napkin** 餐巾 cānjīn
**nappy** 尿裤 niàokù
**nappy rash** 尿裤疹 niàokùzhěn
**national park** 国家公园 guójiā gōngyuán
**nationality** 国籍 guójí
**nature** 大自然 dà zìrán
**nausea** 恶心 ěxīn
**near** 近 jìn
**nearby** 附近 fùjìn
**nearest** 最近 zuìjìn
**necessary** 必要的 bìyào de
**necklace** 项链 xiàngliàn
**nectarine** 油桃 yóutáo
**need** ⓥ 需要 xūyào
**needle (sewing)** 针线 zhēnxiàn
**needle (syringe)** 注射针 zhùshè zhēn
**negative** ⓐ 消极 xiāojí
**neither** 两个都不 liǎngge dōu bù
**net** 网 wǎng
**Netherlands** 荷兰 Hélán
**never** 从来不 cónglái bù
**new** 新 xīn
**New Year's Day** 元旦 yuándàn
**New Year's Eve** 除夕 chúxī
**New Zealand** 新西兰 Xīnxīlán
**news** 新闻 xīnwén
**newspaper** 报纸 bàozhǐ
**next (month)** 下个（月）xiàge (yuè)
**next to** 旁边 pángbiān
**nickname** 昵称 nìchēng
**night** 晚上 wǎnshàng
**no** 不对 bùduì
**no vacancy (restaurants, hotels)** 客满 kèmǎn
**noisy** 吵 chǎo
**nomads** 游牧民 yóumù mín
**none** 一个也没有 yīge yě méiyǒu
**nonsmoking** 不吸烟 bù xīyān
**noodle shop** 面馆 miànguǎn
**noodles** 面条 miàntiáo
**noon** 中午 zhōngwǔ
**north** 北边 běibiān
**Norway** 挪威 Nuówēi
**nose** 鼻子 bízi
**not** 不是 bùshì
**notebook** 笔记本 bǐjì běn
**nothing** 一无所有 yīwú suǒyǒu
**November** 十一月 shíyī yuè
**now** 现在 xiànzài
**nuclear energy** 核能 hé néng
**nuclear testing** 核试验 hé shìyàn
**nuclear waste** 核废物 hé fèiwù
**number** 号码 hàomǎ
**tablet (digital device)** 平板 píngbǎn
**nun** 尼姑 nígū
**nurse** 护士 hùshi
**nut** 果仁 guǒrén

# O

**oats** 燕麦片 yànmài piàn
**occupation** 工作 gōngzuò
**occupied** 有事 yǒushì
**ocean** 大海 dàhǎi
**October** 十月 shíyuè
**off (spoiled)** 过时 guòshí
**office** 办公室 bàngōng shì
**office worker** 白领 báilǐng
**often** 经常 jīngcháng
**oil (food)** 油 yóu
**oil (petroleum)** 汽油 qìyóu
**old** 老 lǎo
**old man (derogatory)** 老头 lǎotóu
**old man (respectful)** 大爷 dàyé
**old woman (derogatory)** 大妈 dàmā
**old woman (respectful)** 老太太 lǎo tàitai
**Olympic Games** 奥运会 Àoyùn huì
**Olympic record** 奥运纪录 Àoyùn jìlù
**omelette** 炒鸡蛋 chǎo jīdàn
**outdoor** 户外 hùwài
**on time** 准时 zhǔnshí
**once** 一次 yīcì
**one** 一个 yīgè
**one-way (ticket)** 单程 dānchéng
**onion** 洋葱 yángcōng
**online (going)** 上网 shàngwǎng
**online (state)** 在线 zàixiàn
**only** 只有 zhǐyǒu
**oolong tea** 乌龙茶 wūlóng chá
**open** ⓐ 开放 kāifàng
**open** ⓥ 打开 dǎkāi
**opening hours** 营业时间 yíngyè shíjiān
**opera (Chinese)** 戏曲 xìqǔ
**opera (Western)** 歌剧 gējù
**opera house** 剧场 jùchǎng
**operation (medical)** 手术 shǒushù
**operator** 操作工 cāozuògōng
**opinion** 看法 kànfǎ
**opposite** 对面 duìmiàn
**optometrist** 验光师 yànguāng shī
**or** 或者 huòzhě
**orange (fruit)** 橙子 chéngzi
**orange (colour)** 橙色 chéngsè
**orange juice** 橙汁 chéngzhī
**organisation** 组织 zǔzhī
**order food delivery** 点外卖 diǎn wàimài
**order (in restaurant)** ⓥ 点菜 diǎncài
**ordinary** 普通 pǔtōng
**orgasm** 高潮 gāocháo
**original work** 原作 yuánzuò
**other** 其他 qítā
**our** 我们的 wǒmende
**out of order** 坏了 huàile
**outside** 外面 wàimian
**ovary** 卵巢 luǎncáo
**oven** 烤箱 kǎoxiāng
**overcoat** 大衣 dàyī
**overdose** 过量 guòliàng
**overnight** 过夜 guòyè
**overseas** 海外 hǎiwài
**owe** 欠 qiàn
**owner** 主人 zhǔrén
**oxygen** 氧气 yǎngqì
**oyster** 蚝 háo
**oyster sauce** 蚝油 háoyóu
**ozone layer** 臭氧层 chòu yǎng céng

# P

**pacemaker** 心律调节器 xīnlǜ tiáojié qì
**pacifier (dummy)** 奶嘴 nǎizuǐ
**package** 包裹 bāoguǒ
**packet (general)** 包 bāo
**padlock** 锁 suǒ
**page** 页 yè
**pagoda** 八角塔 bājiǎotǎ
**pain** 疼 téng
**painful** 很疼 hěnténg
**painkiller** 止痛药 zhǐtòngyào
**painter** 画家 huàjiā
**painting (oils)** 油画 yóuhuà
**painting (the art)** 画画 huàhuà
**pair** 对 duì
**Pakistan** 巴基斯坦 Bājīsītǎn
**palace** 宫殿 gōngdiàn
**pan** 小锅 xiǎoguō

**pancake** 煎饼 jiānbǐng
**panda** 熊猫 xióngmāo
**pants (trousers)** 长裤 chángkù
**panty liners** 卫生巾 wèishēngjīn
**pap smear** 擦片检查 cāpiàn jiǎnchá
**papaya** 木瓜 mùguā
**paper** 纸 zhǐ
**papers (official documents)** 证件 zhèngjiàn
**paperwork** 手续 shǒuxù
**paraplegic** 双肢障 shuāngzhīzhàng
**parcel** 包裹 bāoguǒ
**parents** 父母 fùmǔ
**park** 公园 gōngyuán
**park (a car)** 停 (车) tíng (chē)
**parliament** 议会 yìhuì
**part (component)** 部件 bùjiàn
**part-time** 兼职 jiānzhí
**party (any lively gathering)** 趴 pā
**pack a bag** 收拾行李 shōushi xínglǐ
**party (politics)** 党 dǎng
**pass (mountain)** 关口 guānkǒu
**pass (permit)** 许可证 xǔkězhèng
**pass** 通过 tōngguò
**passenger** 乘客 chéngkè
**passionfruit** 鸡蛋果 jīdàn guǒ
**passport** 护照 hùzhào
**passport number** 护照号码 hùzhào hàomǎ
**past** 过去 guòqù
**pasta** 意大利面 yìdàlì miàn
**pastor** 牧师 mùshī
**pastry (Chinese)** 糕点 gāodiǎn
**path** 小路 xiǎolù
**pavillion** 亭子 tíngzi
**playground (children)** 游乐场 yóulèchǎng
**pay** ⓥ 付 fù
**payment** 付款 fùkuǎn
**pea shoots** 豆苗 dòumiáo
**peace** 和平 hépíng
**peach** 桃子 táozi
**peak (mountain)** 山顶 shāndǐng
**peanut** 花生 huāshēng
**pear** 梨 lí
**peasant** 农民 nóngmín
**pedal** 脚蹬 jiǎodèng
**pedestrian** 行人 xíngrén
**pedicab** 三轮车 sānlúnchē
**Peking duck** 北京烤鸭 Běijīng kǎoyā
**Peking opera** 京剧 jīngjù
**pen (ballpoint)** 钢笔 gāngbǐ
**pencil** 铅笔 qiānbǐ
**penis** 阳具 yángjù
**penknife** 小刀 xiǎodāo
**pensioner** 退休人员 tuìxiū rényuán
**people** 人 rén
**pepper (sweet)** 甜椒 tiánjiāo
**pepper (black or white)** 胡椒 hújiāo
**per (day)** 每 (天) měi(tiān)
**per cent** 百分比 bǎifēnbǐ
**perfect** 完美 wánměi
**performance** 演出 yǎnchū
**perfume** 香水 xiāngshuǐ
**period pain** 痛经 tòngjīng
**permission** 许可 xǔkě
**permit** 许可证 xǔkě zhèng
**persimmon** 柿子 shìzi
**person** 人 rén
**petition** 信访 xìnfǎng
**petrol station** 加油站 jiāyóu zhàn
**pharmacist** 药剂师 yàojì shī
**pharmacy** 药房 yàofáng
**pharmacy** 西药房 xīyào fáng
**phonecard** 电话卡 diànhuà kǎ
**photo** 照片 zhàopiàn
**photographer** 摄影师 shèyǐngshī
**photography** 摄影 shèyǐng
**phrasebook** 常用语手册 chángyòngyǔ shǒucè
**pickles** 咸菜 xiáncài
**picnic** 野餐 yěcān
**pie** 馅饼 xiànbǐng
**piece** 块 kuài
**pig** 猪 zhū
**pigeon** 鸽子 gēzi
**pilgrimage** 朝圣 cháoshèng
**pill** 药片 yàopiàn
**Pill (the)** 避孕药 bìyùn yào
**pillow** 枕头 zhěntou
**pineapple** 菠萝 bōluó

**pink** 粉红色 fěnhóngsè
**pistachio** 开心果 kāixīnguǒ
**PLA (People's Liberation Army)** 解放军 jiěfàng jūn
**place** 地方 dìfāng
**place of birth** 出生地 chūshēng dì
**plane** 飞机 fēijī
**planet** 星球 xīngqiú
**plant** 植物 zhíwù
**plastic** 塑料 sùliào
**plate** 盘子 pánzi
**plateau** 高原 gāoyuán
**platform** 站台 zhàntái
**play (cards)** 打 dǎ
**play (guitar)** 弹 tán
**play (theatre)** 剧 jù
**plug (bath)** 塞子 sāizi
**plug (electricity)** 插头 chātóu
**plum** 梅子 méizi
**pneumonia** 肺炎 fèiyán
**pocket** 口袋 kǒudài
**pocket knife** 折叠刀 zhédié dāo
**podcast** 播客 bōkè
**poetry** 诗歌 shīgē
**point** ⓝ 点 diǎn
**point** ⓥ 指 zhǐ
**poisonous** 有毒 yǒudú
**police** 警察局 jǐngchájú
**police officer** 警察 jǐngchá
**public security officer** 公安 gōng'ān
**police station** 派出所 pàichū suǒ
**policy** 政策 zhèngcè
**politician** 政治家 zhèngzhì jiā
**politics** 政治 zhèngzhì
**pollen** 花粉 huāfěn
**pollution** 污染 wūrǎn
**pollution (air)** 空气污染 kōngqì wūrǎn
**pollution (water)** 水污染 shuǐ wūrǎn
**pomelo** 柚子 yòuzi
**pool (game)** 台球 táiqiú
**pool (swimming)** 游泳池 yóuyǒng chí
**poor** 穷 qióng
**popular** 流行 liúxíng
**pork** 猪肉 zhūròu
**port (sea)** 港口 gǎngkǒu
**portrait sketcher** 画像师 huàxiàng shī
**positive** 正 zhèng
**possible** 有可能 yǒukěnéng
**post code** 邮政编码 yóuzhèng biānmǎ
**post office** 邮局 yóujú
**postage** 邮费 yóufèi
**postcard** 明信片 míngxìnpiàn
**poster** 画报 huàbào
**potato** 土豆 tǔdòu
**pottery** 陶器 táoqì
**pound (money, weight)** 镑 bàng
**poverty** 贫穷 pínqióng
**powder** 粉 fěn
**power** 权利 quánlì
**prawn** 虾子 xiāzi
**prayer** 祈祷 qídǎo
**prayer book** 祈祷书 qídǎo shū
**PRC (People's Republic of China)** 中华人民共和国 Zhōnghuá rénmín gònghé guó
**prefer** 更喜欢 gèng xǐhuān
**pregnancy test kit** 验孕棒 yànyùn bàng
**pregnant** 怀孕 huáiyùn
**prehistoric** 史前 shǐqián
**premenstrual syndrome (PMS)** 经前综合征 jīngqián zōnghé zhēng
**prepare** 准备 zhǔnbèi
**prescription** 药方 yàofāng
**present (gift)** 礼物 lǐwù
**present (time)** 现在 xiànzài
**president** 总统 zǒngtǒng
**pressure** 压力 yālì
**pressure point massage** 经络按摩 jīngluò ànmó
**pretty** 漂亮 piàoliang
**price** 价格 jiàgé
**priest** 神父 shénfù
**prime minister** 首相 shǒuxiàng
**printer (computer)** 打印机 dǎyìnjī
**prison** 监狱 jiānyù
**prisoner** 犯人 fànrén
**private** 私人 sīrén
**produce** ⓥ 生产 shēngchǎn

**profession** 行业 hángyè
**profit** 利润 lìrùn
**programme** 节目 jiémù
**projector** 投影机 tóuyǐngjī
**promise** 承诺 chéngnuò
**protect** 保护 bǎohù
**protected (animal etc)** 受保护动物 shòu bǎohù dòngwù
**protest** ⓝ 游行 yóuxíng
**protest** ⓥ 抗议 kàngyì
**provisions** 预备品 yùbèipǐn
**PSB (Public Security Bureau)** 公安局 gōng'ān jú
**pub (bar)** 酒吧 jiǔbā
**public relations** 公共关系 gōnggòng guānxì
**public toilet** 公厕 gōngcè
**publication** 出版物 chūbǎn wù
**publish** 出版 chūbǎn
**pull** 拉 lā
**pump** ⓝ 打气筒 dǎqìtóng
**pumpkin** 南瓜 nánguā
**pumpkin seeds** 南瓜子 nánguā zi
**puncture** 穿孔 chuānkǒng
**pure** 纯 chún
**purple** 紫色 zǐsè
**purse** 钱包 qiánbāo
**push** 推 tuī
**put** 放 fàng

## Q

**QR code** 二维码 èrwéi mǎ
**quadriplegic** 四肢障 sìzhīzhàng
**qualifications** 资历 zīlì
**qualifications (academic)** 学历 xuélì
**quality** 质量 zhìliàng
**quarantine** 免疫站 miǎnyìzhàn
**quarter** 四分之一 sìfēn zhī yī
**queen** 女王 nǚwáng
**queer (LGBTQI+)** 酷儿 kù'ér
**question** 问题 wèntí
**queue** 排队 páiduì
**quick** 快 kuài
**quiet** 安静 ānjìng
**quit (job)** 辞职 cízhí

## R

**rabbit** 兔子 tùzi
**race (sport)** 比赛 bǐ sài
**racetrack** 赛场 sàichǎng
**racing bike** 公路车 gōnglù chē
**racism** 种族歧视 zhǒngzú qíshì
**racquet** 拍子 pāizi
**radish** 萝卜 luóbo
**railway station** 火车站 huǒchēzhàn
**rain** ⓝ 下雨 xiàyǔ
**raincoat** 雨衣 yǔyī
**raisin** 葡萄干 pútáogān
**rape** ⓝ 强奸 qiángjiān
**rare (uncommon)** 罕见 hǎnjiàn
**rare (about food)** 半生 bànshēng
**rash** 疹子 zhěnzi
**raspberry** 山莓 shānméi
**rat** 老鼠 lǎoshǔ
**rave** 电子舞会 diànzǐ wǔhuì
**raw** 生 shēng
**razor** 剃刀 tìdāo
**read** 读 dú
**reading** 看书 kànshū
**ready** 做好了 zuòhǎole
**real-estate agent** 房产代理 fángchǎn dàilǐ
**realistic** 现实 xiànshí
**rear (seat etc)** 后 hòu
**reason** 原因 yuányīn
**receipt** 发票 fāpiào
**recently** 最近 zuìjìn
**recommend** 推荐 tuījiàn
**recording (audio)** 录音 lùyīn
**recyclable** 可回收 kě huíshōu
**recycle** 回收 huíshōu
**red** 红色 hóngsè
**reel/short video** 视频 shìpín
**referee** 裁判 cáipàn
**reference (letter)** 推荐（信）tuījiàn (xìn)
**reflexology** 反射疗法 fǎnshè liáofǎ
**refrigerator** 冰箱 bīngxiāng
**refugee** 难民 nànmín
**refund** ⓝ 退钱 tuìqián

**refuse** 拒绝 jùjué
**regional** 地方性 dì fāng xìng
**registered mail/post** 挂号 guàhào
**rehydration salts** 补液盐 bǔyèyán
**relationship** 关系 guānxì
**relax** 放松 fàngsōng
**relic** 文物 wénwù
**religion** 宗教 zōngjiào
**religious** 宗教性的 zōngjiào xìngde
**remote** 偏僻 piānpì
**remote control** 遥控 yáokòng
**rent** 租赁 zūlìn
**repair** 修理 xiūlǐ
**republic** 共和国 gònghéguó
**reservation (booking)** 预订 yùdìng
**rest** 休息 xiūxi
**restaurant** 饭馆 fànguǎn
**resumé (CV)** 简历 jiǎnlì
**retired** 退休 tuìxiū
**return (come back)** 回来 huílái
**return (ticket)** 双程（票） shuāngchéng (piào)
**review** ⓝ 复查 fùchá
**rhythm** 节奏 jiézòu
**ribs (beef/pork)** 排骨 páigǔ
**rice (raw)** 大米 dàmǐ
**rice (cooked)** 米饭 mǐfàn
**rice cake** 年糕 niángāo
**rice vinegar (white)** 白醋 báicù
**rich (wealthy)** 有钱 yǒuqián
**ride (horse)** ⓥ 骑 qí
**right (correct)** 对 duì
**right (direction)** 右边 yòubiān
**right-wing** 右派 yòupài
**ring (on finger)** 戒指 jièzhǐ
**ring (phone)** 打（电话） dǎ (diànhuà)
**rip-off** 宰客 zǎikè
**risk** ⓝ 风险 fēngxiǎn
**river** 河/江 hé/jiāng
**road** 道路 dàolù
**road map** 交通地图 jiāotōng dìtú
**rob** 偷 tōu
**rock (stone)** 石头 shítou
**rock (music)** 摇滚 yáogǔn
**rock climbing** 攀岩 pānyán
**roll (bread)** 小面包 xiǎo miànbāo
**rollerblading** 旱冰 hànbīng
**romantic** 浪漫 làngmàn
**room** 房间 fángjiān
**room number** 房间号 fángjiān hào
**rope** 绳子 shéngzi
**round** 圆 yuán
**roundabout** 环岛 huándǎo
**route** 路线 lùxiàn
**rowing** 划船 huáchuán
**rubbish** 垃圾 lājī
**rubella** 德国麻疹 déguó mázhěn
**rug** 地毯 dìtǎn
**rugby** 英式橄榄球 yīngshì gǎnlǎn qiú
**ruins** 废墟 fèixū
**rule** ⓝ 规定 guīdìng
**run** 跑 pǎo
**running (sport)** 跑步 pǎobù
**runny nose** 流鼻涕 liú bítì

## S

**sad** 郁闷 yùmèn
**saddle** 马鞍 mǎ'ān
**safe** 安全 ānquán
**safe sex** 安全性行为 ānquán xìngxíngwéi
**safebox** 保险箱 bǎoxiǎn xiāng
**saint** 圣人 shèngrén
**salad** 沙拉 shālā
**salami** 萨拉米香肠 sàlāmǐ xiāngcháng
**salary** 薪水 xīnshuǐ
**sale (clearance)** 大甩卖 dà shuǎimài
**sales tax** 销售税 xiāoshòu shuì
**salmon** 三文鱼 sānwén yú
**salt** 盐 yán
**same** 一样 yīyàng
**sand** 沙子 shāzi
**sandal** 凉鞋 liángxié
**sanitary napkin** 卫生巾 wèishēngjīn
**sardine** 沙丁鱼 shādīngyú
**COVID** 新冠病毒 xīnguān bìngdú
**Saturday** 星期六 xīngqī liù
**sauce** 酱 jiàng
**sauna** 桑拿 sāngná
**sausage** 香肠 xiāngcháng
**say** 说 shuō
**scarf** 头巾 tóujīn

**scenic area** 风景区 fēngjǐngqū
**school** 学校 xuéxiào
**science** 科学 kēxué
**scientist** 科学家 kēxué jiā
**scissors** 剪刀 jiǎndāo
**score (goal)** 进球 jìnqiú
**Scotland** 苏格兰 Sūgélán
**scrambled (stir-fried)** 炒 chǎo
**sculpture** 雕塑 diāosù
**sea** 海 hǎi
**sea cucumber** 海参 hǎishēn
**seafood** 海鲜 hǎixiān
**seasick** 晕船 yùnchuán
**seaside** 海边 hǎibiān
**season** 季节 jìjié
**seat (place)** 座位 zuòwèi
**seatbelt** 安全带 ānquándài
**second** ⓝ 秒 miǎo
**second** ⓐ 第二 dì'èr
**second-class** 二等 èrděng
**secondhand** 二手 èrshǒu
**secondhand shop** 二手店 èrshǒu diàn
**secretary** 秘书 mìshū
**see** 看见 kànjiàn
**self service** 自助 zìzhù
**self-employed** 个体户 gètǐ hù
**selfish** 自私 zìsī
**sell** 卖 mài
**send** 寄送 jìsòng
**sensible** 有理的 yǒulǐde
**sensual** 官能的 guānguān de
**separate** 分开的 fēnkāide
**September** 九月 jiǔyuè
**serious** 严肃 yánsù
**server (waiter)** 服务员 fúwù yuán
**service** 服务 fúwù
**service charge** 服务费 fúwù fèi
**service station** 加油站 jiāyóu zhàn
**serviette** 纸巾 zhǐjīn
**sesame paste** 芝麻酱 zhīma jiàng
**several** 好几个 hǎo jǐge
**sew (mend)** 补 bǔ
**sew (not mend)** 缝纫 féngrèn
**sex worker** 性工作者 xìnggōngzuò zhě
**sexism** 性别歧视 xìngbié qíshì
**sexual assault** 性侵 xìngqīn
**sexual harrassment** 性骚扰 xìngsāorǎo
**sexual relations** 性关系 xìngguānxì
**sexy** 性感 xìnggǎn
**shade (tree)** ⓝ 树荫 shùyīn
**shadow** 影子 yǐngzi
**shallots** 小葱 xiǎocōng
**shampoo** 洗发水 xǐfàshuǐ
**Shanghai** 上海 Shànghǎi
**shape** ⓝ 形状 xíngzhuàng
**share (with friends)** 分享 fēnxiǎng
**shared** 公用 gōngyòng
**shared bike** 共享单车 gòngxiǎng dānchē
**she** 她 tā
**sheep** 绵羊 miányáng
**sheet (bed)** 床单 chuángdān
**shelf** 架子 jiàzi
**sexual orientation** 性取向 xìng qǔxiàng
**shingles (illness)** 带状泡疹 dàizhuàng pàozhěn
**ship** 船 chuán
**shirt** 衬衫 chénshān
**shoe shop** 鞋店 xiédiàn
**shoes** 鞋子 xiézi
**shoot** 打枪 dǎqiāng
**shop** ⓝ 店 diàn
**shop** ⓥ 买东西 mǎi dōngxi
**shopping** 逛街 guàngjiē
**shopping centre** 商场 shāngchǎng
**short (height)** 矮 ǎi
**short (length)** 短 duǎn
**shortage** 紧缺 jǐnquē
**shorts** 短裤 duǎnkù
**shoulder** 肩膀 jiānbǎng
**shout** 喊 hǎn
**show** 表演 biǎoyǎn
**shower** 浴室 yùshì
**shrine (ancestral hall)** 祠堂 cí táng
**shut** 关 guān
**shy** 害羞 hàixiū
**Sichuan peppercorn** 花椒 huājiāo
**sick** 病 bìng
**sign** 牌子 páizi
**signature** 签名 qiānmíng
**silk** 丝绸 sīchóu

**silver** 银子 yínzi
**silver medal** 银牌 yínpái
**similar** 类似 lèisì
**simple** 简单 jiǎndān
**since (May)** 从(五月) 以来 cóng (wǔ yuè) yǐlái
**sing** 唱歌 chànggē
**Singapore** 新加坡 Xīnjiāpō
**singer** 歌手 gēshǒu
**single (person)** 单人 dānrén
**single room** 单人间 dānrén jiān
**singlet** 背心 bèixīn
**sister (elder)** 姐姐 jiějie
**sister (younger)** 妹妹 mèimei
**sisters** 姐妹 jiěmèi
**sit** 坐下 zuòxià
**size (general)** 大小 dàxiǎo
**skateboarding** 滑板 huábǎn
**ski** ⓥ 滑雪 huáxuě
**skiing** 滑雪 huáxuě
**skin** 皮肤 pífū
**skincare products** 保养品 bǎoyǎng pǐn
**skirt** 裙子 qúnzi
**skull** 头骨 tóugǔ
**sky** 天 tiān
**sleep** 睡觉 shuìjiào
**sleeping bag** 睡袋 shuìdài
**sleeping berth** 卧铺 wòpù
**sleeping car** 卧铺车厢 wòpù chēxiāng
**sleeping pills** 安眠药 ānmián yào
**sleepy** 犯困 fànkùn
**slice (cake)** 蛋糕 dàngāo
**slide (film)** 幻灯片 huàndēng piàn
**slippers** 拖鞋 tuōxié
**slow** 慢 màn
**slowly** 慢慢地 mànmande
**small** 小 xiǎo
**smaller** 更小 gèngxiǎo
**smallest** 最小 zuìxiǎo
**smell** 味道 wèidào
**smile** 微笑 wēixiào
**smoke** 抽烟 chōuyān
**snack** 小吃 xiǎochī
**snail** 蜗牛 wōniú
**snake** 蛇 shé
**snorkelling** 浮潜 fú qiǎn
**snow** 雪 xuě
**snow pea** 荷兰豆 hélán dòu
**snowboarding** 单板滑雪 dānbǎn huáxuě
**soap** 肥皂 féizào
**scan (QR code)** 扫码 sǎomǎ
**social welfare** 社会福利 shèhuì fúlì
**socialism** 社会主义 shèhuì zhǔyì
**socialist** 社会主义战士 shèhuì zhǔyì zhànshì
**sock** 袜子 wàzi
**soft drink** 汽水 qìshuǐ
**soft seat** 软座 ruǎnzuò
**soft sleeper** 软卧 ruǎnwò
**soldier** 军人 jūnrén
**some** 一些 yīxiē
**someone** 某人 mǒurén
**something** 一个什么的 yīge shénme de
**sometimes** 偶尔 ǒu'ěr
**son** 儿子 érzi
**song** 歌曲 gēqǔ
**soon** 快 kuài
**sore** 疮口 chuāngkǒu
**sore throat** 喉咙疼 hóulóngténg
**soup** 汤 tāng
**sour plum drink** 酸梅汤 suānméitāng
**south** 南 nán
**souvenir** 纪念品 jìniàn pǐn
**souvenir shop** 纪念品店 jìniànpǐn diàn
**soybean** 黄豆 huángdòu
**soy milk (fresh)** 豆浆 dòujiāng
**sightseeing** 观光 guānguāng
**soy sauce** 酱油 jiàngyóu
**space** 空间 kōngjiān
**Spain** 西班牙 Xībānyá
**sparkling wine** 起泡酒 qǐpào jiǔ
**speak** 说话 shuōhuà
**special** 特别 tèbié
**specialist** 专家 zhuānjiā
**speed** 速度 sùdù
**speed limit** 最高车速 zuìgāo chēsù
**speedometer** 速度表 sùdù biǎo

**spider** 蜘蛛 zhīzhū
**spinach** 菠菜 bócài
**spirits (Chinese alcohol)** 白酒 báijiǔ
**spoiled (food)** 烂掉了 làndiàole
**spoon** 勺 sháo
**sport** 体育 tǐyù
**sports store** 体育用品店 tǐyù yòngpǐn diàn
**sportsperson** 运动员 yùndòng yuán
**sprain** 扭伤 niǔshāng
**spring (coil)** 弹簧 tánhuáng
**spring (season)** 春天 chūntiān
**Spring Festival** 春节 chūnjié
**square (town)** 广场 guǎngchǎng
**stadium** 体育场 tǐyù chǎng
**stairway** 台阶 táijiē
**stale** 不新鲜 bù xīnxiān
**stamp** 邮票 yóupiào
**standby ticket** 候补票 hòubǔ piào
**star** 星星 xīngxing
**(four-)star** (四)星级 (sì) xīngjí
**star anise** 八角 bājiǎo
**start** ⓝ 开头 kāitóu
**start** ⓥ 开始 kāishǐ
**station** 车站 chēzhàn
**stationer's (shop)** 文具店 wénjù diàn
**statue** 塑像 sùxiàng
**stay (at a hotel)** 住 zhù
**stay (in one place)** 留在 liúzài
**steak (beef)** 排骨 páigǔ
**steal** 偷 tōu
**steamed bun** 馒头 mántou
**steep** 陡 dǒu
**step** 台阶 táijiē
**stereo** 音响 yīnxiǎng
**sticking plaster** 创口贴 chuāngkǒu tiē
**still water** 净水 jìngshuǐ
**stock (broth)** 高汤 gāotāng
**stolen** 盗窃的 dàoqiède
**stomach** 肚子 dùzi
**stomach ache (to have a)** 肚子疼 dùzi téng
**stone** 石头 shítou
**sunbathing** 晒太阳 shài tàiyáng
**stop (bus, tram etc)** 停 tíng
**stop (cease)** 停止 tíngzhǐ
**stop (prevent)** 防止 fángzhǐ
**stop!** 救人! jiùrén!
**storm** 风暴 fēngbào
**story** 故事 gùshi
**stove** 炉子 lúzi
**straight (line, posture)** 直 zhí
**strange** 奇怪 qíguài
**stranger** 陌生人 mòshēngrén
**strawberry** 草莓 cǎoméi
**stream** 溪流 xīliú
**street** 街头 jiētóu
**street market** 街市 jiēshì
**strike** 罢工 bàgōng
**string** 绳子 shéngzi
**stroke (medical)** 中风 zhòngfēng
**stroll** 散步 sànbù
**stroller** 婴儿推车 yīng'ér tuīchē
**strong** 有劲 yǒujìn
**stubborn** 固执 gùzhí
**student** 学生 xuéshēng
**studio** 工作室 gōngzuò shì
**stupid** 愚蠢 yúchǔn
**style** 风格 fēnggé
**subtitles** 字幕 zìmù
**suburb** 郊区 jiāoqū
**subway** 地铁 dìtiě
**suffer** 吃苦 chīkǔ
**sugar** 砂糖 shātáng
**sugar cane** 甘蔗 gānzhè
**suitcase** 旅行箱 lǚxíng xiāng
**summer** 夏天 xiàtiān
**sun** 太阳 tàiyáng
**sunblock** 防晒油 fángshài yóu
**sunburn** 晒伤 shàishāng
**Sunday** 星期天 xīngqītiān
**sunflower seeds** 瓜子 guāzǐ
**sunglasses** 墨镜 mòjìng
**sunny** 很晒 hěnshài
**sunrise** 日出 rìchū
**sunset** 日落 rìluò
**sunstroke** 中暑 zhòngshǔ
**supermarket** 超市 chāoshì
**superstition** 迷信 míxìn
**supporter (politics)** 支持者 zhīchí zhě
**surfboard** 冲浪板 chōnglàng bǎn

**surfing** 冲浪 chōnglàng
**surname** 姓 xìng
**surprise** 惊讶 jīngyà
**sweater** 上衣 shàngyī
**Sweden** 瑞典 Ruìdiǎn
**sweet** 甜 tián
**sweet potato** 地瓜 dìguā
**sweets** 甜点 tiándiǎn
**swim** 游泳 yóuyǒng
**swim cap** 泳帽 yǒngmào
**swimming pool** 游泳池 yóuyǒng chí
**swimsuit** 游泳衣 yóuyǒng yī
**Switzerland** 瑞士 Ruìshì
**swollen** 肿了起来 zhǒngle qǐlái
**synagogue** 犹太教堂 yóutài jiàotáng
**synthetic** 合成的 héchéng de
**syringe** 注射针 zhùshè zhēn

# T

**table** 桌子 zhuōzi
**table tennis** 乒乓球 pīngpāng qiú
**tablecloth** 桌布 zhuōbù
**tail** 尾巴 wěiba
**tailor** 裁缝 cáifeng
**Taiwan** 台湾 Táiwān
**take** 拿走 názǒu
**take a photo** 照相 zhàoxiàng
**talk** 谈话 tánhuà
**tall** 高 gāo
**tampon** 棉条 miántiáo
**Taoism** 道教 Dàojiào
**tap** 水龙头 shuǐlóngtóu
**tap water** 自来水 zìlái shuǐ
**tasty** 好香 hǎoxiāng
**tax** 税 shuì
**taxi** 出租车 chūzū chē
**taxi stand** 出租车站 chūzū chē zhàn
**tea** 茶 chá
**teapot** 茶壶 cháhú
**teacher** 老师 lǎoshī
**teahouse** 茶馆 cháguǎn
**team** 团队 tuánduì
**teeth** 牙齿 yáchǐ
**telephone** ⓝ 电话 diànhuà
**telephone** ⓥ 打电话 dǎ diànhuà
**telescope** 望远镜 wàngyuǎn jìng
**television** 电视 diànshì
**tell** 告诉 gàosu
**temperature (weather)** 温度 wēndù
**temple** 寺庙 sìmiào
**tennis** 网球 wǎngqiú
**tennis court** 网球场 wǎngqiú chǎng
**tent** 帐篷 zhàngpeng
**terrible** 可怕的 kěpà de
**test** 考试 kǎoshì
**thank** 道谢 dàoxiè
**thank you** 谢谢 xièxie
**that (one)** 那个 nàge
**theatre** 剧场 jùchǎng
**their** 他们的 tāmen de
**there** 那边 nàbian
**thermal underwear** 保暖内衣 bǎonuǎn nèiyī
**thermometer (clinical)** 体温计 tǐwēn jì
**thermos** 热水瓶 rèshuǐpíng
**they** 他们 tāmen
**thick** 厚 hòu
**thief** 小偷 xiǎotōu
**thin** 薄 báo
**think** 想 xiǎng
**third** 第三 dìsān
**thirsty (to be)** 渴 kě
**this (month)** 这个（月）zhège (yuè)
**this (one)** 这个 zhège
**thread** 棉线 miánxiàn
**neck** 脖子 bózi
**thrush (health)** 鹅口疮 ékǒuchuāng
**thunderstorm** 雷雨 léiyǔ
**Thursday** 星期四 xīngqī sì
**Tibet** 西藏 Xīzàng
**ticket** 票 piào
**ticket collector** 售票员 shòupiào yuán
**ticket office** 售票处 shòupiàochù
**tide (sea)** 潮汐 cháoxī
**tight** 很紧 hěnjǐn
**time** 时间 shíjiān
**time difference** 时差 shíchā
**timetable** 时刻表 shíkè biǎo
**tin (can)** 罐头 guàntou
**tin opener** 开罐器 kāiguànqì
**tiny** 微小 wēixiǎo

**tip (gratuity)** 小费 xiǎofèi
**tired** 累 lèi
**tissues** 纸巾 zhǐjīn
**to (go to, come to)** 到 dào
**toast** 烤面包 kǎo miànbāo
**tobacco** 烟丝 yānsī
**tobacco and liquor store** 烟酒店 yānjiǔ diàn
**today** 今天 jīntiān
**toe** 脚指头 jiǎo zhǐtou
**tofu** 豆腐 dòufu
**together** 一起 yīqǐ
**toilet** 厕所 cèsuǒ
**toilet paper** 卫生纸 wèishēng zhǐ
**tomato** 西红柿 xīhóngshì
**tomato sauce** 番茄酱 fānqié jiàng
**tomb** 坟墓 fénmù
**tomorrow** 明天 míngtiān
**tonight** 今天晚上 jīntiān wǎnshàng
**too (expensive etc)** 太 tài
**tooth** 牙齿 yáchǐ
**toothache** 牙齿疼 yáchǐ téng
**toothbrush** 牙刷 yáshuā
**toothpaste** 牙膏 yágāo
**toothpick** 牙签 yáqiān
**torch (flashlight)** 手电筒 shǒudiàntǒng
**touch** 触摸 chùmō
**tour** 向导游 xiàngdǎo yóu
**tourist** 旅客 lǚkè
**tourist office** 游客服务中心 yóukè fúwù zhōngxīn
**towards** 向 xiàng
**towel** 毛巾 máojīn
**tower (telecoms)** (电视)塔 (diànshì) tǎ
**toxic** 有毒 yǒudú
**toxic waste** 有毒废料 yǒudú fèiliào
**toy shop** 玩具店 wánjù diàn
**track (sport)** 田径 tiánjìng
**tracks (railway)** 轨道 guǐdào
**traffic** 交通 jiāotōng
**traffic light** 红绿灯 hónglǜdēng
**trail** 步道 bùdào
**train** 火车 huǒchē
**train station** 火车站 huǒchē zhàn
**tram** 电车 diànchē
**trans** 跨性别 kuaxingbie
**transit lounge** 转机室 zhuǎnjī shì
**translate** 翻译 fānyì
**transport** 运输 yùnshū
**travel** 旅游 lǚyóu
**travel agency** 旅行社 lǚxíng shè
**travel sickness** 晕车 yùnchē
**travellers cheque** 旅行支票 lǚxíng zhīpiào
**tree** 树 shù
**trip (journey)** 旅程 lǚchéng
**trolley** 车子 chēzi
**trousers** 裤子 kùzi
**truck** 卡车 kǎchē
**trust** 信用 xìnyòng
**try** ⓥ 尝试 chángshì
**T-shirt** T恤 tīxù
**tube (tyre)** 内胎 nèitāi
**Tuesday** 星期二 xīngqī èr
**tumour** 肿瘤 zhǒngliú
**tuna** 金枪鱼 jīnqiāngyú
**tune** 曲调 qǔdiào
**turkey** 火鸡 huǒjī
**turn (motion)** 转 zhuǎn
**TV** 电视 diànshì
**tweezers** 镊子 nièzi
**twice** 两次 liǎngcì
**twin room** 双人房 shuāngrén fáng
**twins** 双胞胎 shuāngbāo tāi
**two** 两个 liǎngge
**type** 类型 lèixíng
**tyre** 轮胎 lúntāi

# U

**ultrasound** 超声检查 chāoshēng jiǎnchá
**umbrella** 雨伞 yǔsǎn
**uncle** 叔叔 shūshu
**uncomfortable** 不舒服 bù shūfu
**understand** 懂 dǒng
**underwear** 内衣 nèiyī
**unemployed** 失业 shīyè
**unfair** 不公平 bù gōngpíng
**uniform** 制服 zhìfú
**universe** 宇宙 yǔzhòu

**university** 大学 dàxué
**unleaded** 无铅 wúqiān
**unsafe** 不安全 bù ānquán
**until (Friday etc)** 一直到 yīzhí dào
**unusual** 反常 fǎncháng
**up** 上 shàng
**uphill** 上坡 shàngpō
**urgent** 紧急 jǐnjí
**urinary tract infection** 尿路感染 niàolù gǎnrǎn
**USA** 美国 Měiguó
**useful** 有用的 yǒuyòng de
**usually** 通常 tōngcháng

## V

**vacancy (room)** 空房 kōngfáng
**vacant** 空的 kōngde
**vacation** 度假 dùjià
**vaccination** 免疫针 miǎnyì zhēn
**vagina** 阴道 yīndào
**validate** 确认 quèrèn
**valley** 山谷 shāngǔ
**valuable** 贵重 guìzhòng
**value (price)** 实价 shíjià
**van** 面包车 miànbāo chē
**veal** 小牛肉 xiǎo niúròu
**vegetable** 蔬菜 shūcài
**vegetarian** 吃素的 chīsù de
**vein (blood vessel)** 血管 xuèguǎn
**venereal disease** 性病 xìngbìng
**venue** 地点 dìdiǎn
**vermicelli** 粉丝 fěnsī
**very** 很 hěn
**Vietnam** 越南 Yuènán
**view** 视野 shìyě
**villa** 别墅 biéshù
**village** 村庄 cūnzhuāng
**vine (creeper)** 攀藤 pānténg
**vinegar** 醋 cù
**vineyard** 葡萄园 pútáo yuán
**virus** 病毒 bìngdú
**visa** 签证 qiānzhèng
**visit** 拜访 bàifǎng
**vitamins** 维生素 wéishēngsù
**vodka** 伏特加 fútèjiā
**voice** 声音 shēngyīn
**volleyball (sport)** 排球 páiqiú
**volume** 音量 yīnliàng
**vote** 投票 tóupiào

## W

**wage** 工资 gōngzī
**wait (for)** 等 děng
**waiting room** 等候室 děnghòu shì
**wake (someone) up** 叫醒 jiàoxǐng
**walk** 走路 zǒulù
**wall (outer)** 墙壁 qiángbì
**want** 想要 xiǎngyào
**war** 战争 zhànzhēng
**wardrobe** 衣柜 yīguì
**warehouse** 仓库 cāngkù
**warm** 暖和 nuǎnhuo
**warn** 警告 jǐnggào
**wash** 洗 xǐ
**wash cloth (flannel)** 毛巾 máojīn
**washing machine** 洗衣机 xǐyī jī
**watch** ⓝ 手表 shǒubiǎo
**watch** ⓥ 观望/看 guānwàng/kàn
**water** 水 shuǐ
**water bottle (hot)** 热水袋 rèshuǐ dài
**waterfall** 瀑布 pùbù
**watermelon** 西瓜 xīguā
**waterproof** 防水 fángshuǐ
**water purification tablets** 清水药 qīngshuǐyào
**waterskiing** 滑水 huáshuǐ
**wave** 海浪 hǎilàng
**way** 道 dào
**we** 我们 wǒmen
**weak** 弱 ruò
**wealthy** 富裕 fùyù
**wear** 穿 chuān
**weather** 气候 qìhòu
**wedding** 婚礼 hūnlǐ
**wedding cake** 喜饼 xǐbǐng
**wedding gift (monetary)** 红包 hóngbāo
**Wednesday** 星期三 xīngqī sān
**week** 星期 xīngqī
**(this) week** (这个)礼拜 (zhège) lǐbài
**weekend** 周末 zhōumò

**weigh** 称 chēng
**weight** 重量 zhòngliàng
**weight training** 重量训练 zhòngliáng xùnliàn
**welcome** 欢迎 huānyíng
**welfare** 福利 fúlì
**well** 很好 hěnhǎo
**west** 西 xī
**wet** 湿 shī
**what** 什么 shénme
**wheel** 车轮 chēlún
**wheelchair** 轮椅 lúnyǐ
**when** 什么时候 shénme shíhòu
**where** 哪里 nǎli
**which** 哪个 nǎge
**whisky** 威士忌 wèishìjì
**white** 白色 báisè
**who** 谁 shéi
**wholemeal bread** 全麦面包 quánmài miànbāo
**why** 为什么 wèi shénme
**wide** 宽 kuān
**wife** 太太 tàitai
**win** 胜利 shènglì
**wind** 风 fēng
**window** 窗 chuāng
**windscreen** 挡风玻璃 dǎngfēng bōli
**windsurfing** 滑浪风帆 huálàng fēngfān
**wine** 葡萄酒 pútáo jiǔ
**wings** 翅膀 chìbǎng
**winner** 胜利者 shènglìzhě
**winter** 冬天 dōngtiān
**wire** 金属丝 jīnshǔ sī
**wish** ⓥ 祝愿 zhùyuàn
**with** 跟 gēn
**within (an hour)** (一个小时)以内 (yīge xiǎoshí) yǐnèi
**without** 以外 yǐwài
**wok** 锅 guō
**woman** 女人 nǚrén
**wonderful** 奇妙 qímiào
**wonton noodles** 馄饨面 húntūn miàn
**wonton soup** 馄饨 húntun
**wood** 木头 mùtou
**wood (as material)** 木材 mùcái
**wool** 羊毛 yángmáo
**work** ⓝ 工作 gōngzuò
**work** ⓥ 打工 dǎgōng
**work experience** 工作经历 gōngzuò jīnglì
**work permit** 工作证 gōngzuò zhèng
**workout** 健身 jiànshēn
**workshop** 工作室 gōngzuòshì
**world** 世界 shìjiè
**world record** 世界纪录 shìjiè jìlù
**worm** 蚯蚓 qiūyǐn
**worried** 着急 zháojí
**worship** 崇拜 chóngbài
**wrist** 手腕 shǒuwàn
**write** 写 xiě
**writer** 作家 zuòjiā
**wrong** 错 cuò

## Y

**year** 年 nián
**(this) year** (今)年 (jīn) nián
**yellow** 黄色 huángsè
**yes** 是 shì
**yesterday** 昨天 zuótiān
**(not) yet** 还(没有) hái (méiyǒu)
**yoga** 瑜伽 yújiā
**yoghurt** 酸奶 suānnǎi
**you** sg inf 你 nǐ
**you (Beijing)** pol 您 nín
**you** pl 你们 nǐmen
**young** 年轻 niánqīng
**your** 你的 nǐde
**youth hostel** 青年旅社 qīngnián lǚshè

## Z

**zip/zipper** 拉链 lāliàn
**zodiac (Western)** 星座 xīngzuò
**zoo** 动物园 dòngwù yuán
**zucchini** 西葫芦 xī húlu

# DICTIONARY

## Mandarin to English

普通话 – 英文

The Mandarin-English dictionary is arranged according to the number of strokes in the first character of the Chinese word. Thus, the dictionary starts with 一个 yīgè 'one' (the character 一 yī has one stroke), and ends with 罐头 guàntóu (罐 guàn has 24 strokes). As there are many first characters with the same number of strokes, the characters within this number-of-strokes classification system are then ordered according to radical – the element of a character which conveys the meaning of a word.

The symbols ⓝ, ⓐ and ⓥ (noun, adjective and verb) have been added for clarity where this is not clear from the English word itself. Where necessary, inf (informal) and pol (polite) forms are also indicated.

### 一画 1 stroke

一个 yīgè one
一无所有 yīwú suǒyǒu nothing
一切 yīqiè everything
一月 yīyuè January
一直到 yīzhí dào until (Friday etc)
一起 yīqǐ together
一顿饭 yīdùn fàn meal

### 二画 2 strokes

二月 èryuè February
二等 èrděng second class ⓝ
十一月 shíyī yuè November
十二月 shí'èr yuè December
十月 shíyuè October
T-恤 tīxù T-shirt
七月 qīyuè July
人 rén mankind
人参 rénshēn ginseng
入口 rùkǒu entry
入场费 rùchǎng fèi cover charge
八月 bāyuè August
儿子 érzǐ son
九月 jiǔyuè September
刀 dāo knife

### 三画 3 strokes

三月 sānyuè March
干 gān dry
干净 gānjìng clean ⓥ
干部 gānbù communist party official
上 shàng up
上衣 shàngyī jumper/sweater
工人 gōngrén factory worker
工作 gōngzuò job

工程师 gōngchéng shī engineer
工程学 gōngchéng xué engineering
下(车) xiàchē get off (a train etc)
下个 xiàgè next (month)
(今天)下午 (jīntiān) xiàwǔ (this) afternoon
下雨 xiàyǔ rain ⓝ
下面 xiàmiàn down
大 dà big
大小 dàxiǎo size ⓝ
大夫 dàfū doctor
大巴 dàbā bus (city)
大米 dàmǐ rice (raw)
大衣 dàyī coat ⓝ
大佛 dàfó Buddha
大使 dàshǐ ambassador
大使馆 dàshǐguǎn embassy
大学 dàxué university
大麻 dàmá cannabis ⓝ
川 chuān river
小 xiǎo small
小刀 xiǎodāo penknife
小心! xiǎoxīn! careful!
小吃 xiǎochī snack ⓝ
小时 xiǎoshí hour
小卖部 xiǎo màibù convenience store • kiosk
小姐 xiǎojiě Ms/Miss
小娃娃 xiǎo wáwa baby
小路 xiǎolù path
口 kǒu mouth
口红 kǒuhóng lipstick
山 shān mountain
门票钱 ménpiàoqián admission price • fare
勺 sháo spoon ⓝ
广东话 Guǎngdōng huà Cantonese (language) ⓝ
女人 nǚrén woman
女士 nǚshì Mrs and Ms
女同性恋 nǚ tóngxìng liàn lesbian ⓝ
女性 nǚxìng female
女朋友 nǚpéngyǒu girlfriend
女孩子 nǚháizi girl
已婚 yǐ hūn married
卫生巾 wèishēngjīn panty liners • sanitary napkins
叉子 chāzi fork
广场 guǎngchǎng square (town)
飞 fēi fly ⓥ
飞机 fēijī aeroplane
飞机场 fēijī chǎng airport
乡下 xiāngxià countryside

## 四画 4 strokes

开车 kāichē drive ⓥ
开放 kāifàng open ⓐ
开罐器 kāiguàn qì can/tin opener
无聊 wúliáo boring
元旦 yuándàn New Year's Day
艺术 yìshù art
艺术馆 yìshùguǎn art gallery
艺术家 yìshùjiā artist
不可能 bù kěnéng impossible
不对 búduì no
不同 bùtóng different
不吸烟 bù xīyān nonsmoking
不舒服 bù shūfú uncomfortable
长 cháng long
长城 Chángchéng Great Wall
长途车 chángtú chē bus (intercity)
长途车站 chángtú chēzhàn intercity bus station
长袜 chángwà pantyhose
长裤 chángkù pants (trousers)
木柴 mùchái wood
支票 zhīpiào cheque/check
太阳 tàiyáng sun
比赛 bǐsài match (sports) ⓝ
五月 wǔyuè May
车子 chēzi trolley
车号 chēhào car registration
车灯 chēdēng headlights
车闸 chēzhá brakes
车站 chēzhàn bus stop/station ⓝ
车租赁 chē zūlìn car hire
牙齿疼 yáchǐ téng toothache
牙医 yáyī dentist
牙刷 yáshuā toothbrush
牙膏 yágāo toothpaste
切 qiē cut ⓥ
止痛药 zhǐtòngyào painkiller
少 shǎo less
中午 zhōngwǔ midday

中文 Zhōngwén Chinese (language)
中心 zhōngxīn centre ⓝ
中国 Zhōngguó China
中华人民共和国 Zhōnghuá rénmín gònghé guó People's Republic of China (PRC)
中医 Zhōngyī Chinese medicine doctor
中药 Zhōngyào Chinese medicine
日本 Rìběn Japan
日出 rìchū dawn ⓝ
日常 rìcháng daily
日期 rìqī date (day)
日程表 rìchéng biǎo itinerary
日出 rìchū sunrise
日落 rìluò sunset
月 yuè month
水 shuǐ water ⓝ
水龙头 shuǐlóngtóu tap/faucet
水果 shuǐguǒ fruit ⓝ
内衣 nèiyī underwear
牛仔裤 niúzǎi kù jeans
牛奶 niúnǎi milk
牛肉 niúròu beef
午饭 wǔfàn lunch ⓝ
午夜 wǔyè midnight
气 qì chi
手 shǒu hand
手工艺 shǒugōngyì handicrafts
手工的 shǒugōng de handmade
手电筒 shǒudiàntǒng flashlight/torch
手袋 shǒudài handbag
手提包 shǒutíbāo briefcase
手机 shǒujī mobile/cell phone
手套 shǒutào glove
手纸 shǒuzhǐ toilet paper
手续 shǒuxù paperwork
手表 shǒubiǎo watch ⓝ
毛巾 máojīn towel
毛衣 máoyī jumper/sweater
毛毯 máotǎn blanket
斤 jīn jin (measure)
什么时候 shénme shíhòu when
反胃 fǎnwèi nausea
父亲 fùqīn father
从 cóng from
父母 fùmǔ parents
火车 huǒchē train ⓝ
火车站 huǒchēzhàn railway station
火柴 huǒchái matches (for lighting)
今天 jīntiān today
今天晚上 jīntiān wǎnshàng tonight
分 fēn fen (measure)
分钟 fēnzhōng minute ⓝ
公斤 gōngjīn kilogram
公司 gōngsī company (business)
公用 gōngyòng share ⓥ
公园 gōngyuán park ⓝ
公安 gōng'ān police officer (in country)
公安局 gōng'ān jú Public Security Bureau (PSB)
公里 gōnglǐ kilometre
公厕 gōngcè public toilet
公寓 gōngyù apartment (upmarket)
风俗 fēngsú custom
风水 fēngshuǐ feng shui
方向 fāngxiàng direction
六月 liùyuè June
文具店 wénjù diàn stationer's (shop)
心脏 xīnzàng heart
心脏病 xīnzàngbìng heart condition
为什么 wèi shénme why
双边插座 shuāngbiān chāzuò adaptor
双人床 shuāngrén chuáng double bed
双人间 shuāngrén jiān double room
双人房 shuāngrén fáng twin room
双程（票）shuāngchéng (piào) return (ticket)
书 shū book ⓝ
幻灯片 huàndēng piàn slide (film)
订 dìng book (make a booking)
订满 dìngmǎn booked out

## 五画 5 strokes

未婚夫 wèihūnfū fiancé
未婚妻 wèihūnqī fiancée
去 qù go
玉米 yùmǐ corn
打开 dǎkāi open ⓥ
打火机 dǎhuǒjī cigarette lighter
打电话 dǎ diànhuà telephone ⓥ
打印机 dǎyìnjī printer (computer)
打扫 dǎsǎo clean ⓐ

打扮 dǎbàn to do oneself up ⓥ
打针 dǎzhēn injection
古代 gǔdài ancient
古典 gǔdiǎn classical
古董 gǔdǒng antique ⓝ
古董市场 gǔdǒng shìchǎng antique market
艾滋病 àizībìng AIDS
节日 jiérì festival
左边 zuǒbiān left (direction)
右边 yòubiān right (direction)
石头 shítóu rock, stone
头 tóu head ⓝ
头巾 tóujīn scarf
头疼 tóuténg headache
头等舱 tóuděng cāng first class
商务舱 shāngwù cāng business class
东方 dōngfāng east
北边 běibian north
北京烤鸭 Běijīng kǎoyā Peking duck
以上 yǐshàng on
以外 yǐwài beyond, other than
以后 yǐhòu after • later
目的地 mùdì dì destination
兄弟 xiōngdì brother
叫 jiào call ⓥ
叫醒 jiàoxǐng wake (someone) up
(美)元 (Měi) yuán (American) dollar
号码 hàomǎ number ⓝ
电脑 diànnǎo computer
电子用品店 diànzǐ yòngpǐn diàn electrical store
电邮 diànyóu email ⓝ
电子舞会 diànzǐ wǔhuì rave ⓝ
电风扇 diànfēngshàn electrical fan
电池 diànchí battery ⓝ
电视 diànshì television
电话 diànhuà telephone ⓝ
电话卡 diànhuà kǎ phonecard
电梯 diàntī lift/elevator
电影 diànyǐng movie
电影院 diànyǐngyuàn cinema
平板 píngbǎn tablet (digital device)
四月 sìyuè April
生日 shēngrì birthday
生意 shēngyì business ⓝ
皮革 pígé leather ⓝ
付款 fùkuǎn payment
代理费 dàilǐ fèi commission
他 tā he, him
他的 tāde his
乐队 yuèduì band (music)
冬天 dōngtiān winter
外套 wàitào jacket
外国人 wàiguó rén foreigner
外面 wàimiàn outside
包 bāo bag • packet
包子 bāozi steamed dumpling
包括 bāokuò including
包裹 bāoguǒ package • parcel ⓝ
写 xiě write
市中心 shìzhōngxīn city centre
市场 shìchǎng market ⓝ
白天 báitiān day
白色 báisè white
半个 bàngè half
礼物 lǐwù gift ⓝ
记者 jìzhě journalist
民主主义 mínzhǔ zhǔyì democracy
出口 chūkǒu exit ⓝ
出去 chūqù go out
出发 chūfā departure
出生日 chūshēngrì date of birth
出生证 chūshēngzhèng birth certificate
出纳 chūnà cashier
出事了chūshì le an accident has occurred
出差 chūchāi business trip
出租车 chūzū chē taxi ⓝ
出租车站 chūzū chē zhàn taxi stand
奶奶 nǎinai grandmother (paternal)
奶酪 nǎiluò cheese
奶油 nǎiyóu butter
加油站 jiāyóu zhàn service station
加拿大 Jiānádà Canada
加油站 jiāyóu zhàn petrol station
发动机 fādòngjī engine
发烧 fāshāo fever
发票 fāpiào receipt
边界 biānjiè border ⓝ
圣诞节 shèngdànjié Christmas
台阶 táijiē stairway

台湾 Táiwān Taiwan
母亲 mǔqīn mother ⓝ
幼儿园 yòu'éryuán childminding ⓝ
丝绸 sīchóu silk ⓝ

## 六画 6 strokes

买 mǎi buy ⓥ
买东西 mǎi dōngxī shop ⓥ
亚麻布 yàmá bù linen (material)
交换 jiāohuàn exchange ⓝ
价格 jiàgé cost • price ⓝ
休闲裤 xiūxián kù track pants
休息 xiūxī intermission ⓝ
会议 huìyì conference (big)
会合 huìhé converge, assemble
伤害 shānghài injury
先生 xiānshēng Mr
光 guāng light ⓝ
先后 xiānhòu chronology
共产主义 gòngchǎn zhǔyì communism
关 guān shut
关口 guānkǒu pass (mountain)
关门 guānmén closed
关闭 guānbì turn off, shut down
再一个 zài yīge another
再见 zàijiàn goodbye
军人 jūnrén soldier
农民 nóngmín farmer (peasant)
冰 bīng ice ⓝ
冰冻 bīngdòng frozen
冰箱 bīngxiāng refrigerator
动物 dòngwù animal ⓝ
动物园 dòngwù yuán zoo
危险 wēixiǎn dangerous
吃饭 chīfàn eat
吃的 chīde food
吃素的 chīsù de vegetarian ⓐ
同样 tóngyàng same, identical
同伙 tónghuǒ companion
同志（吧）tóngzhì (bā) gay (bar)
同事 tóngshì colleague
同性恋 tóngxìng liàn homosexual ⓝ
名字 míngzì given name • name
后 hòu rear (seat etc)
后天 hòutiān day after tomorrow
团体旅行 tuántǐ lǚxíng guided tour
回复 huífù reply, response
回来 huílái return (come back)
在……上 zài ... shàng aboard/atop the
在……里面 zài ... lǐmiàn inside the
地方 dìfāng local
地址 dìzhǐ address ⓝ
地图 dìtú map ⓝ
地铁 dìtiě subway
地铁站 dìtiě zhàn subway station
地震 dìzhèn earthquake
（网球）场 (wǎngqiú) chǎng court (tennis)
多 duō more
她 tā she/her
她的 tāde hers
好 hǎo good
好香 hǎoxiāng tasty, aromatic
字幕 zìmù subtitles
存钱 cúnqián deposit (bank)
孙女 sūnnǚ granddaughter
孙子 sūnzǐ grandson
安全 ānquán safe ⓐ
安全性交 ānquán xìngjiāo safe sex
安全带 ānquándài seatbelt
安静 ānjìng quiet
导游 dǎoyóu tourguide
年 nián year
年龄 niánlíng age ⓝ
忙得很 máng dé hěn very busy
收费公路 shōufèi gōnglù motorway (tollway)
收音机 shōuyīnjī radio ⓝ
收银台 shōuyín tái cash register
早 zǎo early
早上 zǎoshàng morning ⓝ
早饭 zǎofàn breakfast ⓝ
有毛病 yǒu máobìng faulty
约会 yuēhuì appointment or date
有事 yǒushì engaged (occupied)
有空 yǒukòng free (available)
有空调的 yǒu kōngtiáo de air-conditioned
有保证 yǒu bǎozhèng guaranteed
有病 yǒubìng ill
有暖气 yǒu nuǎnqì heated
机场税 jīchǎng shuì airport tax

杂技 zájì acrobatics
灰色 huīsè grey/gray
爷爷 yéye grandfather (paternal)
百货商店 bǎihuò shāngdiàn department store
米 mǐ metre
米饭 mǐfàn rice (cooked)
红色 hóngsè red
纪念品 jìniàn pǐn souvenir
纪念品店 jìniànpǐn diàn souvenir shop
网吧 wǎngbā internet cafe
网球 wǎngqiú tennis
网球场 wǎngqiú chǎng tennis court
羊毛 yángmáo wool
羊肉 yángròu mutton or goat meat
耳朵 ěrduǒ ear
老 lǎo old
老公 lǎogōng husband
老师 lǎoshī teacher
老百姓 lǎobǎixìng common people
老婆 lǎopó wife
肉 ròu meat
肉店 ròudiàn butcher's shop
自动取款机 zìdòng qǔkuǎn jī automated teller machine (ATM)
自行车 zìxíngchē bicycle ⓝ
自行车骑手 zìxíngchē qíshǒu cyclist
自助 zìzhù self service
血型 xuèxíng blood group
血液 xuè yè blood
行李 xínglǐ luggage
行李寄存 xínglǐ jìcún luggage lockers
行李领取处 xínglǐ lǐngqǔ qù baggage claim
衣服 yīfú clothing
西 xī west, western
西药房 xīyào fáng pharmacy
西班牙 Xībānyá Spain
西藏 Xīzàng Tibet
许可证 xǔkězhèng pass (permit)
过时 guòshí outmoded, invalid, stale
过夜 guòyè overnight
超重(行李) chāozhòng xínglǐ excess (baggage)
那个 nàgè that (one)
那边 nàbiān there
防晒油 fángshài yóu sunblock

## 七画 7 strokes

两个 liǎnggè two
两个都 liǎnggèdōu both
住宿 zhùsù accommodation
体育用品店 tǐyù yòngpǐn diàn sports store/shop
体育场 tǐyù chǎng stadium
运动员 yùndòng yuán athlete
佛寺 fósì monastery (Buddhist)
佛教 Fójiào Buddhism
佛教徒 Fójiào tú Buddhist
你 nǐ you inf
克 kè gram
免疫针 miǎnyì zhēn vaccination
免费 miǎnfèi free (gratis)
免费行李 miǎnfèi xínglǐ baggage allowance
兑现 duìxiàn cash (a cheque)
兑换率 duìhuàn lǜ exchange rate
冷 lěng cold (temperature)
医学 yīxué medicine (study, profession)
医药 yīyào medicine (medication)
医院 yīyuàn hospital
吵 chǎo noisy
帐单 zhàngdān bill (restaurant etc)
帳戶 zhànghù account (bank, social media)
听 tīng listen (to)
坏了 huàile out of order
坟地 féndì cemetery
尿裤 niàokù nappy/diaper
层 céng floor (storey)
岛 dǎo island
床 chuáng bed
床单 chuángdān bed linen
弟弟 dìdi brother (younger)
快 kuài fast • soon
快乐 kuàilè happy
快递 kuàidì courier
怀孕 huáiyùn pregnant
我 wǒ I • me
我们的 wǒmende ours
我的 wǒde my

戒指 jièzhi ring (on finger)
扶梯 fútī escalator
投诉 tóusù complaint
折扣 zhékòu discount ⓝ
抗菌素 kàngjūnsù antibiotics
护士 hùshì nurse ⓝ
护照 hùzhào passport
护照号码 hùzhào hàomǎ passport number
扭伤 niǔshāng sprain ⓝ
报纸 bàozhǐ newspaper
抛锚 pāomáo broken down (car)
时刻表 shíkè biǎo timetable ⓝ
时差反应 shíchā fǎnyìng jet lag
更大 gèngdà bigger
更小 gèngxiǎo smaller
更好 gènghǎo better
更衣室 gēngyīshì changing room
来信 láixìn mail (letters)
步行 bùxíng hike ⓥ
每(天) měi(tiān) per (day)
每个 měigè each
每个人 měigè rén everyone
每次 měicì every
沙滩 shātān beach
沙漠 shāmò desert
汽油 qìyóu petrol
没空 méikòng occupied, busy
没有订位 méiyǒu dìngwèi haven't made reservation
男人 nánrén man (male person)
男朋友 nánpéngyou boyfriend
男孩子 nán háizi boy
社会主义 shèhuì zhǔyì socialism
私人 sīrén private
纸巾 zhǐjīn tissues
纸币 zhǐbì banknote
罕见 hǎnjiàn rare (uncommon)
肚子 dùzi stomach
肚子疼 dùzi téng indigestion • stomach ache
肠胃炎 chángwèiyán gastroenteritis
花园 huāyuán garden ⓝ
花粉热 huāfěn rè hay fever
苏格兰 Sūgélán Scotland
证件 zhèngjiàn official ID document)
词典 cídiǎn dictionary
豆浆 dòujiāng soy milk
豆腐 dòufu tofu
走廊 zǒuláng aisle (on plane)
走路 zǒulù walk ⓥ
足够 zúgòu enough
足球 zúqiú football (soccer)
身份证 shēnfēn zhèng identification card (ID)
近 jìn near
这个 zhègè this (one)
这里 zhèlǐ here
进港口 jìngǎngkǒu port of arrival
远 yuǎn far
连衣裙 liányīqún dress ⓝ
连接 liánjiē connection
迟到 chídào to be late
邮电 yóudiàn mail (postal system)
邮政编码 yóuzhèng biānmǎ post code
邮局 yóujú post office
邮票 yóupiào stamp ⓝ
针灸 zhēnjiǔ acupuncture
针线 zhēnxiàn needle (sewing)
阿姨 āyí aunt
阿斯匹林 āsīpǐlín aspirin
附近 fùjìn nearby
饭馆 fànguǎn restaurant
饮料 yǐnliào drink ⓝ
鸡 jī chicken
鸡蛋 jīdàn egg (chicken)

## 八画 8 strokes

现代 xiàndài modern
现在 xiànzài now
现金 xiànjīn cash ⓝ
表演 biǎoyǎn performance
武术（中国功夫）wǔshù (Zhōngguó gōngfū) martial arts (Chinese kung fu)
其他 qítā other
取消 qǔxiāo cancel
取代 qǔdài replace
抽烟 chōuyān smoke ⓥ
拉稀 lāxī diarrhoea
拉链 lāliàn zip/zipper
事故 shìgù accident
卧室 wòshì bedroom
卧铺车厢 wòpù chēxiāng sleeping carriage (on train)

直接 zhíjiē direct
直播 zhíbō livestream
苦 kǔ bitter
英文 Yīngwén English
英文老师 Yīngwén lǎoshī English teacher
英国 Yīngguó England
英俊 yīngjùn handsome
雨伞 yǔsǎn umbrella
雨衣 yǔyī raincoat
杯子 bēizi cup ⓝ
枕头 zhěntóu pillow
画 huà painting (a work)
画画儿 huàhuàr painting (the art)
画家 huàjiā painter
厕所 cèsuǒ toilet
矿泉水 kuàngquán shuǐ mineral water
转机室 zhuǎnjī shì transit lounge
软卧 ruǎnwò soft sleeper
软座 ruǎnzuò soft seat
轮椅 lúnyǐ wheelchair
轮胎 lúntāi tyre
欧元 Ōuyuán euro
欧洲 Ōuzhōu Europe
到 dào to (go to, come to)
到达 dàodá arrive
垃圾 lājī garbage
垃圾箱 lājī xiāng garbage can
周末 zhōumò weekend
味道 wèidào smell ⓝ
咖啡 kāfēi coffee
咖啡色 kāfēi sè brown
咖啡馆/咖啡店 kāfēi guǎn/kāfēi diàn cafe
性别友善 xìngbié yǒushàn gender-inclusive
国家 guójiā country (nation)
明天 míngtiān tomorrow
明天下午 míngtiān xiàwǔ tomorrow afternoon
明天早上 míngtiān zǎoshàng tomorrow morning
明天晚上 míngtiān wǎnshàng tomorrow evening
明信片 míngxìnpiàn postcard
朋友 péngyǒu friend
服务 fúwù service ⓝ
服务员 fúwù yuán server, attendant
服务费 fúwù fèi service charge
服装店 fúzhuāngdiàn clothing store
肥皂 féizào soap
图书馆 túshū guǎn library
账单 zhàngdān invoice
账单 zhàngdān check (bill)
钓鱼 diàoyú fishing
刮痧 guāshā cupping (therapy)
季节 jìjié season ⓝ
岳父 yuèfù father-in-law
岳母 yuèmǔ mother-in-law
昏迷 hūnmí unconscious
昏倒 hūndǎo to faint, lose consciousness
货币兑换 huòbì duìhuàn currency exchange
往后退 wǎnghòutuì to back away
炸 zhá deep fry, deep-fried
炒菜 chǎocài cook ⓥ
贪污 tānwū corrupt
鱼 yú fish ⓝ
鱼摊 yútān fish stall
狗 gǒu dog
京剧 jīngjù opera (Chinese)
夜店 yèdiàn entertainment venue that's open at night (dance club, karaoke lounge, bar)
店 diàn shop ⓝ
废墟 fèixū ruins
闹钟 nàozhōng alarm clock
宝贝 bǎobèi child
实惠 shíhuì cheap
空 kōng empty
空房 kōngfáng vacancy
法国 Fǎguó France
法律 fǎlǜ law (study, professsion)
注射针 zhùshè zhēn needle (syringe)
浅色 qiǎnsè light (of colour)
单人 dānrén single (person)
单人间 dānrén jiān single room
单程 dānchéng one-way (ticket)
学生 xuéshēng student
房东 fángdōng landlord
房地产公司 fángdìchǎn gōngsī estate agency
房间 fángjiān room
房间号 fángjiān hào room number

肩膀 jiānbǎng shoulder
衬衫 chènshān shirt
视野 shìyě view, vision, vista
建筑师 jiànzhùshī architect
建筑学 jiànzhùxué architecture
录像机 lùxiàng jī video recorder
妹妹 mèimei sister (younger)
姐姐 jiějie sister (elder)
姓 xìng family name
驾照 jiàzhào driver's licence
纸 zhǐ paper
经络按摩 jīngluò ànmó pressure point massage
经济舱 jīngjì cāng economy class

## 九画 9 strokes

春天 chūntiān spring (season)
毒品 dúpǐn drug (illicit)
玻璃杯 bōlí bēi glass (drinking)
玻璃 bōlí glass (material)
帮助 bāngzhù help ⓝ
帮 bāng help ⓥ
城市 chéngshì city
项链 xiàngliàn necklace
挂号 guàhào registered mail/post ⓝ
指 zhǐ point ⓥ
指头 zhǐtóu finger
指南 zhǐnán guidebook
按摩 ànmó massage ⓝ
按摩师 ànmó shī masseur • masseuse
垫子 diànzi mattress
政治 zhèngzhì politics
胡同 hútòng alleyway
点心 diǎnxīn dim sum, snack
药片 yàopiàn pill
药方 yàofāng prescription
药剂师 yàojì shī pharmacist
药房 yàofáng pharmacy
药品 yàopǐn drug (medication)
茶馆 cháguǎn teahouse
南 nán south ⓝ
要紧 yàojǐn urgent
树荫 shùyīn shade of a tree
迷路 mílù lost (one's way)
厘米 límǐ centimetre
残疾 cánjí disabled
面包 miànbāo bread
面馆 miànguǎn noodleshop
面条 miàntiáo noodles
止泻药 zhǐxiè yào anti-diarrhea medicine
轻 qīng light (not heavy)
背 bèi back (body)
背包 bèibāo backpack
背面 bèimiàn behind
尝试 chángshì to attempt
新加坡 Xīnjiāpō Singapore
星期 xīngqī week
星期一 xīngqī yī Monday
星期二 xīngqī èr Tuesday
星期三 xīngqī sān Wednesday
星期四 xīngqī sì Thursday
星期五 xīngqī wǔ Friday
星期六 xīngqī liù Saturday
星期天 xīngqī tiān Sunday
哪里 nǎlǐ where
哪个 nǎgè which
是 shì yes
昨天 zuótiān yesterday
贵 guì expensive
罚款 fákuǎn fine (penalty)
贵重 guìzhòng valuable
钥匙 yàoshi key ⓝ
钢笔 gāngbǐ pen (ballpoint)
重 zhòng heavy ⓐ
重要 zhòngyào important
香烟 xiāngyān cigarette
香港 Xiānggǎng Hong Kong
秋天 qiūtiān autumn/fall
科学 kēxué science
科学家 kēxué jiā scientist
复活节 fùhuójié Easter
饺子 jiǎozi dumpling (boiled)
便秘 biànmì constipation
保险 bǎoxiǎn insurance
修理 xiūlǐ repair ⓥ
信 xìn letter (mail)
信用 xìnyòng credit
信用卡 xìnyòng kǎ credit card
信息 xìnxī text message
信徒 xìntú believers of a religion
信心 xìn xīn confidence, faith
信箱 xìnxiāng mailbox
徒步旅行 túbù lǚxíng to travel on foot

很硬 hěn yìng hard (not soft)
律师 lǜshī lawyer
疼 téng pain
食品 shípǐn food products
受伤 shòushāng injured
独自一个人 dúzì yīge rén alone
急救车 jíjiù chē ambulance
急急忙忙 jíji mángmang hectic
急救装备 jíjiù zhuàngbèi first-aid kit
临时保姆 línshí bǎomǔ babysitter
亭子 tíngzi pavillion
疮口 chuāngkǒu wound, open sore
度假 dùjià vacation
音乐会 yīnyuè huì concert
音乐 yīnyuè music
音乐祭/音乐节 yīnyuè jì/yīnyuè jié music festival
皇帝 huángdì emperor
皇后 huánghòu empress
美丽 měilì beautiful
姜 jiāng ginger
美国 Měiguó USA
首饰 shǒushì jewellery
前一个 qián yīgè last (previous) ⓐ
前天 qiántiān day before yesterday
宫殿 gōngdiàn palace
客户 kèhù client
洪水 hóngshuǐ flood
洋(货) yáng (huò) foreign (goods)
洗 xǐ wash (something)
洗衣店 xǐyī diàn launderette
洗衣服 xǐyīfú laundry (clothes)
洗衣机 xǐyī jī washing machine
洗碗 xǐwǎn wash the dishes
测光表 cèguāng biǎo light meter
派出所 pàichū suǒ police station
语言 yǔyán language
祖先 zǔxiān ancestors
说明书 shuōmíng shū instruction manual
退休职工 tuìxiū zhígōng pensioner
退钱 tuìqián refund ⓝ
退货 tuìhuò return goods/a purchase
孩子们 háizimen children
除夕 chúxī New Year's Eve

## 十画 10 strokes

换 huàn change • exchange
换钱 huànqián change (money)
热 rè hot ⓐ
热气 rèqì heat ⓝ
热水瓶 rèshuǐpíng thermos
热水袋 rèshuǐ dài hot water bottle
哥哥 gēge brother (elder)
恭喜 gōngxǐ congratulations
荷兰 Hélán Netherlands
桥 qiáo bridge
粉紅色 fěnhóng sè pink
夏天 xiàtiān summer
党员 dǎngyuán communist (party member)
轿车 jiàochē sedan
晒伤 shàishāng sunburn(t)
晕船/晕车 yùnchuán/ yùnchē seasickness/motion sickness
晚上 wǎnshàng evening • night
晚上活动 wǎnshàng huódòng night-time event
晚饭 wǎnfàn dinner
胳膊 gēbo arm ⓝ
胶卷 jiāojuǎn film (for camera)
胸 xiōng chest (body)
脆弱 cuìruò fragile
脏 zāng dirty
钱 qián money
钱包 qiánbāo purse
铅笔 qiānbǐ pencil
乘客 chéngkè passenger
租赁 zūlìn rent ⓥ
透镜 tòujìng lens
预订 yùdìng reservation (cake, dish or banquet)
饿 è hungry (to be)
笔记本 bǐjì běn notebook
健身房 jiànshēn fáng gym (place)
烟丝 yānsī tobacco
烤面包 kǎo miànbāo toast ⓝ
烧伤 shāoshāng burn injury
烧焦 shāojiāo burnt
爱 ài love ⓥ
爱尔兰 Ài'ěrlán Ireland
爱情 àiqíng love ⓝ

逛街 guàngjiē to windowshop
酱油 jiàngyóu soy sauce
离开 líkāi depart (leave)
离婚 líhūn divorce
高 gāo high ⓐ
高铁 gāotiě express train
高铁站 gāotiě zhàn express train station
高尔夫场 gāo'ěrfū chǎng golf course
高速公路 gāosù gōnglù highway
准时 zhǔnshí on time
座位 zuòwèi seat (place) ⓝ
病 bìng sick
病人 bìngrén patient (person)
旁边 pángbian beside
站台 zhàntái platform
站台票 zhàntái piào standby ticket
资本主义 zīběn zhǔyì capitalism
旅客 lǚkè tourists
旅客服务中心 lǚkè fúwù zhōngxīn tourist service centre
旅行社 lǚxíng shè travel agency
旅行团 lǚxíng tuán tour group
旅游保险 lǚyóu bǎoxiǎn travel insurance
旅館/旅栈 lǚguǎn/lǚzhàn hostel
旅程 lǚchéng journey
航班动态 hángbān dòngtài flight status
航空公司 hángkōng gōngsī airline
航班 hángbān flight
家 jiā home
家具 jiājù furniture
家庭 jiātíng family
宾馆 bīnguǎn guesthouse
酒吧 jiǔbā bar ⓝ
酒店 jiǔdiàn hotel
酒 jiǔ drink (alcoholic)
酒精 jiǔjīng alcohol
消毒剂 xiāodújì antiseptic
消费 xiāofèi tip (gratuity) ⓝ
海 hǎi sea
海外 hǎiwài overseas
海关 hǎiguān customs (airport)
海拔 hǎibá altitude above sea level
浴室 yùshì bathroom • shower ⓝ
浴缸 yùgāng bath
润滑油 rùnhuá yóu lubricant
(电)流 (diàn) liú current (electricity)
递送 dìsòng deliver
浪漫 làngmàn romantic
瓶子 píngzi bottle ⓝ
瓶装 píng zhuāng bottled (beer, water)
谁 shéi who
袜子 wàzi sock
剧 jù play (theatre)
剧场 jùchǎng theatre
展览 zhǎnlǎn exhibition
展览厅 zhǎnlǎn tīng exhibition hall
陶瓷 táocí ceramics
娱乐指南 yúlè zhǐnán entertainment guide

## 十一画 11 strokes

理发 lǐfà to get a haircut
理发店 lǐfà diàn hair salon
推荐 tuījiàn recommend
博物馆 bówù guǎn museum
搭便车 dā biànchē hitchhike
票 piào ticket ⓝ
票房 piàofáng ticket office
黄色 huángsè yellow
黄金 huángjīn gold ⓝ
剪刀 jiǎndāo scissors
剪指刀 jiǎnzhǐ dāo nail clippers
菊花 júhuā chrysanthemum
菜单 càidān menu
营业时间 yíngyè shíjiān opening hours
非典 fēidiǎn SARS
雪 xuě snow ⓝ
救人! jiùrén! help!
厨师 chúshī chef, cook
厨房 chúfáng kitchen
奢侈 shēchǐ luxury
插头 chātóu plug (electricity)
帽子 màozi hat
喝 hē drink
啤酒 píjiǔ beer
啤酒摊 píjiǔ tān liquor store
眼睛 yǎnjīng eye(s)
眼镜 yǎnjìng glasses (spectacles)
累 lèi tired
脖子 bózi neck
脚 jiǎo foot

脚踝 jiǎohuái ankle
脸 liǎn face
野餐 yěcān picnic ⓝ
银子 yínzi silver ⓝ
银行 yínháng bank (money)
银行账户 yínháng zhànghù bank account
甜 tián sweet
剩余额 shèngyú é balance (account)
停(车) tíngchē park (a car) ⓥ
您 nín you pol
假期 jiàqī holidays
领事馆 lǐngshìguǎn consulate
象棋 xiàngqí chess (Chinese)
猪肉 zhūròu pork
猫 māo cat
毫米 háomǐ millimetre
深色 shēnsè dark (of colour)
痒 yǎng itch(y)
麻将 májiàng mah-jong
商人 shāngrén businessman • businesswoman
商场 shāngchǎng shopping centre
盗窃的 dàoqiède theft, stolen
船 chuán boat
奥运会 Àoyùn huì Olympic Games
盘 pán dish (food item)
盘子 pánzi plate
寄存处 jìcúnqù cloakroom • left-luggage office
寄特快 jì tèkuài express mail (by)
清洁 qīngjié cleaning
清真 qīngzhēn halal
清真寺 qīngzhēn sì mosque
隐形眼镜 yǐnxíng yǎnjìng contact lenses
绷带 bēngdài bandage ⓝ
绿色 lǜsè green
骑马 qímǎ horse riding
骑自行车 qí zìxíngchē cycle ⓥ

## 十二画 12 strokes

裁缝 cáiféng tailor ⓝ
超市 chāoshì supermarket
越南 Yuènán Vietnam
朝鲜 Cháoxiǎn Korea (North)
葡萄酒 pútáo jiǔ wine
韩国 Hánguó Korea (South)
棉条 miántiáo tampon
森林 sēnlín forest
硬币 yìngbì coins
硬卧 yìngwò hard sleeper
硬座 yìngzuò hard seat
确认 quèrèn validate, confirm
确定 quèdìng confirm (a booking)
紫色 zǐsè purple
最大 zuìdà biggest
最小 zuìxiǎo smallest
最后的 zuìhòude last (final)
最好的 zuìhǎode best
最近 zuìjìn nearest
最高车速 zuìgāo chēsù speed limit
晾干 liànggān dry (clothes)
遗失物 yíshī wù lost property
黑白(片) hēibái (piàn) B&W (film)
黑色 hēisè black
黑暗 hēi'àn dark
锁 suǒ padlock
锁上 suǒshàng lock ⓥ
锁上了 suǒshàng le locked (door)
锅 guō wok, pot, cauldron
锅贴 guōtiē potstickers (dumplings)
等 děng wait (for)
等候室 děnghòu shì waiting room
街头 jiētóu street
街市 jiēshì street market
舒服 shūfu comfortable
短 duǎn short (length)
短裤 duǎnkù shorts
窗 chuāng window
短语集 duǎnyǔ jí phrasebook
湖 hú lake
温度 wēndù temperature (weather)
渴 kě thirsty (to be)
滑雪 huáxuě skiing
渡船 dùchuán ferry
游泳 yóuyǒng swim ⓥ
游泳池 yóuyǒng chí swimming pool
游泳衣 yóuyǒng yī swimsuit
普通话 pǔtōnghuà Mandarin
道教 Dàojiào Taoism
道路 dàolù road
裙子 qúnzi skirt
谢谢 xièxie thank you
登 dēng board (a plane, ship etc) ⓥ

登记台 dēngjì tái check-in (desk)
登机牌 dēngjī pái boarding pass

## 十三画 13 strokes

摄影 shèyǐng photography
摄影师 shèyǐng shī photographer
摇滚 yáogǔn rock (music)
蒙古 Ménggǔ Mongolia
蓝色 lánsè blue
零钱 língqián change (coins)
楼 lóu building
楼房 lóufáng apartment (downmarket)
感光度 gǎnguāngdù film speed
感冒 gǎnmào cold or flu
感冒药 gǎnmào yào cold or flu medicine
感染 gǎnrǎn infection
感谢 gǎnxiè grateful
碗 wǎn bowl ⓝ
暖气 nuǎnqì heater/heating
照片 zhàopiàn photo
暖 nuǎn warm
照相 zhàoxiàng take a photo
照相机 zhàoxiàng jī camera
睡觉 shuìjiào sleep ⓥ
睡袋 shuìdài sleeping bag
腿 tuǐ leg
跳舞 tiàowǔ dance
矮 ǎi short (height)
筷子 kuàizi chopsticks
签证 qiānzhèng visa
车锁 chēsuǒ lock (for vehicle)
微波炉 wēibō lú microwave (oven) ⓝ
解放军 jiěfàng jūn People's Liberation Army (PLA)
煤气 méiqì gas (for cooking)
遥控 yáokòng remote control
新 xīn new
新西兰 Xīnxīlán New Zealand
新闻 xīnwén news
新鲜 xīnxiān fresh
塑像 sùxiàng statue, figurine
塑胶 sùjiāo plastic
满 mǎn full

## 十四画 14 strokes

酷儿 kùér queer (LGBTQ)
磁带 cídài tape (recording) ⓝ
棒 bàng great (fantastic)
慢慢地 mànmande slowly
墨镜 mòjìng sunglasses
舞蹈 wǔdǎo dance (art form)
辣椒 làjiāo chili
辣椒酱 làjiāo jiàng chili sauce
鼻子 bízi nose
演出 yǎnchū performance
演员 yǎnyuán actor
蜜月 mìyuè honeymoon
熊猫 xióngmāo panda

## 十五画 15 strokes

蔬菜 shūcài vegetable
醉 zuì drunk
鞋 xié shoe
鞋店 xiédiàn shoe shop
膝盖 xīgài knee
镊子 nièzi tweezers
镑 bàng pound (money, weight)
箱子 xiāngzi box ⓝ
德国 Déguó Germany
摩托车 mótuō chē motorcycle ⓝ
颜色 yánsè colour
澳大利亚 Àodàlìyà Australia

## 十六至二十四画 16 to 24 strokes

橙色 chéngsè orange (colour)
糖尿病 tángniàobìng diabetes
赠(票) zèng (piào) complimentary (tickets)
穆斯林 Mùsīlín Muslim
避孕套 bìyùntào condom
餐巾 cānjīn napkin
餐车 cānchē dining car (on a train)
翻译 fānyì interpreter • translator
警察 jǐngchá police • police officer (in city)
罐头 guàntou can/tin

# INDEX

For topics that are covered in several sections of this book, we've indicated the most relevant page number in bold.


## A

abbreviations ... 3
accidents ... 162
accommodation ... 66
addresses ... 57, **63**, 122
adjectives (grammar) ... 18
adverbs of time (grammar) ... 29
age ... 118
airplane ... 44, **51**
alcoholic drinks ... 187
allergies ... **170**, 196
alphabet (Roman) ... 16
alternative medicine ... 171
ambulance ... 162
amounts ... 37
animals ... 159
apologies ... 112
appointments ... 97, 138
art ... 103
articles (grammar) ... 19
ATMs ... 96

## B

babysitters ... 109
baggage ... 50
banking ... 63, **95**
bar (drinking) ... 135, 187, **189**
bargaining ... 80
be (verb) ... 19
beach ... 158
Beijing dialect ... 11
beliefs ... 145
bicycle ... 58
bills ... 79, 81, **94**
bills (restaurant) ... 184
boat ... 44, 47, **54**
body language ... **142**, 147
body parts (diagram) ... 172
booking (accommodation) ... 67
booking (restaurant) ... 178
booking (transport) ... **46**, 56
books ... 82
border crossing ... 61
breakfast ... 70, 176
bus ... 44, **52**
business ... 97

## C

calendar ... 39
camera ... 84-5
camping ... 75
car hire ... 56
careers ... 118
cell phone ... 90
changing money ... 71, **95**
characters (script) ... 7, **17**, 48
checking in (accommodation) ... 67
checking in (transport) ... 50
checking out (accommodation) ... 74
checks ... 79, 81, **94**
checks (restaurant) ... 184
chemist ... 166, **173**
children ... 62, 103, **108**, 121
Chinglish ... 7
cinema ... 126
classifiers (grammar) ... 20
clothes ... 84
coffee ... **186**, 187
communication problems ... **32**, 48
comparatives (grammar) ... 18
compass points ... 65
complaints ... 72, 182
compliments ... 74, 77, 182
computers ... **88**, 99
concerts ... 124, 136
conferences (business) ... 97
conjunctions (grammar) ... 21
consonant sounds ... 12
consulate ... 165

contact details ........ 122
contraception ........ 170
conversation starters ........ 115, 119
cooking ........ 182, 194
counters (grammar) ........ 20
credit card ........ 79, 94
cuisines ........ 190, 199
cultural differences ........ 146
currency exchange ........ 96
customs (border crossing) ........ 62
customs (cultural) ........ 146
cycling ........ 58

## D

dates (calendar) ........ 40
dating (going out) ........ 140
days of the week ........ 40
demonstratives (grammar) ........ 21
dentist ........ 173
diagrams ........ 59, 65, 73, 172, 183
dialects (Mandarin) ........ 7, 11
dictionary English–Mandarin ........ 209
dictionary Mandarin–English ........ 239
diets (special) ........ 196
directions ........ 63
disabilities, travellers with ........ 106
discounts ........ 80, **103**, 108
diseases ........ 168
dishes (menu decoder) ........ 199
doctor ........ 162, **166**
drinks ........ 185, 187
driving ........ **56**, 63
drugs (illegal) ........ 139, 165
drugs (prescription) ........ 165, 167, **173**
dynasties ........ 60

## E

eating in ........ 192
eating out ........ 176
elevator ........ **71**, 107
email ........ **88**, 122
embassy ........ 165
emergencies ........ 162
emotions ........ 128
entertainment ........ 124, **134**, 139
environment ........ **132**, 159
etiquette (business) ........ 98, 99, 147
etiquette (food) ........ 77, 184, 186
etiquette (general) ........ 116, 142, 147
exchange (currency) ........ 96

## F

face (social standing) ........ 147
family ........ 108, 114, **120**
fares (hire car & taxi) ........ 56
farewells ........ 115, 121
faulty things ........ 80
fauna ........ 159
feelings ........ 128
ferry ........ 54, **55**
film (camera) ........ 84, 86
flora ........ 159
food ........ 175, 199
food allergies ........ 196
fractions (numbers) ........ 36
friends, addressing ........ 116
future (grammar) ........ 29, 30
future (time) ........ 42

## G

games ........ 127
gay travellers ........ 135, 144
gender (grammar) ........ 24
going out ........ 134
goodbyes ........ 115, 121
grammar ........ 18
greetings ........ 113
*guānxi* ........ 99
guide (hiking) ........ 157
guide (sightseeing) ........ 100, 104

## H

halal food ........ 197
have (verb) ........ 22
health ........ 166
help (emergencies) ........ 162
hiking ........ 156
hiring (bicycle) ........ 58
hiring (car & taxi) ........ 56
hiring (sports equipment) ........ 154
hobbies ........ 123
holidays ........ 61, 116
homestays ........ 76
hospital ........ 166
hotel ........ 66
hotel room (diagram) ........ 73

## I

illnesses ........ 168
imperatives (grammar) ........ 22
injuries ........ 152, 162, **169**
interests ........ 123

internet ... **88**, 99
interrogatives (grammar) ... 27
introductions (meeting people) ... **112**, 114
invitations ... 136

## J

jobs ... 118, **119**

## K

kissing ... 141
kinship terms ... 116, **120**
kosher food ... 197

## L

language difficulties ... **32**, 48
laundry service ... 71
leaving ... 74, 115, 121
legal problems ... 164
lesbian travellers ... 135, 144
life jackets ... 54
lift (elevator) ... **71**, 107
literature ... 80, **83**
local expressions ... **9**, 99, 105, 116, 119, 132, 184
lockers (luggage) ... 51
lost (luggage) ... 51
lost (valuables) ... 165
lost (disorientated) ... 105, 158, 163
love ... 144
luggage ... 50

## M

mail ... 92
maps ... **64**, 100, 156
marital status ... 120
martial arts ... 150, 155
meal requests ... 178, **180**, 196
meals ... 176
medical assistance ... 166
medication ... 165, 167, **173**
meeting up ... 138
menu ... **179**, 181, 185, 199
misunderstandings ... 32
mobile phone ... 90
Modern Standard Chinese ... 7, 11
money ... **94**, 96
months ... 40
movies ... 126, 127
museums (art) ... 103
music ... 124

## N

names ... 114
nationalities ... 117
nature ... 132, 159
need (verb) ... 23
negatives (grammar) ... 24
no (grammar) ... 7, **112**
nonsmoking section ... 49, 179
nouns (grammar) ... 24
numbers ... 34

## O

occupations ... 118
older travellers ... 106
opinions ... 129
ordering (drinks) ... 189
ordering (food) ... **179**, 197
outdoor pursuits ... 156

## P

particles (grammar) ... 24
past (grammar) ... 29
past (time) ... 4
pastimes ... **123**, 12
payment (methods of) ... 94
pharmacy ... 166, **173**
phone ... 70, **90**, 122, 163
photography ... **84**, 85, 10
pick-up lines ... 14
PIN numbers ... 9
Pinyin ... 7, 8, **1**
plane ... 44, **5**
plants ... 15
play (theatre) ... 12
playing sport ... 148, **15**
police ... 16
politics ... 13
possessive pronouns (grammar) ... 2
post office ... 9
prepositions (grammar) ... 2
prescriptions (medical) ... 165, 167, **17**
present (grammar) ... 2
present (time) ... 4
problems (health) ... 16
problems (language) ... 3
pronouns (grammar) ... 21, **2**
pronunciation ... 1
PSB ... 57, 67, **16**
punctuality ... 9
puncture (bicycle) ... 5

## Q


uantities .......... **37**, 193
uestions (grammar) .......... 27


## R


eceipts .......... 71, **79**, 168
efunds .......... 80, 95
egional variations
ronunciation) .......... 11, 33
ejections (romantic) .......... 141
elatives .......... 120
eligion .......... 145
enting (accommodation) .......... 76
epairs .......... 58, **87**
equests (accommodation) .......... 70
equests (dining) .......... 178, **180**, 196
eservations .......... *see* booking
estaurant .......... 135, 176, **178**, 186, 197
everse-charge calls .......... 91
oman alphabet .......... 16
omance .......... 140
oom (diagram) .......... 73
outes (transport) .......... 44


## S


afe (for valuables) .......... 71
easons .......... 41, 159
eating (restaurant) .......... 109, **178**, 179
eating (transport) .......... 45, 49
elf-catering .......... 192
enior travellers .......... 106
ex .......... 142
hopping (general) .......... 78
hopping (groceries) .......... 192
gns .......... 62, 70, 163, 171, 185
M card .......... 90
zes (clothes) .......... 83
nall talk .......... 112, 115, 119
noking .......... 49, 139, 167, 179
noking section .......... 49, 179
nacks .......... 184, 188
occer .......... 148
ocial issues .......... 130
ouvenirs .......... 87
pelling things out .......... 16
pitting .......... 171
port .......... 148
ation (train) .......... 53
reet food .......... 177, 184, **188**
reet scene (diagram) .......... 65
studies .......... 118, **120**
subway .......... **53**, 64
superstitions (numbers) .......... 98
swimming .......... 71, 109, 153, 158
symptoms (medical) .......... 168


## T


table tennis .......... 149, **154**
tailor .......... 83
taxi .......... **56**, 74, 191
tea (types of) .......... 187
telephone .......... 71, **90**, 122, 163
telling the time .......... 38
tense (grammar) .......... 29
thanking people .......... 74, 77, **112**
theatre .......... 126
tickets (transport) .......... 46
time .......... **38**, 98
titles (for people) .......... 115
toilets .......... 50, 54, 72, **162**, 191
tones (pronunciation) .......... 6, 13, 33
tongue twisters .......... 14, 33
tourist sites (in Mandarin) .......... 102
tours .......... 104
train .......... 44, 46, **53**
transport .......... 44
travellers cheques .......... 94
trekking .......... 156


## V


vacations .......... 61, 116
vaccinations .......... 168
vegetarian food .......... 196
verbs (grammar) .......... 28
verbs (sport) .......... 148
visas .......... 61
vowel sounds .......... 11


## W


walking (hiking) .......... 156
want (verb) .......... 30
weather .......... 158
wheelchair .......... 106
women's health .......... 170
word order (grammar) .......... 30
work .......... 97, **118**
writing system (Mandarin) .......... 17


## Y


yes (grammar) .......... 7, **112**

# 10 Ways

## TO START A SENTENCE

|  |  |  |
|---|---|---|
| When does (the next bus) leave? | (下一趟车)几点走? | (Xià yītàng chē) jǐdiǎn zǒu? |
| Where's (the tourist office)? | (旅行社)在哪儿? | (Lǚxíng shè) zài nǎr? |
| How much is (the deposit)? | (押金)多少? | (Yājīn) duōshǎo? |
| Do you have (a room)? | 有没有(房)? | Yǒuméiyǒu (fáng)? |
| Is there (heating)? | 有(暖气)吗? | Yóu (nuǎnqì) má? |
| I'd like (that one). | 我要(那个)。 | Wǒ yào (nàgè). |
| Please give me (the menu). | 请给我(菜单)。 | Qǐng gěiwǒ (càidān). |
| Can I (sit here)? | 我能(坐这儿)吗? | Wǒ néng (zuòzhèr) má? |
| I need (a can opener). | 我想要(一个开罐器)。 | Wǒ xiǎngyào (yīgè kāiguàn qì). |
| Do we need (a guide)? | 需要(向导)吗? | Xūyào (xiàngdǎo) má? |